THE NEW CHILDREN'S ENCYCLOPEDIA

Claudia Martin, Giles Sparrow,
Clare Hibbert, Honor Head,
Michael Leach, and Meriel Lland

ARCTURUS

Picture Credits

Every attempt has been made to clear copyright. Should there be any inadvertent omission, please apply to the publisher for rectification.

Alamy: 100–101 (Greg Vaughn), 101cr (Xinhua), 110–111 (Sean Pavone), 113cl (World History Archive, 144–145 (David Fleetham), 163cr (Fernando Quevedo de Oliveira), 180–181 (Suzi Eszterhas/Minden Pictures), 188br (Scott Camazine), 192b (Nature Picture Library), 202–203 (Richard Becker), 221 (Rawf8); **alexfreire:** 60br; **Alex Hindle:** 196–197; **Arcturus Publishing:** 160br, 236cr, 241r, 247t, 248–249, 250–251, 250br (Stefano Azzalin), 234–251 profile box icons, 234–235, 238–239, 240–241, 242–243 (Mat Edwards), 235t (Val Walerczuk), 236–237, 245cr (Juan Calle), 238l, 246–247 (Martin Bustamante), 244–245 (Rudolf Farkas), 245tl (Kunal Kundu); **Ardea:** 185c (Anthony Mercieca/Science Source); **ESA:** 74–75 (D. Ducros), 86–87; **ESO.org:** 43tr; **EUMETSAT:** 74b; **FLPA:** 156–157 (Frans Lanting), 164–165 (Karl Van Ginderdeuren), 165bl (Juan-Carlos Munoz), 168–169 (Norbert Wu), 170–171 (Christopher Swan/Biosphoto), 172cr (Photo Researchers), 172cl (Christian Ziegler), 176–177 (Erica Olsen), 178–179 (Frans Lanting), 178cl (Juergen & Christine Sohns/Minden Pictures), 184–185 (Tim Zurowski, BIA/Minden Pictures), 186–187 (Artur Cupak/Imagebroker), 186bl (Paul van Hoof/ Minden Pictures), 194–195 (Imagebroker), 195br (Richard Hermann/Minden Pictures), 198–199 (Peter Schwarz, BIA/Minden Pictures), 198bl (Piotr Naskrecki/Minden Pictures), 199cr (Michel Gunther/Biosphoto), 201cr (Reinhard Dirscherl); **Getty Images:** 34–35 (Education Images/UIG), 68–69 (Roger Ressmeyer/Corbis/VCG), 75b (Detlef van Ravenswaay), 104–105 (Carsten Peter/Speleoresearch and Films), 108–109 (CESAR MANSO/AFP), 122–123 (Sylwia Duda), 124–125 (Oliver Henze/EyeEm), 125b (Ryan McGinnis), 136–137 (David Merron Photography), 142–143 (Ralph Lee Hopkins), 230–231 (Peathegee Inc/Blend Images), 232–233 (Echo); **Keck Observatory:** 63cr (NRC-HIA, Christian Marois); **LASERPHACO/Dr Patricia Bath:** 228bl; **Lawrence Livermore National Laboratory:** 90–91; **Library of Congress:** 41tr (Oren Jack Turner); **NASA Images:** 17br, 29cr, 38br (JPL-Caltech), 41c (ESA/Judy Schmidt), 42cl (SOHO/ESA), 46bl (JPL), 46r, 50tr, 50cr, 51tl (JPL-Caltech/ASU), 52cl (JPL-Caltech/UCLA/MPS/DLR/IDA/Justin Cowart), 53tr (JPL/MPS/DLR/IDA/Björn Jónsson), 54cl, 56cl, 57tr, 60c (AEI/ZIB/M Koppitz & L Rezzolla), 58c, 64br (ESA/Hubble Heritage Team), 62b (ESA/ESO/L Ricci), 63tc (CXC/M Weiss), 66c (WMAP Science Team), 67bl, 72br, 73tr, 75r, 76–77 (JPL-Caltech), 76c (JPL/Space Science Institute), 77r (JHU APL/SwRI/Steve Gribben); **Pikaia Imaging:** 58–59; **Science Photo Library:** 6–7 (Photo Insolite Realite), 11cl (Tony McConnell), 12cl (Dr Gary Settles), 14l (GIPhotoStock), 18–19 (Matthew Oldfield), 22–23 (Patrice Loiez, CERN), 31br, 40–41 (Nicolle R Fuller), 42–43 (NASA/JPL), 49b (Mark Garlick), 58–59 (Chris Butler), 66br (Carlos Clarivan), 78b (Universal History Archive/UIG), 82–83 (David Parker), 84–85 (Samuel Ashfield), 84cl (US Army), 88tr (Dr Gary Settles), 92–93 (Nicolle R Fuller), 92cr (Philippe Plailly), 98cr, 121br, 128c (Gary Hincks), 100cr (Henning Dalhoff), 102cl, 113br (Spencer Sutton), 119cr (Carlos Clarivan), 127 (Mikkel Juul Jensen), 148tr (Kateryna Kon), 156c (Smetek), 160–161 (Jose Antonio Penas), 218–219 (KH Fung), 218b (Eye of Science), 220cl (Anatomical Travelogue), 222–223 (Jellyfish Pictures), 226c (Natural History Museum, UK), 230br (CNRI), 232cr (John Bavosi), 232br (Prof P Motta/Dept of Anatomy/University "La Sapienza", Italy); **Shutterstock:** 3tr (M Aurelius/NASA), 3bl, 36cl (kasezo), 3br, 44bl (Jurik Peter), 4tl, 92tr (Forance), 4tr (Sergey Lavrentev), 4bl, 122cr (Samak Bootsinoi), 4br, 167br (Photo by Lola), 5tl, 184b (Erick Houli), 5tr (David Roland), 5bl, 226–227 (Cipolina), 5br, 206–207, 221tr (Life science), 6tr (adriaticfoto), 6c (Neal Pritchard Media), 6br (YC_Chee), 7tr (adike), 7br (NASA Images), 8–9 (ZinaidaSopina), 8tr (MicroOne), 8bl (sandatlas.org), 9bl (kaer_stock), 10–11, 105c, 97tr (Sebastian Janicki), 10cl (grafvision), 11bl (Macrovector), 12–13 (Digital Storm), 12bl (MilanMarkovic78), 13tl (Evgeniya Chertova), 14–15 (Fredy Thuerig), 15cr (Inna Bigun), 15bl, 17tl, 116t, 118bl, 208tr (NoPainNoGain), 16–17 (Maximilian Laschon), 18cl (Taras Vyshnya), 18bl, 114cl, 58tr, 148c, 149cr, 216cr (Designua), 19bl (CE Wagstaff/ Georgios Kolidas), 20–21 (cyo bo), 20tr (haryigit), 21cr (patx64), 22bl (Andrea Danti), 23cr (MichaelTaylor), 23bl (mila kad), 24–25 (3Dsculptor), 24cr (Sombat Muycheen), 25bl (freevideophotoagency), 26–27 (Cassiohabib), 26cr (Roberto Cerruti), 26c (JonathanC Photography), 26bl (StockSmartStart), 27cr (Aspen Photo), 28–29 (Sky Antonio), 28c (TES_PHOTO, MatiasDelCarmine, Genestro), 28bl, 36bl, 157bl (MatiasDelCarmine), 30–31 (Little Dog Korat), 30cl (Kosta Iliev), 30bc (pandapaw), 31tl (Morphart Creation), 32–33 (Gabor Kenyeres), 32tr (Littlekidmoment), 32c (SkyPics Studio), 32bl (Fouad A Saad), 34c (Zigzag Mountain Art), 35br (ShutterStockStudio), 36–37 (Kobby Dagan), 38–39 (Jag_cz), 38tr (Fouad A Saad), 39tl (ALXR), 41bl (Meowu), 44–45 (Amanda Carden), 44r (koya979), 45t, 47b, 50b 52b, 55tr, 56b (21), 46–47 b/g (nienora), 47, 57c, 57br (NASA), 48–49 (godrick, vovan/NASA), 48cl (Castleski/NASA), 48bl (Monkey_Fish), 50–51 (Vadim Sadovski/NASA), 52–53 (Andrea Danti), 54–55, 54cr (Vadim Sadovski/NASA), 54–55 b/g (Yuriy Kulik), 54br (Tristan3D), 56–57 (manjik/NASA), 56–57 b/g (Triff/NASA), 58bl (Maria Zvonkova), 58cl (vectortatu), 60–61 (Vadim Sadovski), 61br, 242b (Catmando), 62–63 (Giovanni Benintende), 66–67 (Andrea Danti), 68b (Georgios Kollidas/R Hart), 69tr (VectorPot), 69cr, 151bl, 220bl (BlueRingMedia), 69br (Olga Rutko), 70–71 (3Dsculptor), 70c (Fred Mantel), 70br (stoyanh), 71tr (Georgios Kollidas), 72–73 (Naeblys/NASA), 72bl, 73br (PavloArt Studio), 74c (Johan Swanepoel), 76bl (MawRhis), 78–79 (Maryna Kulchytska), 78tr (SherSS), 79bl (NPavelN), 80–81 (mekcar), 80bl (Photomontage), 81cr (andrea crisante), 82c (fotografos), 82bl (Luisa Fumi), 83br (tomas devera photo), 85tr (Volodymyr Krasyuk), 86bl (Chris Singshinsuk), 87cr (asharkyu), 87bl (Blan-k), 88–89 (satit_srihin), 88bl (Peppy Graphics), 89bl (Gabor Miklos), 90c (Martin Lisner), 90bl (Blue Ring Media), 91bl (udaix), 92bl (Shmitt Maria), 94–95 (Vadim Sadovski/NASA), 94tr (Diego Barucco), 94cr (Marc Ward/NASA), 96–97 (Mark Agnor), 97tl (yongyut rukkachatsuwa), 97bl (Andrey Kuzmin), 98–99 (Jakub Cejpek), 98bl (M Scheja), 100bl (robin2), 102–103 (Daniel Prudek), 102br (Kotenko Oleksandr), 103tr (bteimages), 104c (Mivr), 104br, 105tl, 105tr, 105br, 106c (Albert Russ), 105cl (PNSJ88), 105bl (Bascar), 106–107 (saiko3p), 106br (Sunshine Seeds), 107tr (yurchello108), 107br (worradirek), 108c (AlessandroZocc), 108br (Sasha Samardzija), 109b (fotosub), 110l (IxMaster), 111tr (John And Penny), 111br (Panwasin seemala), 112–113 (Therato), 112bl (Palau), 114–115 (S. Borisov), 114br (OHishiapply), 115br (Sasin Tipchai), 116bl (dalmingo), 117tr (BoJe10), 118–119 (Harvepino), 118c (sumikophoto), 120–121 (beeboys), 120c (VectorMine), 120br (Dave Greenberg), 122tr (Akexey Kijatov), 122 (Andrea Danti), 123t (Datskevich Aleh), 123ct (Dariusz Leszczynski), 123cb (ClownxgMeng), 123b (samray), 124c (Niccolò Ubalducci Photographer - Stormchaser), 126–127 (lavizzara), 126tr (All Stock Photos), 128–129 (Erik Mandre), 128br (Alexander Demyanov), 129c (sergemi), 130–131 (Ghiuz), 130l (Alexey Stiop), 130br (Matt Makes Photos), 131r (Tom Roche), 132–133 (Andrzej Kubik), 132c (Luiz Kagiyama), 132br (Ksenia Ragozina), 133tr (Ron Ramtang), 134–135 (PhotocechCZ), 134c (Christian Roberts-Olsen), 134b (Baranov E), 135br (PunyaFamily), 136l (Gregory A. Pozhvanov), 136br (Ondrej Prosicky), 137r (longtaildog), 138–139 (Brian Lasenby), 138tr (Westend61), 138bl (Pongsiri), 138bc (Traveller Martin), 138br (Pavel Svoboda Photography), 139br (lavizzara), 140tr (Dani O'Brien), 140cr (Anan Kaewkhammul), 140br (Steve Heap), 142c, 153ct, 153bc (Rich Carey), 142b (Jag-cz), 143tr (Phuong D. Nguyen), 144cr (Lightspring), 144bc (Susan Schmitz), 146–147 (hamdee), 146l (Calmara), 147cr (koya979), 148–149 (ranjith ravindran), 150–151 (Brannon_Naito), 150cr (Sakura), 150br (Molly NZ), 152tr (tcareob72), 152trbl (hillmanchaiyaphum), 152trbr (Popova Tetiana), 152ct, 152ctr (schankz), 152c (Andrey Armyagov), 152cbr (F Neidl), 152cb (Gerald Robert Fischer), 152bl (dangdumrong), 152br (Jolanta Wojcicka), 153tlb (Romeo Andrei Cana), 153tc (Victor Tyakht), 153tr (Zety Akhzar), 153ctr (Salparadis), 153cb (scubaluna), 153br (Laura Dinraths), 154–155 (sebi_2569), 154cl (Bildagentur Zoonar GmbH), 154bl (Christos Georghiou), 155cr (yougoigo), 158–159 (Hedrus), 158bl (Esteban De Armas), 159tl, 182b, 217bl (Panda Vector), 160cl (Tatsiana Salayuova), 161bl (kalen), 162bl (Victor Lapaev), 163br, 164br, 177br, 200br (Spreadthesign), 165cr (hansenexposed), 166–167 (Sergey Uryadnikov), 166cl (sirtravelalot), 167tr (elmm), 168cl, 169cr (vladsilver), 169br, 175tr (Maquiladora), 170cl (Michael Smith/ITWP), 170br (Kurilin Gennadiy Nikolaevich), 171b (Tory Kallman), 172–173 (Worraket), 173tr (Mush322), 174–175 (Nuamfolio), 174tr (Utopia_88), 175cr (Nivlac921), 177tl (T Wilbertz), 177c (MarciSchauer), 178br (Noahsu), 179br (Yana Kazuar), 180c (Andril Slonchak), 180br (Creative Mood), 181cr (Jason Benz Bennee), 182–183 (Nick Fox), 182cl (Jill Richardson King), 183br (Jon_Clark), 185tr (Aniko Gerendi Enderle), 187cr (Abhindia), 187br (RinArte), 188–189 (Shane Myers Photography), 188c (Martha Marks), 189tr (Dream_master), 190–191 (wildestanimal), 190cl (Grant M Henderson), 191tr (Adisom Chaikit), 191br (Voinau Pavel), 192–193 (Kjersti Joergensen), 192cl (Vladimir Wrangel), 193br (Bonezboyz), 194c (pr2is), 194br (Voinau Pavel), 196cr (Dewald Kirsten), 196b (stefanphotozemun), 197br (VectorPot), 199br (Alastair Wallace), 200–201 (Sergey Lavrentev), 200c (Anest), 202c (Sally Wallis), 202br (foodonwhite), 203br (Kostiantyn Kravchenko), 204–205 (Sirisak_baokaew), 204cr, 216–217, 217cr (Sebastian Kaulitzki), 205bl (eenoki), 206cl (Christos Georghiou), 206bl (NotionPic), 207br (VILevi), 208–209 (Biomedical), 208bl (stihii), 209bl (LynxVector), 210–211 (adike), 210tr (yodiyim), 210c (wavebreakmedia), 211bl, 212cl, 222c (Tefi), 212–213 (Michal Knitl), 213cr (Robert J Gatto), 213bl (Everett Historical), 214–215 (Nerthuz), 214cl (nobeastsofierce), 214bl (EstherQueen999), 215cr (bitt24), 216cl (deepadesigns), 218cr (Vasilyeva Larisa), 219tl (eranicle), 220cr (okili77), 222bl (Double Brain), 223br (Olya Vusochyn), 224–225 (Juan Gaertner), 224c (Kateryna Kon), 224bl (GraphicsRF), 225br (by pap), 227b (Ermolaev Alexander), 228cr (snapgalleria), 228c (Peter Hermes Furian), 229 (air009), 230cr (Alexander_P), 231bl (Sakurra), 241b (MikhailSh), 248b (Linda Bucklin), 251cr (Warpaint); **thehistoryblog.com:** 147bl; **Wellcome Images:** 205tl; **Wikimedia Commons:** 21tl (Christian Albrecht Jensen), 24bl (Justus Sustermans, National Maritime Museum), 34bl (Frederick Bedell's *The Principles of the Transformer* (1896)), 37tr (Niabot), 42bl (Adler Planetarium and Astronomy Museum, Chicago/Brahe's *Astronomiae instauratae*), 65bl (Harvard University Library), 84bl (Science Museum, London/Mrjohncummings), 89tl (www.jedliktarsasag.hu), 94bl (Davorka Herak and Marijan Herak), 99bl (Scottish National Gallery/Henry Raeburn), 102cr (United States Meteorological Survey), 145tl (Alexander Roslin, Nationalmuseum, Stockholm, Sweden), 148bl (Robert Hooke, *Micrographia*, National Library of Wales), 153tl (Maija Karala), 156bl (Charles Darwin and John Gould: *The Voyage of the Beagle*), 159br (Mendel: *Principles of Heredity: A Defence*/Bateson, William), 226bl (DBCLS/BodyParts3D), 231tl (Joe Haupt), 239t (Didier Descouens), 246l (Allie Caulfield/Los Angeles Museum of Natural History), 249tr (Daderot/Natural History Museum of Utah), 122br, 124br, 127tr.

Front cover: Paul Oakley; **back cover** all from Shutterstock. tl Salparadis, bl NASA Images, c Lightspring, tr PunyaFamily, br MDGRPHCS

ARCTURUS

This edition published in 2024 by Arcturus Publishing Limited
26/27 Bickels Yard, 151–153 Bermondsey Street,
London SE1 3HA

Copyright © Arcturus Holdings Limited

All rights reserved. No part of this publication may be reproduced, stored in a retrieval system, or transmitted, in any form or by any means, electronic, mechanical, photocopying, recording or otherwise, without prior written permission in accordance with the provisions of the Copyright Act 1956 (as amended). Any person or persons who do any unauthorised act in relation to this publication may be liable to criminal prosecution and civil claims for damages.

Authors: Claudia Martin, Giles Sparrow, Clare Hibbert, Honor Head, Michael Leach, and Meriel Lland
Designers: Lorraine Inglis and Amy McSimpson
Front cover design: Paul Oakley

ISBN: 978-1-3988-0944-4
CH008275NT
Supplier 29, Date 0724, Print run 00007624

Printed in China

THE NEW CHILDREN'S ENCYCLOPEDIA

CONTENTS

Introduction — 6

CHAPTER 1: MATTER AND MATERIALS
- Phases of Matter — 8
- Solid Materials — 10
- Liquids and Gases — 12
- Elements — 14
- Periodic Table — 16
- Chemistry At Work — 18
- Electrical Properties — 20
- Inside The Atom — 22

CHAPTER 2: FORCES AND ENERGY
- Physics Is Everywhere — 24
- Newton's Laws of Motion — 26
- Gravity — 28
- Waves — 30
- Heat and Energy — 32
- Electricity and Magnetism — 34
- Secrets of Light — 36
- Invisible Rays — 38
- Einstein's Universe — 40

CHAPTER 3: SPACE
- The Solar System — 42
- The Sun — 44
- Mercury and Venus — 46
- Earth and Moon — 48
- Mars — 50
- The Asteroid Belt — 52
- Jupiter — 54
- Saturn, Uranus, and Neptune — 56
- Stars and The Galaxy — 58
- Black Holes — 60
- Exoplanets — 62
- The Universe — 64
- The Big Bang and Beyond — 66
- Telescopes — 68
- Rockets — 70
- International Space Station — 72
- Satellites — 74
- Space Probes — 76

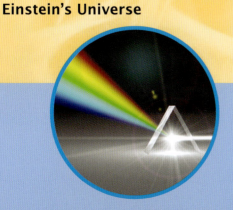

CHAPTER 4: TECHNOLOGY

Simple Machines	78
Engines, Motors, and Generators	80
Electronics	82
Computers	84
Connected World	86
Flying Machines	88
Nuclear Energy	90
Nanotechnology	92

CHAPTER 5: PLANET EARTH

Inside The Earth	94
Rocks and Minerals	96
Earth's Crust	98
Volcanoes and Earthquakes	100
Mountains	102
Crystals	104
Metals	106
Fossils	108
Fossil Fuels	110

CHAPTER 6: WEATHER, CLIMATE, AND HABITAT

The Atmosphere	112
Seasons	114
Day and Night	116
Earth's Water	118
Weather Systems	120
Storms and Precipitation	122
Tornadoes	124
Hurricanes	126
Climate Zones	128
Deserts	130
Grasslands	132
Forests	134
Polar Regions	136
Wetlands	138
Farmland	140
Climate Change	142

CHAPTER 7: LIFE ON EARTH

Kingdoms of Life	144
Story of DNA	146
Cell Machinery	148
Plants	150
Animals	152
Web of Life	154
Darwin's Theory	156
Evolution At Work	158
History of Life	160
Cats	162
Foxes	164
Bears	166
Seals	168
Whales and Dolphins	170
Bats	172
Elephants	174
Giraffes	176
Apes	178

Marsupials	180
Vultures	182
Hummingbirds	184
Frogs	186
Turtles	188
Sharks	190
Seahorses	192
Cephalopods	194
Jellyfish	196
Spiders and Scorpions	198
Slugs and Snails	200
Bees	202

CHAPTER 8: THE HUMAN BODY

Amazing Body	204
Inside The Brain	206
Bone and Muscle	208
Nervous System	210
Skin and Hair	212
Digestive System	214
Heart, Blood, and Lungs	216
The Liver	218
Kidneys and Urine	220
Making Babies	222
Fighting Disease	224
Touch	226
Eyes and Sight	228
Ears and Hearing	230
Smell and Taste	232

CHAPTER 9: DINOSAURS AND RELATIVES

Dinosaurs and Relatives	234
Tyrannosaurus	236
Spinosaurus	238
Archaeopteryx	240
Sauroposeidon	242
Parasaurolophus	244
Triceratops	246
Stegosaurus	248
Quetzalcoatlus	250
Glossary	252
Index	254

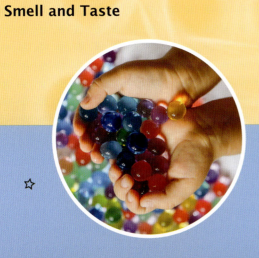

Introduction

We humans are naturally curious creatures. When our ancestors gazed up at the night sky or watched the changing seasons, they would have wondered why the stars shone, or why leaves fell from trees. Today, we are in the happy position of being able to answer these, and many other questions.

Learning About Our World

This book draws together knowledge from many different disciplines—including physics, chemistry, biology, geography, cosmology, geology, and paleontology. Each of these subject areas is like a different lens through which we can see our Universe.

Physical Science

Physical science is the study of anything non-living. This includes much of chemistry, which is the branch of science that investigates materials, from atoms to elements. Physics, on the other hand, is the scientific study of energy, forces, mechanics, and waves.

A scientist observes a chemical reaction under a microscope.

Chimpanzees are one of around 7.8 million species of living animals.

Many forms of energy are involved in a storm.

Life on Earth

Natural history is the study of living things—the plants, animals, and other creatures that inhabit Earth now or that existed in the past. It studies how these organisms are influenced by each other and their environment. It also looks at the complex process of evolution—gradual change from one generation to the next.

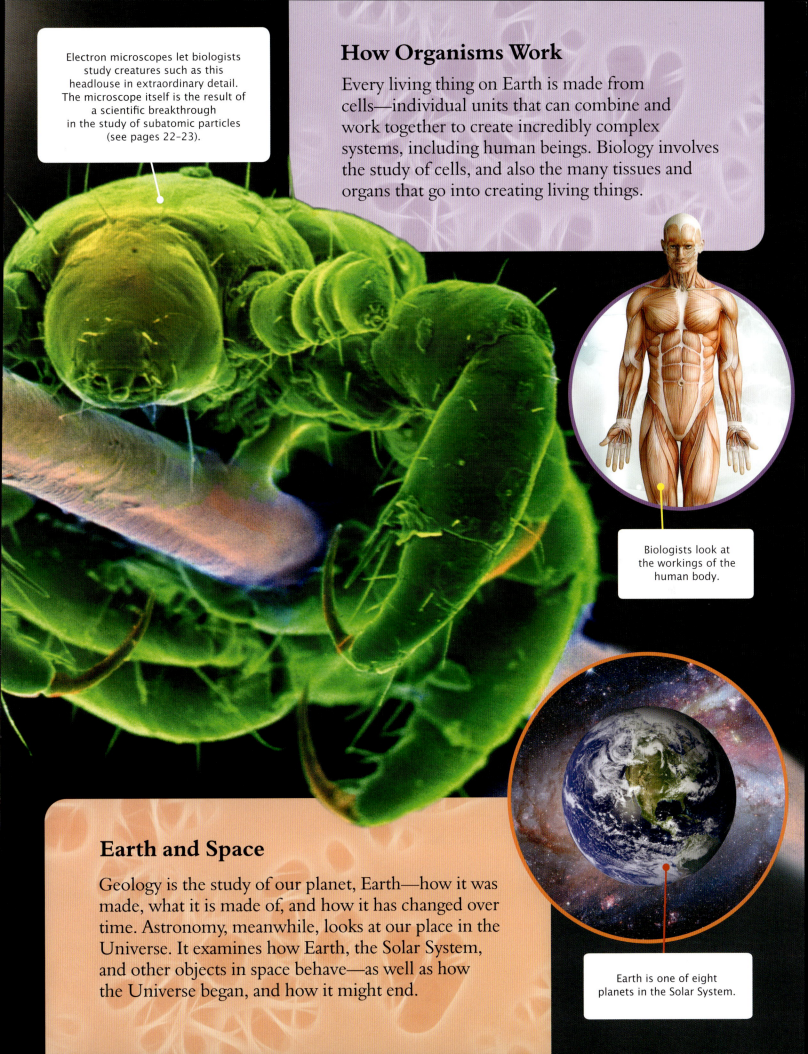

Electron microscopes let biologists study creatures such as this headlouse in extraordinary detail. The microscope itself is the result of a scientific breakthrough in the study of subatomic particles (see pages 22–23).

How Organisms Work

Every living thing on Earth is made from cells—individual units that can combine and work together to create incredibly complex systems, including human beings. Biology involves the study of cells, and also the many tissues and organs that go into creating living things.

Biologists look at the workings of the human body.

Earth and Space

Geology is the study of our planet, Earth—how it was made, what it is made of, and how it has changed over time. Astronomy, meanwhile, looks at our place in the Universe. It examines how Earth, the Solar System, and other objects in space behave—as well as how the Universe began, and how it might end.

Earth is one of eight planets in the Solar System.

CHAPTER 1: MATTER AND MATERIALS

Phases of Matter

Matter is the stuff that makes up the Universe. It is built from countless tiny particles called atoms and molecules. Depending on how these particles arrange themselves and join together, matter can take one of three forms: solid, liquid, or gas. These forms are called phases.

Material Bonds

Solid substances are made up of particles joined by strong, rigid bonds. Particles in liquids have looser bonds, which constantly break and reform. Gases are very loose collections of atoms or molecules that have extremely weak bonds. The strength of a material's bonds affects its ability to keep its shape.

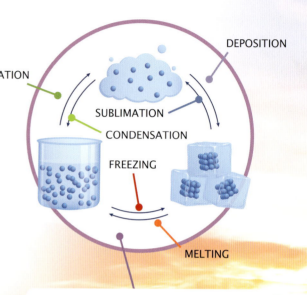

Water can be a solid (ice), liquid, or gas (steam). When it's solid, it stays the same shape whatever container it's put in. As a liquid, its molecules flow outward to spread across surfaces. Steam spreads to fill its container or heads in all directions.

Changing Phases

The phase of a substance is affected by how much energy its individual particles have to move around, and this energy depends on the material's temperature. Heating a solid material enough loosens its bonds and makes it melt. Heating a liquid will cause particles to boil or evaporate into a gas.

Different substances have different melting and boiling points. The melting point of rock is very high, so molten lava rapidly turns solid when it erupts from a volcano and begins to cool.

DID YOU KNOW? The metal mercury is usually in liquid form. Its freezing point is −38.8°C (−37.8°F) and its boiling point is 356.7°C (674°F), both are the lowest of any metal.

A geyser is created where matter suddenly changes its phase.

As the steam meets the cold air above, it cools and turns back to liquid water droplets.

Wherever the water finds a way through cracks to the surface, it suddenly and violently boils into steam.

Below ground, hot rocks heat liquid water higher than the boiling point but trap it so it cannot turn to steam.

AMAZING DISCOVERY

Scientist: James Thomson
Discovery: Triple point of water
Date: 1873
The story: Thomson was an engineer specializing in water transport. He showed that pure water can coexist as a solid, liquid, and gas at a particular pressure and temperature: 0.01°C (32.01°F).

Solid Materials

Most objects are made of solid matter. The atoms or molecules that make up a solid are held together very strongly. There are lots of very different solids, but they all share certain features.

Solid Properties

In some solids, the atoms form regular patterns called crystals. Quartz and salt have a crystal structure. In other solids—for example, polythene—the atoms bond in more of a jumble. Some of these shapeless solids can change shape by stretching—this is called being ductile.

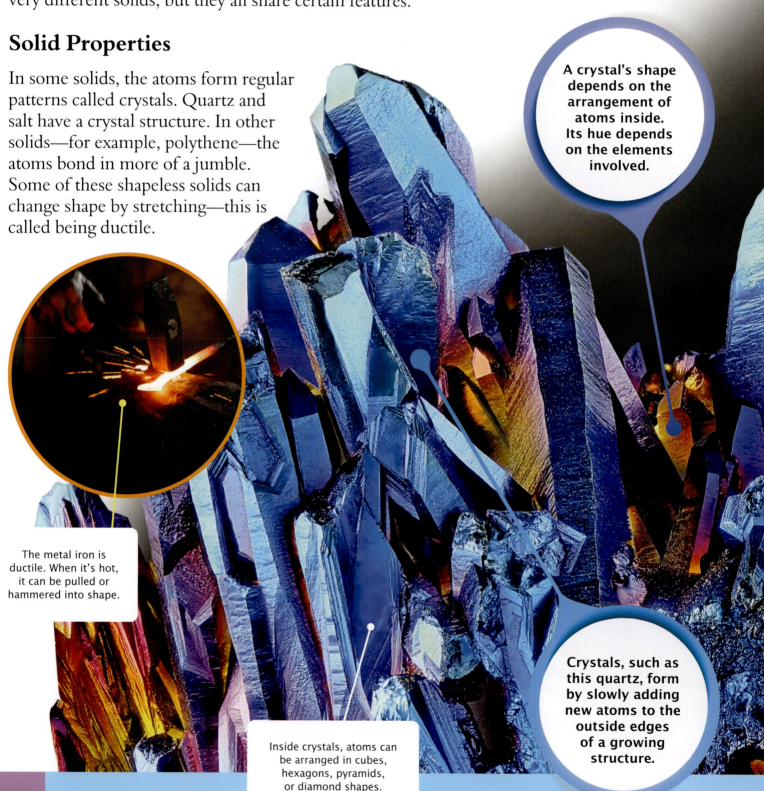

A crystal's shape depends on the arrangement of atoms inside. Its hue depends on the elements involved.

The metal iron is ductile. When it's hot, it can be pulled or hammered into shape.

Inside crystals, atoms can be arranged in cubes, hexagons, pyramids, or diamond shapes.

Crystals, such as this quartz, form by slowly adding new atoms to the outside edges of a growing structure.

Conducting Heat

Solids respond to being heated in different ways. Some solids, including many metals, carry the heat rapidly from one atom to the next. They are called conductors. Others, such as wood or plastic, do not pass on heat. They are called insulators.

In nature, large crystals can can take millions of years to grow. These quartz crystals were grown artificially in just a few hours.

A metal pan conducts heat rapidly through its base to the food inside. However, a wooden spoon (purple and cool in this thermal image) insulates the cook's hand from the heat.

AMAZING DISCOVERY

Scientists: Metalworkers in what is now Turkey
Discovery: Steel
Date: c.2000 BCE
The story: Iron Age metalworkers found that adding other materials to a metal created an alloy that was more useful than the pure metal. For example, people in ancient Turkey found that adding charcoal to iron produced strong steel.

DID YOU KNOW? Tungsten, used in high-performance aircraft, has the highest melting point of any metal. It remains solid up to an amazing 3,414°C (6,277°F).

Liquids and Gases

Most substances are only liquid in a narrow range of temperatures between their solid and gas phases. Atoms or molecules inside liquids are more loosely bonded than those in solids. In gases, their bonds are even weaker.

Moving Particles

In everyday language, we use "fluid" to mean a liquid. In science, it covers both liquids and gases because their particles can flow more or less freely. Water molecules run very freely but those in molasses are more strongly bonded and flow slower. Slow-moving, thick liquids are described as "viscous."

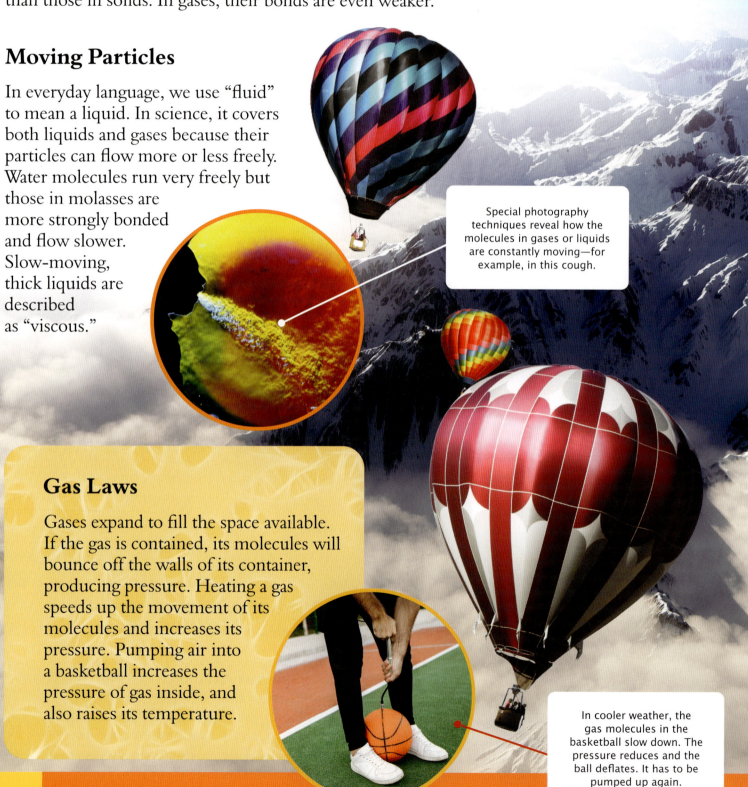

Special photography techniques reveal how the molecules in gases or liquids are constantly moving—for example, in this cough.

Gas Laws

Gases expand to fill the space available. If the gas is contained, its molecules will bounce off the walls of its container, producing pressure. Heating a gas speeds up the movement of its molecules and increases its pressure. Pumping air into a basketball increases the pressure of gas inside, and also raises its temperature.

In cooler weather, the gas molecules in the basketball slow down. The pressure reduces and the ball deflates. It has to be pumped up again.

AMAZING DISCOVERY

Scientist: Daniel Bernoulli
Discovery: Bernoulli's principle
Date: 1738
The story: Swiss mathematician Bernoulli discovered that fluids flowing at fast speeds create less pressure than slow-moving ones. The design of an aircraft wing uses this principle to create lift—its shape forces air to move quickly as it passes over its upper surface, resulting in the upward force of lift.

Hot-air balloons work because hot gases rise up through cooler ones. That's because heat moves through fluids by convection—a process where hot parts of the substance expand and flow into colder areas.

The air in the balloon is warmer and lighter than the surrounding cold air, so the balloon floats upward.

The warm air molecules expand and put pressure on the balloon's inner walls so they bulge outward.

DID YOU KNOW? Solid carbon dioxide, or "dry ice," can change from being a solid to a gas without passing through a liquid phase.

13

Elements

Elements are the most basic substances. They are made up of tiny identical particles called atoms and they cannot be split into simpler substances. Each element's atoms have unique properties.

Properties, Mixtures, and Compounds

There are 94 elements found in nature. Seventeen are non-metals. They include carbon, oxygen, and nitrogen. Most of the others are metals, apart from six metalloids—elements that sometimes behave like metals and sometimes like non-metals. Two or more elements can be mixed together without their atoms bonding. This is a mixture. They can also be combined in a chemical reaction so their atoms bond. This is a compound.

An element's melting and boiling points decide whether we find it as a solid, liquid, or gas.

Sulfur combines with other elements to form chemical compounds. When it combines with oxygen from the air it forms sulfur dioxide.

This is a mixture of the elements iron and sulfur. Their atoms have not bonded. The iron atoms are magnetic but the sulfur atoms are not. This makes them easy to separate when a magnet is near.

This is iron sulfide, a compound of iron and sulfur. Its atoms cannot be separated without destroying the compound. Iron sulfide is not magnetic, so none of its atoms is attracted to the magnet.

Pure sulfur can have many different forms, depending on the way its atoms bond to form crystals.

DID YOU KNOW? Oxygen is Earth's most common element. Most of it is locked up in rocks—it accounts for 47 percent of the mass of Earth's crust.

The crater of Ethiopia's Dallol Volcano is covered in sulfur-based chemical compounds, and different forms of pure sulfur.

Atomic Bonds

When atoms bond together, they make larger particles called molecules. The way they bond depends on how many particles called electrons they contain (see page 22). Certain numbers of electrons are more stable than others. Atoms gain or share electrons to reach these stable numbers.

A sodium (Na) atom has one electron in its outer shell. A chlorine (Cl) atom has space for one more. When they bond to form sodium chloride (salt), the sodium gives its outer electron to the chlorine.

When two chlorine (Cl) atoms bond to form a chlorine molecule, they share a pair of electrons. Now each chlorine atom's outer shell has a more stable number of electrons.

AMAZING DISCOVERY

Scientist: John Dalton
Discovery: Atomic theory
Date: 1803
The story: Dalton said that all matter is made of atoms, and that atoms are indivisible and indestructible. He observed that all atoms of a given element have the same properties. He also described how compounds are formed by a combination of two or more different kinds of atom.

15

Periodic Table

The periodic table is a way to display the properties of all 118 elements that have been discovered so far. It lets chemists predict what characteristics an element has just by knowing where it is in the table.

The shape of the periodic table reflects the arrangement of electrons inside atoms. Electrons are the subatomic particles that control chemical reactions between elements.

Periods and Groups

The elements are arranged in seven rows in order of their atomic number—the number of protons that one atom of that element has in its nucleus. Each row is called a period. Elements that share similar properties are arranged in columns called groups. There are 18 groups.

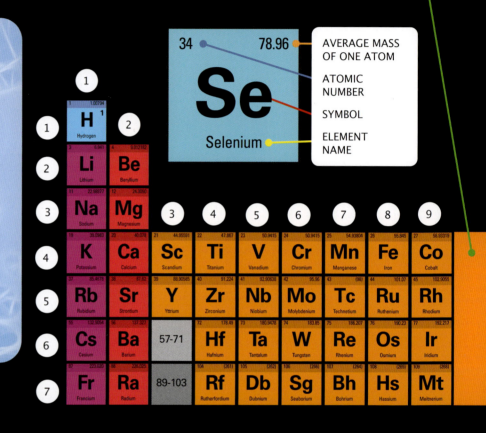

There are too many elements to fit in Period 6 of Group 3, so they are here:

There are too many elements to fit in Period 7 of Group 3, so they are here:

Atoms tend to get heavier from left to right in each period (row), and from top to bottom in each group (column).

KEY
- ALKALI METALS
- ALKALI EARTH METALS
- TRANSITION METALS
- BASIC METALS
- SEMI-METALS
- NON-METALS
- HALOGENS
- NOBLE GASES
- LANTHANIDES
- ACTINIDES

AMAZING DISCOVERY

Scientist: Dmitri Mendeleev
Discovery: The periodic table
Date: 1869
The story: Mendeleev was one of the first chemists to spot repeating patterns in the chemistry of elements with different masses. This allowed him to draw up the first periodic table and predict the discovery and properties of new elements.

All the elements in a group have the same number of electrons in their outer shell.

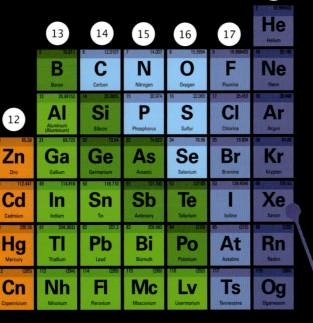

New Elements

Scientists can make new elements in special nuclear reactors. They fire extra particles at the central nuclei of the heaviest elements. More than 20 new elements have been made this way, but they are all unstable and fall apart after just a short time. This is why they are not found in nature.

The elements in Group 18 are called the noble gases and are non-reactive. They all have a full outer shell of electrons.

Physicists build new elements by nuclear fusion—the same process that combines elements inside the Sun.

DID YOU KNOW? Atoms of oganesson, the heaviest element, are so unstable that they disintegrate in less than one-thousandth of a second.

Chemistry at Work

Chemical reactions rearrange atoms and molecules to create new substances. The substances at the start of a chemical reaction are called reactants. During the reaction their particles break apart, join together, or swap places. They create a new set of substances called products.

How Reactions Work

All chemical reactions take in or give out energy, often in the form of heat, light, or sound. Combustion is an explosive reaction that produces more energy than it takes in. A catalyst is a substance that speeds up a reaction without using energy and without changing itself.

Combustion is used for fireworks. Gunpowder reacts with oxygen in the air and releases intense heat and bright light. Adding metal salts gives different effects—strontium carbonate produces red fireworks, barium chloride makes green, and calcium chloride creates orange.

Organic Chemistry

The structure of carbon atoms lets them form four strong chemical bonds—the most of any common element. As a result, carbon combines with itself and other atoms to make many different and complex molecules known as organic chemicals. These include the building blocks of life itself.

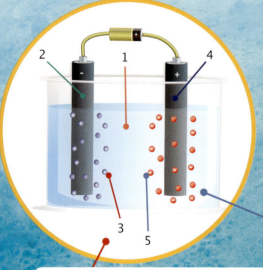

Electrolysis uses electrical energy to start a reaction. Electric current is passed through a solution that contains dissolved particles of the reactants.

1. Chemicals break apart into positively and negatively charged particles called ions.
2. The negative electrode is a source of electrons.
3. Positive ions combine with electrons to form atoms.
4. The positive electrode draws in electrons.
5. Negative ions give up electrons to form atoms.

Seawater is a chemical solution—a mixture of pure water with floating molecules of different chemical compounds.

Chemical reactions are helping to create artificial reefs. The "biorock" forms when a reaction attracts the rocky mineral calcium carbonate to objects—in this case, bikes.

The biorock process is started by electrolysis—passing a small electric current through the seawater.

Corals begin to grow on the buildup of calcium carbonate. Soon other reef creatures will come.

AMAZING DISCOVERY

Scientists: Mikhail Lomonosov and Antoine Lavoisier (left)
Discovery: Balance in reactions
Date: 1748–1774
The story: Chemists Lomonosov and Lavoisier showed that the total mass of substances present before and after a chemical reaction (including any gases released) is the same. This convinced later chemists that reactions involve rearranging fixed numbers of atoms.

DID YOU KNOW? Baking a cake involves chemical reactions, such as when heat helps the baking powder create bubbles of gas so the cake rises.

Electrical Properties

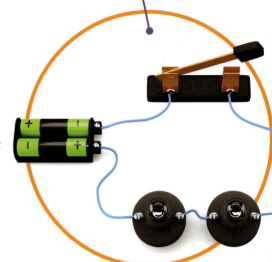

When a switch is closed to complete this circuit, electricity will flow. The current will heat the wire in the lamp so it glows.

Electricity is a form of energy. Every atom has a balance of electric charge in its particles—positive charge in its protons and negative in its electrons. If an atom gains or loses electrons, those charges are no longer balanced. The object becomes electrically charged.

Conductors, Currents, and Circuits

Any electrically charged object has an electromagnetic field around it, which attracts or repels other charged objects. Electricity flows when electrons or other charged particles move. Materials that let electricity flow through them are called electrical conductors. Most metals are good conductors. Charge flowing through a conductor is called an electric current. An electric circuit is a loop of conducting wire that carries current through components with different functions.

A maglev train hovers above the rails, lifted by the repelling force between superconductors and magnets.

The maglev's track is made of very powerful electrical conductors called superconductors.

Maglev is short for "magnetic levitation."

DID YOU KNOW? Electricity from batteries is direct current (DC)—it flows in one direction. Electric sockets provide alternating current (AC) that changes direction many times a second.

AMAZING DISCOVERY

Scientist: Hans-Christian Ørsted
Discovery: Electromagnetic fields
Date: 1820
The story: Danish physicist Ørsted discovered that switching an electric current off and on caused the needle of a nearby magnetic compass to flicker. This was the first evidence that changing currents produce changing magnetic fields around themselves.

Electricity Supply

Electricity from power stations travels along a network of cables. The current travels at high voltages (with high electrical force) to stop too much power being lost along the way. Devices called transformers step up the voltage as the electricity leaves the power station, and then they reduce it to a safe level before it enters our homes, schools, and factories.

Transformers at this electrical substation change high-voltage electricity to suitable lower voltages. Homes need low-voltage electricity, while railways need high voltage.

Coils of conducting wire in the track create an electromagnetic field that pushes the train forward.

Maglev trains like this one in Shanghai can reach speeds of up to 430 kph (267 mph).

Inside the Atom

Atoms are the building blocks of everyday matter, and they are the smallest amount of an individual element that can exist. But each atom is made up of even smaller particles. Together, these subatomic particles—protons, neutrons, and electrons—create the atom's overall structure.

Particle Properties

Subatomic particles have particular features. Protons have almost as much mass as a hydrogen atom and carry a positive electric charge. Neutrons have a similar mass but no electric charge. Electrons have much less mass than the other particles and carry a negative electric charge equal and opposite to the proton's charge.

This amazing photograph shows tracks left behind by subatomic particles as they move through fluid. Scientists smash atoms together to create subatomic particles.

The positive charge of protons (red) in an atom's nucleus is usually balanced by the negative charge of electrons (blue) orbiting around it. The atom's mass comes from a combination of protons and neutrons (white).

Particles follow different paths depending on their mass and electric charge.

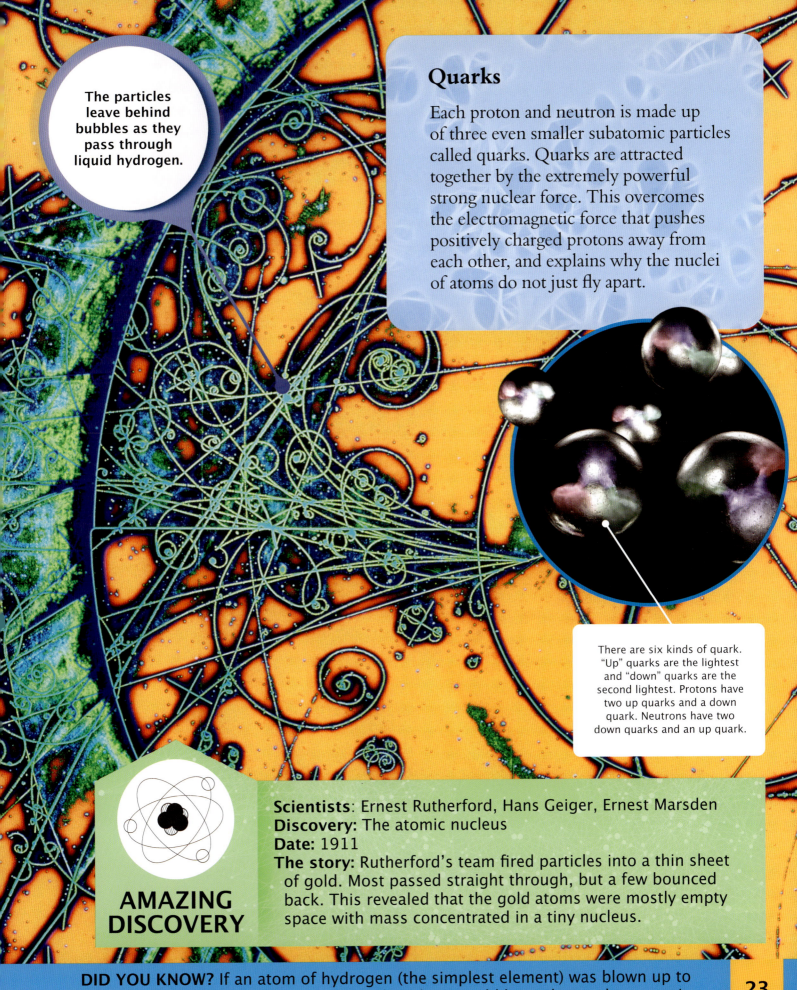

The particles leave behind bubbles as they pass through liquid hydrogen.

Quarks

Each proton and neutron is made up of three even smaller subatomic particles called quarks. Quarks are attracted together by the extremely powerful strong nuclear force. This overcomes the electromagnetic force that pushes positively charged protons away from each other, and explains why the nuclei of atoms do not just fly apart.

There are six kinds of quark. "Up" quarks are the lightest and "down" quarks are the second lightest. Protons have two up quarks and a down quark. Neutrons have two down quarks and an up quark.

AMAZING DISCOVERY

Scientists: Ernest Rutherford, Hans Geiger, Ernest Marsden
Discovery: The atomic nucleus
Date: 1911
The story: Rutherford's team fired particles into a thin sheet of gold. Most passed straight through, but a few bounced back. This revealed that the gold atoms were mostly empty space with mass concentrated in a tiny nucleus.

DID YOU KNOW? If an atom of hydrogen (the simplest element) was blown up to the size of a football stadium, its central nucleus would be no larger than a pea!

CHAPTER 2: FORCES AND ENERGY

Physics is Everywhere

> Physics tells us that the velocity or speed of the rocket will depend on its mass.

Physics is the science that explains the workings of everything in the Universe, from the tiniest to the largest scales. Its rules guide all the other branches of science, and we can see them at work everywhere in the world around us.

Understanding of physics lets us build amazing machines. We can achieve tasks as complex as launching rockets into space.

Forces and Work

We're all influenced by forces. Gravity pulls things toward the ground, while friction slows objects down when they rub together. Without forces, nothing in the Universe would ever change. A force can alter an object's speed, change its direction, or even change its shape. When a force applied to an object moves the object, that is called work. Work changes energy from one form to another or transfers energy from one object to another.

The man uses a pulling force to move the basket forward. The chemical energy in his body changes into kinetic, or movement, energy.

Other forces work on the basket, too: friction (resistance from the ground) and gravity (see pages 28–29).

AMAZING DISCOVERY

Scientist: Galileo Galilei
Discovery: Principle of relativity
Date: 1632
The story: Italian scientist Galileo's principle of relativity says it is not possible to tell whether you are on a body moving at a constant speed or a body that's not moving at all. He was thinking about whether the Earth revolves around the Sun or the Sun around the Earth.

The speed needed to escape Earth's gravity is called escape velocity. It is about 40,270 kph (25,020 mph).

The rocket speeds up as long as the force pushing it up (thrust) is greater than the forces pulling it down (gravity and drag).

Made to Measure

Forces are measured in units called newtons. When we hold a 1-kg (2.2-lb) bag of sugar, we feel a downward force of almost 10 newtons thanks to the pull of gravity. Work is measured in joules. When a force of 1 newton moves an object through 1 m (3.3 ft), the work completed is 1 joule.

To work out the overall forward force on this speedboat, take away the drag or friction force created by pushing through the water from the thrust force made by the engine.

DID YOU KNOW? At take off, the Space Shuttle's main engines produced 1.86 million newtons of force to lift the spacecraft against the pull of Earth's gravity.

Newton's Laws of Motion

Scientist Isaac Newton laid the foundations of modern physics with three laws of motion that he identified in the late 1600s. These laws describe the way that objects move, how they react to each other, and how forces can affect their motion.

First and Second Laws

Newton's first law says that objects will always stay still or keep moving with the same velocity (speed in one direction) unless they are affected by a force. His second law states that the bigger that force on the object, the greater the change in its momentum. Momentum is an object's mass times its velocity.

When the downward force of gravity acts on the rollercoaster, it changes its momentum.

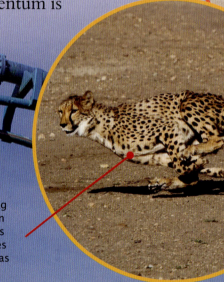

This cheetah weighs about 74 kg (163 lb), but the bull weighs ten times as much. The cheetah has a top speed or velocity five times faster than the bull, but it still has only half of its momentum.

AMAZING DISCOVERY

Scientist: Isaac Newton
Discovery: Laws of motion
Date: 1679–1687
The story: Philosopher Newton wanted to understand the elongated orbits of comets around the Sun. He realized they were obeying simple laws of motion—they were being influenced by the powerful force of the Sun's gravity.

According to Newton's first law, an object stays as it is unless a force acts on it. The force that gets the rollercoaster started is provided by the mechanical chain that pulls it to its first high point.

The downward stretches of the rollercoaster ride demonstrate Newton's second law. The mass of the cars and riders combines with the force of gravity to make the cars speed up down the track.

As the riders push down on their seats, the seats push back at them in an equal and opposite reaction.

Action and Reaction

Newton's third law of motion is that an object reacts to the force acting on it. The force of this reaction is equal to the original force, but in the opposite direction. If the masses of the two objects are the same, they push away from each other at the same velocity.

When a heavy bat applies force to a lightweight ball, it boosts the ball to high velocity. The bat recoils with a much lower velocity. The velocities aren't equal because the bat and ball have different masses.

DID YOU KNOW? Newton's second law explains why objects of different masses fall at the same rate—gravity makes them speed up at a rate of 9.8 m (32.2 ft) per second.

Gravity

Gravity pulls skydivers down. When their parachutes open, the force of friction will slow them down.

Gravity is the force that keeps our planet going around the Sun and keeps our feet on the ground. It is a force of attraction between objects with mass. Between small masses, it is too weak to notice. Between larger objects, gravity is so powerful that it can stretch across space and affect the shape of the Universe.

The Everyday Force

Isaac Newton was the first person to suggest that the same force that makes an apple fall from a tree also keeps the Moon in orbit around the Earth. He noticed that objects with a larger mass had more gravitational pull. If two objects both have large mass, then the force between them is even stronger. However, the strength of an object's gravity gradually gets weaker as you move farther away.

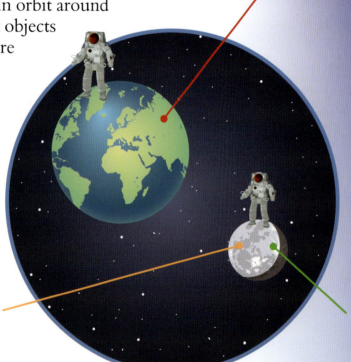

EARTH

MOON

The Moon has a lower mass and smaller size than Earth. Its gravity is just one-sixth of Earth's, so astronauts can jump around there despite their bulky spacesuits.

Gravity is pulling the aircraft toward the Earth, but its wings create a lifting force to stop it falling.

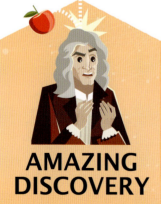

AMAZING DISCOVERY

Scientists: Robert Hooke and Isaac Newton (left)
Discovery: Universal gravitation
Date: 1666–1687
The story: Hooke, Newton's rival, was the first to suggest that all massive objects produce a gravitational field that stretches into space. Newton showed that this could explain the curving orbits of planets.

Earth acts as if all its mass is at its core because it is a sphere. Its gravity pulls the skydivers toward its core.

Weightlessness

Astronauts in orbit experience weightlessness. It is not because there is no gravity on a space station. They experience almost the same pull of gravity toward Earth as we do. The difference is that everything else around them is moving at the same rate—the space station's orbital velocity, or the speed it is moving around the Earth.

Mass and weight are not the same. The skydiver's mass is how much matter their body contains. Their weight is a measure of the force of gravity acting on that mass.

This astronaut and the contents of the space station are not floating—they are falling. The station's orbital speed means it falls *around* the Earth instead of *down* to it.

Newton's second law (pages 26–27) tells us that two skydivers together fall at the same rate as one skydiver.

DID YOU KNOW? Objects called black holes have such strong gravity that nothing can ever move fast enough to escape them—not even light!

Waves

A wave is a disturbance that transfers energy or movement in a particular direction. Waves are everywhere in physics. The most familiar types in everyday life are water and sound waves.

Measuring Waves

There are three ways to measure a wave: wavelength, frequency, and amplitude. Wavelength is the distance from one peak of the wave disturbance to the next. Frequency is the number of peaks passing a single point each second. A wave's overall speed is equal to its wavelength times its frequency. Amplitude is the strength of the wave disturbance itself.

Ripples spread out from the spot where the stone hit the water. These are waves and they are carrying energy. Ocean waves carry energy, too.

When two waves meet, their effects add up. The waves get stronger where they line up neatly, but they disappear where they don't—an effect called interference.

The ripples are evenly spaced. Each one is a separate, circular wavefront.

AMAZING DISCOVERY

Scientist: Christiaan Huygens
Discovery: Huygens' principle
Date: 1678
The story: Dutch mathematician Huygens was the first person to describe how light moves in the form of waves. He also suggested that, at every point on the front of the light wave, tiny wavelets spread out in all directions.

These water waves are transverse. They're carrying energy across the surface as they move up and down.

Wave Properties

There are two main types of wave: transverse and longitudinal. Each has a wavelength, frequency, and amplitude, but each moves in a different way. Nearly all waves need a material to carry them, a substance called a medium.

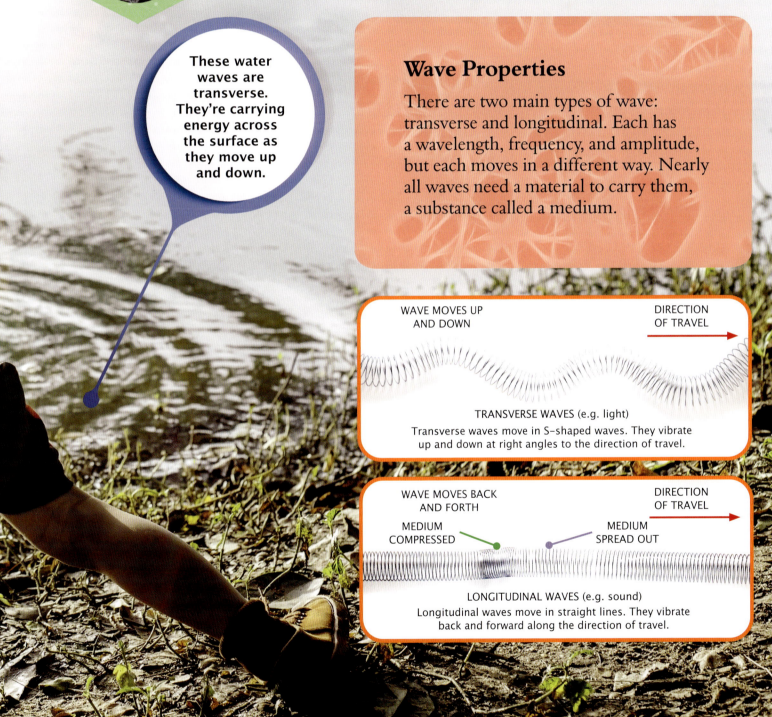

WAVE MOVES UP AND DOWN — DIRECTION OF TRAVEL
TRANSVERSE WAVES (e.g. light)
Transverse waves move in S-shaped waves. They vibrate up and down at right angles to the direction of travel.

WAVE MOVES BACK AND FORTH — DIRECTION OF TRAVEL
MEDIUM COMPRESSED — MEDIUM SPREAD OUT
LONGITUDINAL WAVES (e.g. sound)
Longitudinal waves move in straight lines. They vibrate back and forward along the direction of travel.

DID YOU KNOW? Sound, a longitudinal wave, travels 343 m (1,125 ft) per second at 20°C (68°F). Light waves, which are transverse, travel almost a million times faster.

Heat and Energy

Energy is the ability to do work and make things happen. Energy cannot be created or destroyed, but it is always changing from one form to another. Heat is a form of energy that makes the individual atoms in a material vibrate or jostle around. Other types of energy often get "lost" as heat and then cannot be recovered.

Forms of Energy

Energy can take many forms. Moving objects have kinetic energy. Potential energy is energy that is stored and ready to be used to do work in the future. Chemical energy is released when bonds form in a chemical reaction (see page 18).

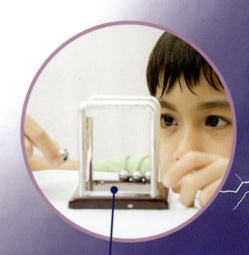

This is a Newton's cradle. The three balls on the right have no potential energy and no kinetic energy. The ball on the left has potential energy, because it has been lifted, but no kinetic energy. When the boy releases the ball, it will move and have kinetic energy.

Heat Transfer

There are three main ways that heat energy moves from one place to another. Conduction happens in solids (see page 11). The energy travels from one atom to the next. Metals conduct heat better than wood. Convection happens in liquids and gases. It is a circular movement where hot areas expand and flow into cooler ones. Heat also travels as infrared (see page 38).

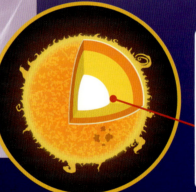

The Sun moves heat in all three ways. Conduction takes the energy from atom to atom. Convection makes hotter particles expand and rise to take the place of ones with less energy. Radiation carries the heat away into space.

AMAZING DISCOVERY

Scientists: Sadi Carnot and others
Discovery: Entropy
Date: 1824–1897
The story: In the 1800s engineers and physicists discovered that it is impossible to move energy from one form to another without losing some, often as heat. The lost energy can no longer do useful work, a state called entropy.

A single flash of lightning releases around five billion joules of energy.

Lightning heats the surrounding air to temperatures of more than 27,000°C (48,632°F).

A lightning strike has four main types of energy: electrical energy, heat, light, and sound.

DID YOU KNOW? At −273.15°C (−459.67°F), all atoms stop moving and have no kinetic energy. This is the lowest possible temperature and is called absolute zero.

Electricity and Magnetism

The flow of electric current and a magnet's ability to pick up metal objects may look like very different things, but they're both aspects of a single force—electromagnetism. They both generate force fields that attract objects or push them away.

Electromagnetism at Work

Any object with electric charge generates an electromagnetic field around it, which attracts objects with the opposite charge, and repels those with the same charge. A changing electromagnetic field, meanwhile, can cause an electric current to move through a conducting material.

COILED WIRE

IRON CORE

In this simple electromagnet, electric current flows through a coiled wire to produce the magnetic field. The iron core in the middle of the coil makes the magnetic force more powerful.

AMAZING DISCOVERY

Scientist: Michael Faraday
Discovery: Electromagnetic induction
Date: 1831
The story: Faraday discovered induction while experimenting with wire coils on opposite sides of an iron ring. Passing current through one coil briefly magnetized the iron, and the changing magnetic field caused a brief current to flow in the other coil.

DID YOU KNOW? Every few hundred thousand years, the direction of Earth's magnetic field reverses completely.

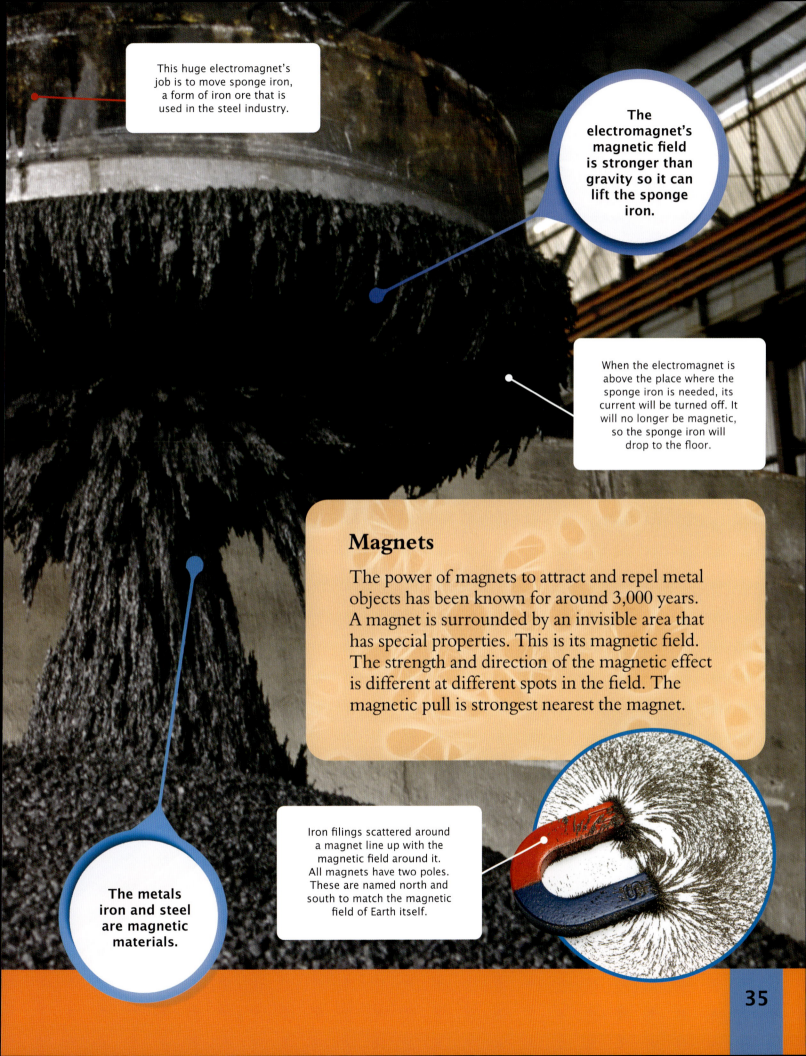

This huge electromagnet's job is to move sponge iron, a form of iron ore that is used in the steel industry.

The electromagnet's magnetic field is stronger than gravity so it can lift the sponge iron.

When the electromagnet is above the place where the sponge iron is needed, its current will be turned off. It will no longer be magnetic, so the sponge iron will drop to the floor.

Magnets

The power of magnets to attract and repel metal objects has been known for around 3,000 years. A magnet is surrounded by an invisible area that has special properties. This is its magnetic field. The strength and direction of the magnetic effect is different at different spots in the field. The magnetic pull is strongest nearest the magnet.

The metals iron and steel are magnetic materials.

Iron filings scattered around a magnet line up with the magnetic field around it. All magnets have two poles. These are named north and south to match the magnetic field of Earth itself.

35

Secrets of Light

Light is a form of energy that travels as a series of tiny waves. Most of our light comes from the Sun or from electric lights. It moves extremely fast—in fact, nothing in the Universe can travel faster than the speed of light.

Seeing Light

Light is a mix of wavelengths, which our eyes see as different hues. Red light has the longest wavelengths, and blue and violet have the shortest. A red T-shirt looks red because dye molecules in the fabric absorb light from the blue-violet end of the spectrum, and only red light is reflecting back.

At night, when light from the Sun does not reach us, we use artificial electric lighting. The first electric street lights were invented in 1875.

What we see as white light is made up of many hues. When white light passes through a prism, we can see this visible spectrum, which has blue and red at opposite ends.

AMAZING DISCOVERY

Scientist: Isaac Newton
Discovery: The spectrum of visible light
Date: 1672
The story: Newton split a beam of sunlight into a spectrum (rainbow) using a prism, and then he brought that spectrum back together to form white light. He showed for the first time that the prism was not somehow "adding" the different hues to light.

DID YOU KNOW? Light travels at 299,793 km (186,000 miles) per second—that's fast enough to reach the Moon in around 1.3 seconds.

Tricks with Light

Light travels in a straight line from its source and bounces off objects (which lets us see them). Microscopes and telescopes use lenses to refract (bend) light and mirrors to reflect it. They can gather more light than our eyes alone, and they also produce magnified images.

A magnifying glass bends the paths of light rays coming from the words. It creates a closer and larger virtual version of the words.

The light is behind this tree, which means the area in front of the tree will be in a shadow.

Neon lights are tubes containing neon, an element that is a gas. When electricity passes through the gas, it gives off light in a particular hue.

Lights make our cities safer, but they also stop us from being able to see the night sky.

Invisible Rays

Visible light is just one type of electromagnetic radiation. It has a narrow range of wavelengths that our eyes can detect. Beyond it, there are other forms of radiation that are invisible to us. They carry energy from objects much hotter or colder than those that give off visible light.

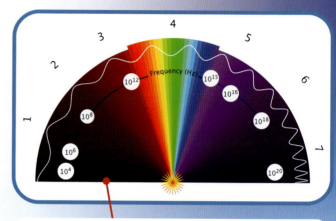

Electromagnetic Spectrum

Radio waves have the longest wavelengths and come from the coolest, lowest-energy objects. We use them for broadcasting and for radio telescopes. Microwaves are next along the spectrum. We use them to send cellphone signals. Infrared radiation is produced by anything warm. Next comes visible light. Finally there are ultraviolet (UV) radiation, X-rays, and super-energetic, short-wavelength gamma rays.

The different types of radiation are divided into a spectrum from long waves that carry little energy to short ones that carry lots. Visible light is just a small part of this electromagnetic spectrum.

RADIATION TYPES
1. RADIO WAVE
2. MICROWAVE
3. INFRARED
4. VISIBLE LIGHT
5. ULTRAVIOLET (UV)
6. X-RAY
7. GAMMA RAY

Rays in Action

The view from Earth telescopes is distorted by our atmosphere, which is why stars twinkle. Space telescopes can give astronomers a clearer view. As well as visible rays, they collect invisible rays, such as infrared, X-rays, and gamma rays from stars and other objects.

Infrared telescopes use protective shields to block the Sun, and they use cold gas to cool their instruments. This lets them see weak rays coming from cool dust and gas in space.

DID YOU KNOW? Radio waves have the lowest frequency in the electromagnetic spectrum and the longest wavelengths—more than 100 km (62 miles).

AMAZING DISCOVERY

Scientist: William Herschel
Discovery: Infrared radiation
Date: 1800
The story: Astronomer Herschel passed light through a prism and took the temperature of each hue. Just past the red part of the spectrum, where there was no visible light, he found the temperature was even higher. He realized there must be a type of light there that we cannot see. He called it infrared.

Radiation from the Sun covers the whole electromagnetic spectrum, from radio waves to gamma rays.

The body produces heat that radiates out as infrared. Protective clothing stops this heat from escaping into the atmosphere and being lost.

Goggles shield this mountaineer's eyes from harmful UV radiation from the Sun.

Einstein's Universe

Newton's laws of gravity and motion describe most of physics in the everyday world, but they break down in some extreme situations. In the early 1900s, Albert Einstein came up with an idea called relativity that offered a more accurate picture of how the Universe really works.

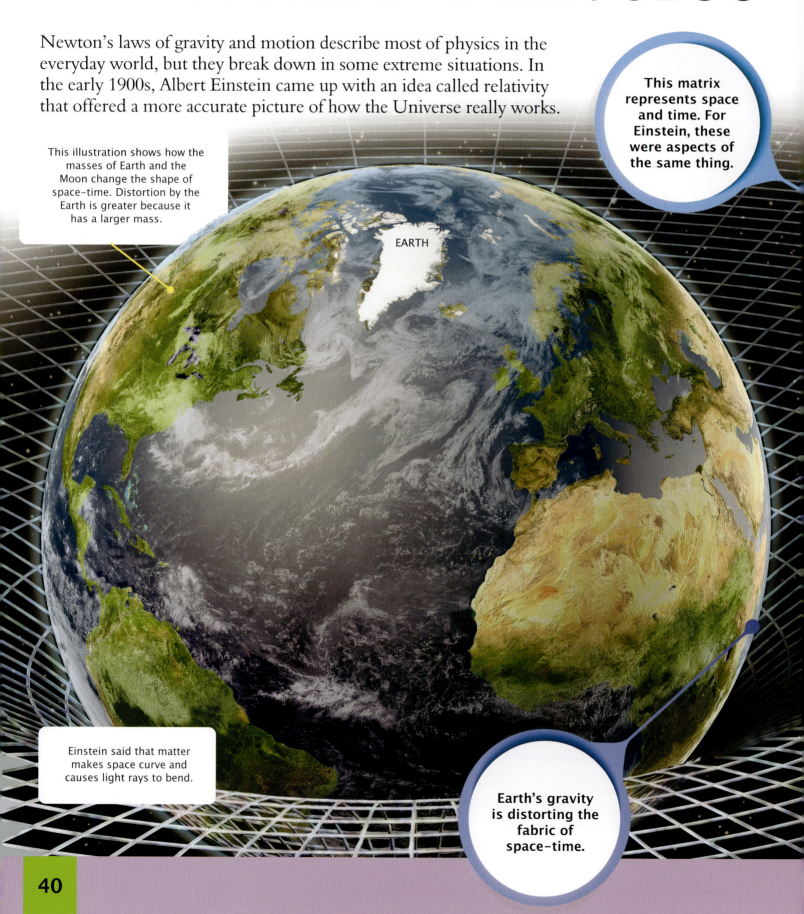

This illustration shows how the masses of Earth and the Moon change the shape of space-time. Distortion by the Earth is greater because it has a larger mass.

This matrix represents space and time. For Einstein, these were aspects of the same thing.

EARTH

Einstein said that matter makes space curve and causes light rays to bend.

Earth's gravity is distorting the fabric of space-time.

Special and General Relativity

Einstein's special theory of relativity (1905) describes how physics changes when objects travel at speeds close to the speed of light. His general theory (1915) explains how physics behaves in situations with extreme gravity. Einstein explained that space has a structure that can be warped out of shape by large masses.

German-born Einstein was just 26 years old when he published his special theory of relativity.

MOON

Distortions of space-time caused by large masses such as Earth hold smaller ones like the Moon in orbit around them.

Proofs of Relativity

The ideas of special and general relativity have been proved in many experiments. Special relativity causes clocks carried on fast-moving satellites to run slower than those that remain on Earth. General relativity explains how large masses can deflect the path of light that passes close to them.

Blue light from a distant galaxy has its path changed as it passes nearer galaxies (yellow) that are bending space around them. The light reaches Earth as a series of distorted images.

AMAZING DISCOVERY

Scientist: Arthur Eddington
Discovery: Gravitational lensing
Date: 1919
The story: By photographing a total solar eclipse (when the Moon briefly hides the disc of the Sun), Eddington showed how the Sun's gravity deflects the path of starlight, proving Einstein's theory of general relativity.

DID YOU KNOW? Astronauts on a six-month mission to the *International Space Station* age about 0.007 seconds less than if they stayed on Earth because of their orbital speed.

CHAPTER 3: SPACE

The Solar System

Earth is the third of eight planets orbiting our local star, the Sun. The part of space caught in the Sun's pull is called the Solar System. As well as the planets, it contains countless smaller worlds—rocky asteroids in the inner solar system and frozen comets and ice dwarf planets farther out.

The Planets

Mercury, Venus, Earth, and Mars are closest to the Sun. Earth is the largest of these rocky planets. Farther out lie the giant planets—Jupiter (the biggest of all), Saturn, Uranus, and Neptune. Each of the giant planets has rings and a family of moons.

NEPTUNE

URANUS

Saturn's bright ring system is made up of countless icy fragments in orbit around it.

The Sun is a massive, fiery ball of gas, about 1.4 million km (870,000 miles) across. It contains 99.8 percent of the Solar System's mass, and it provides heat and light to all of the planets.

SOLAR SYSTEM PROFILE

Planets: Eight
Radius of orbit of most distant planet, Neptune:
 4.5 billion km (2.8 billion miles)
Radius of heliosphere:
 18 billion km (11.2 billion miles)
Region ruled by Sun's gravity:
 Four light-years across

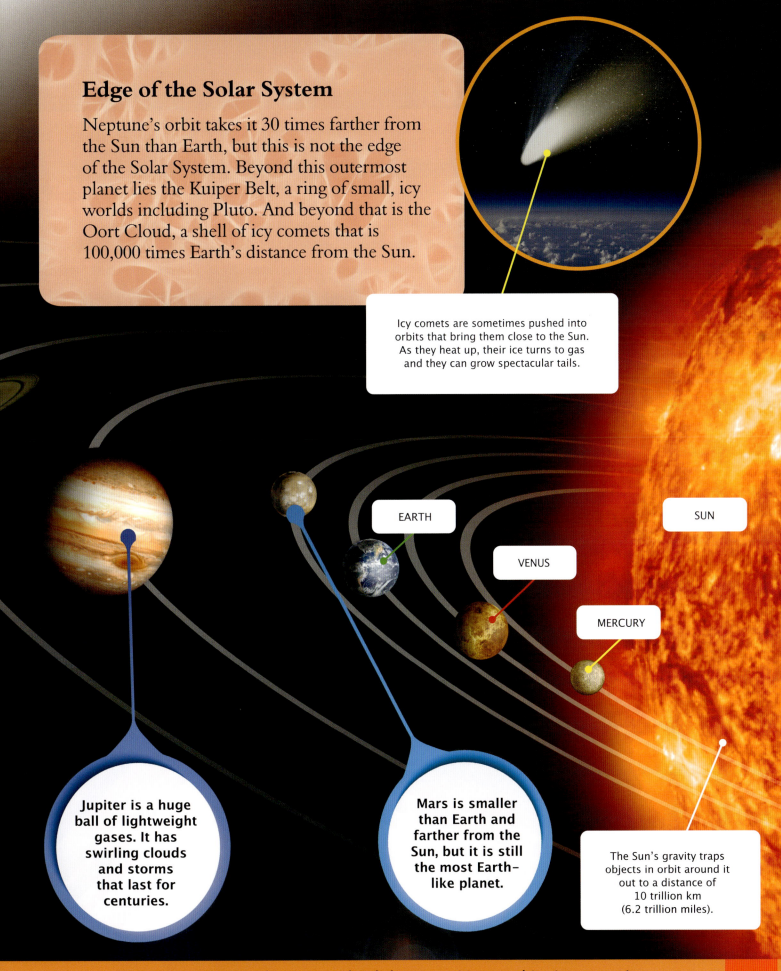

Edge of the Solar System

Neptune's orbit takes it 30 times farther from the Sun than Earth, but this is not the edge of the Solar System. Beyond this outermost planet lies the Kuiper Belt, a ring of small, icy worlds including Pluto. And beyond that is the Oort Cloud, a shell of icy comets that is 100,000 times Earth's distance from the Sun.

Icy comets are sometimes pushed into orbits that bring them close to the Sun. As they heat up, their ice turns to gas and they can grow spectacular tails.

EARTH

SUN

VENUS

MERCURY

Jupiter is a huge ball of lightweight gases. It has swirling clouds and storms that last for centuries.

Mars is smaller than Earth and farther from the Sun, but it is still the most Earth-like planet.

The Sun's gravity traps objects in orbit around it out to a distance of 10 trillion km (6.2 trillion miles).

DID YOU KNOW? The Asteroid Belt between Mars and Jupiter contains about 1.5 million space rocks that are bigger than 1 km (0.6 miles) across.

The Sun

Our Sun is a fairly average, middle-aged star. It doesn't stand out, compared to other stars we know, but the heat, light, and streams of particles it pours out across the Solar System set the conditions on Earth and all the other planets.

Solar Features

The Sun's surface is made up of extremely hot gas, with a temperature of around 5,500°C (9,900°F). Hot gas from inside the Sun rises to the surface, cools down by releasing light, and then sinks back toward the core. A nonstop stream of particles is also released from the surface, forming a solar wind that blows across the Solar System.

Some particles are led toward Earth's poles, creating the aurorae, or northern and southern lights.

Earth's magnetic field shields it from the passing solar wind.

The Solar Cycle

Some features on the Sun come and go over time. Dark areas called sunspots form and then disappear, and so do huge loops of gas, called prominences, that rise high above the Sun. Most impressive of all are outbursts called solar flares, which release huge amounts of radiation (energy) and hot gas. All this activity repeats itself every 11 years because of changes in the Sun's magnetic field.

Never look directly at the Sun—it's so bright that you risk damaging your eyes. Astronomers study it with special telescopes.

Prominences are created when gas flows along loops of magnetic field that stick out of the Sun's surface. There is usually a sunspot group at each end.

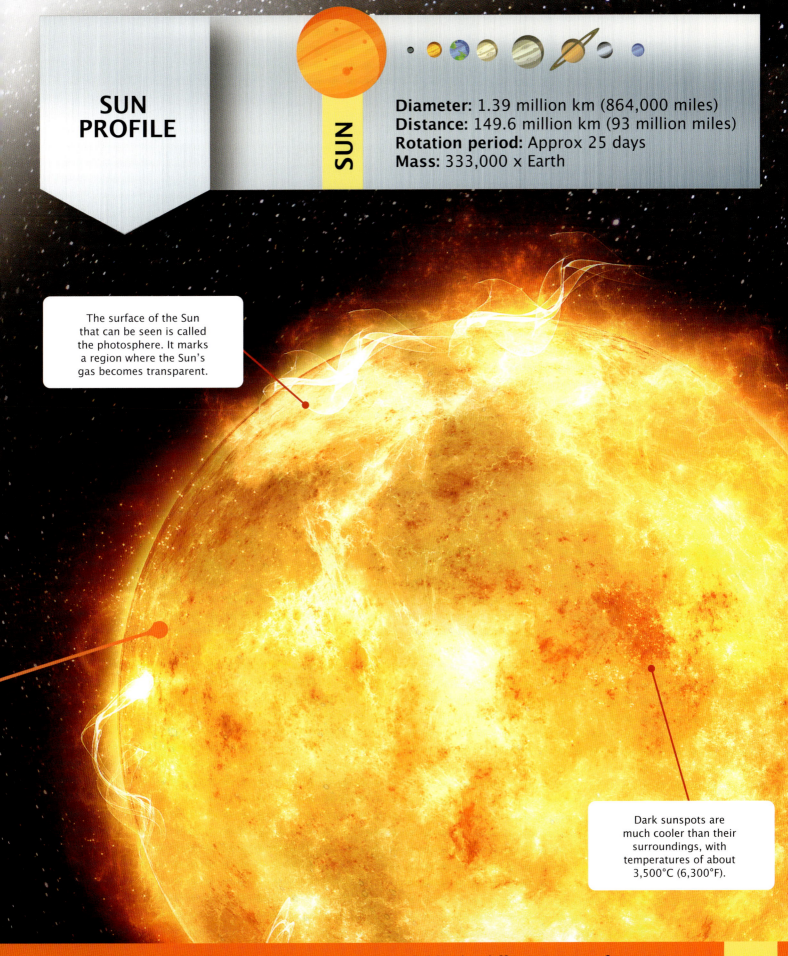

SUN PROFILE

SUN

Diameter: 1.39 million km (864,000 miles)
Distance: 149.6 million km (93 million miles)
Rotation period: Approx 25 days
Mass: 333,000 x Earth

The surface of the Sun that can be seen is called the photosphere. It marks a region where the Sun's gas becomes transparent.

Dark sunspots are much cooler than their surroundings, with temperatures of about 3,500°C (6,300°F).

DID YOU KNOW? Because the Sun is not a solid body, different parts of it rotate (spin around) at different rates—its equator spins faster than the polar regions.

Mercury and Venus

Two scorching-hot rocky planets orbit closer to the Sun than Earth. Venus is almost the same size as Earth but with a very different atmosphere. Mercury is a tiny world much like our Moon, which speeds around the Sun in just 88 days.

Roasted Surfaces

Temperatures on both Mercury and Venus reach more than 430°C (800°F), but Venus is actually hotter than Mercury although it is farther from the Sun. That is because Venus's atmosphere traps heat. This means that the temperature is about 460°C (860°F) both day and night. Mercury has no atmosphere, so temperatures on its night side can drop to -170°C (-280°F).

Mercury's surface has many craters (holes) like our Moon. This picture has been treated to reveal surface features.

This 3D view shows a Venusian volcano called Maat Mons.

Visiting Venus

Venus's atmosphere is 100 times thicker than Earth's, and it is mostly made up of toxic carbon dioxide with sulfuric acid rain. Any human trying to land there would be choked, crushed, and cooked at the same time. Even heavily shielded robot space probes have lasted only for a few minutes. Astronomers have mapped Venus's landscape without landing there, using radar beams that pass through the clouds and bounce back from the surface to show its features.

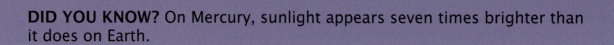

DID YOU KNOW? On Mercury, sunlight appears seven times brighter than it does on Earth.

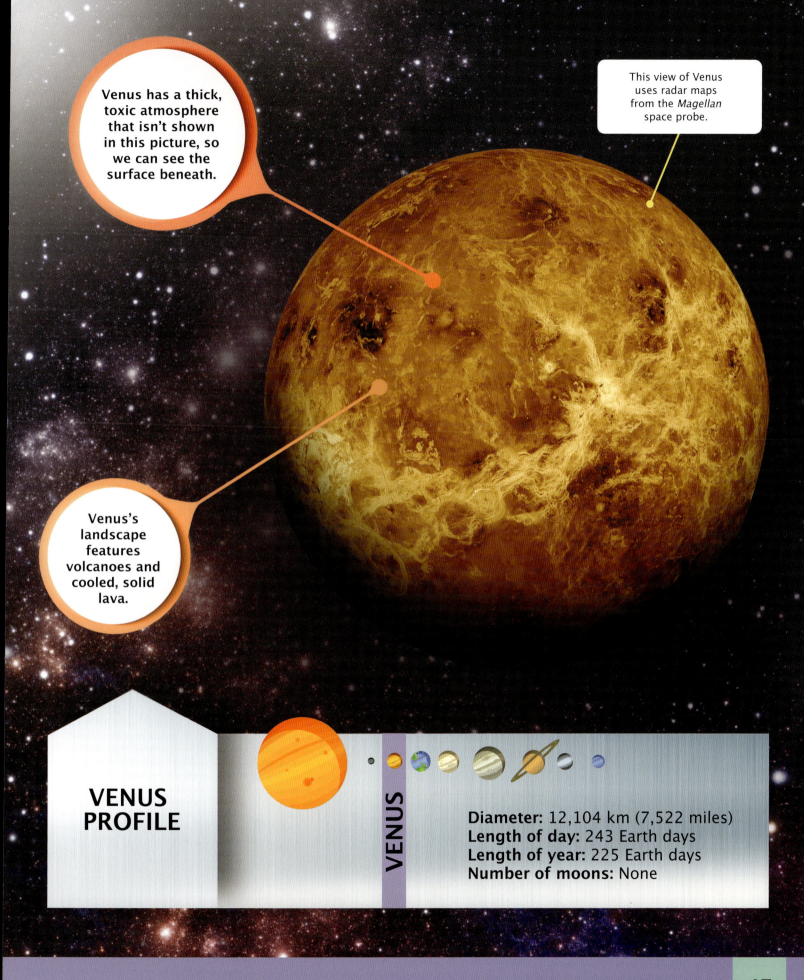

Venus has a thick, toxic atmosphere that isn't shown in this picture, so we can see the surface beneath.

This view of Venus uses radar maps from the *Magellan* space probe.

Venus's landscape features volcanoes and cooled, solid lava.

VENUS PROFILE

VENUS

Diameter: 12,104 km (7,522 miles)
Length of day: 243 Earth days
Length of year: 225 Earth days
Number of moons: None

Earth and Moon

Earth is not alone on its journey through space. A rocky satellite world we call the Moon orbits our planet every 27.3 days. At 3,474 km (2,160 miles) across, the Moon is a quarter of Earth's diameter. It is up to 400,000 km (248,548 miles) away—close enough to have a great influence on our planet.

A Lifeless World

The Moon's small size and gravity mean it cannot hold onto an atmosphere, and it has no life, surface water, or tectonic plates (see page 98). Its main features are bright highlands and dark, smooth "seas" of solidified lava from ancient volcanoes. The highlands are covered in craters from when the Moon was bombarded by space rocks early in its history.

Volcanic activity ended on the Moon about 3 billion years ago. Since then, only a few new craters have appeared from asteroid impacts.

Dust thrown out during asteroid impacts forms bright streaks across the surface.

The Moon does not have its own light—it reflects the Sun's. As it orbits us, we see different amounts of the lit-up side and it seems to change shape. The different shapes are called the phases of the Moon.

EARTH PROFILE

EARTH

Diameter: 12,742 km (7,918 miles)
Length of day: 23 h 56 m
Length of year: 365.25 days
Number of moons: One

DID YOU KNOW? Energy from Earth's tides makes the Moon move about 3.8 cm (1.5 in) farther away from us each year.

The Moon has no air to protect it. Temperatures range from 127°C (260°F) in sunlight to –173°C (–280°F) in darkness.

Darker "seas" show where volcanic lava filled huge craters on the Moon's surface.

Time and Tide

The Moon's gravity pulls on the near side of Earth. This creates bulges in Earth's oceans directly beneath, and opposite, the Moon. As Earth rotates each day under these bulges, the seas rise and fall.

Tidal bulges cancel each other out, resulting in weak tides.

Tidal bulges join together, resulting in especially strong tides.

The Sun's gravity creates its own tidal bulge. It can either work against the Moon's pull (1) or with it (2).

49

Mars

The outermost rocky planet is also the one most like Earth. Mars today is a cold desert with a thin, toxic atmosphere, but the newest discoveries have shown that it used to be much more welcoming, and that it might be again in the future.

Desert Planet?

Mars owes its famous red sands to large amounts of iron oxide, better known as rust. But sand dunes are only one part of the varied Martian landscape. Mars is also home to the largest volcano in the Solar System (Olympus Mons, which is currently not active), and the deepest canyon, a huge crack in the surface called the Mariner Valley.

Rocks reveal traces of past water.

NASA's Curiosity rover has covered more than 24 km (15 miles) of the Martian surface.

Martian Explorers

Mars is the most explored of all the other planets in the Solar System. Many countries have sent space probes to map it from orbit, while NASA has landed wheeled rovers on the surface. Together, the different space agencies have shown that large amounts of water used to flow on Mars (it is now locked away as ice in the upper layers of soil). Is it possible there used to be life on this planet?

MARS PROFILE

Diameter: 6,789 km (4,217 miles)
Length of day: 24 h 37 m
Length of year: 1.88 Earth years
Number of moons: Two

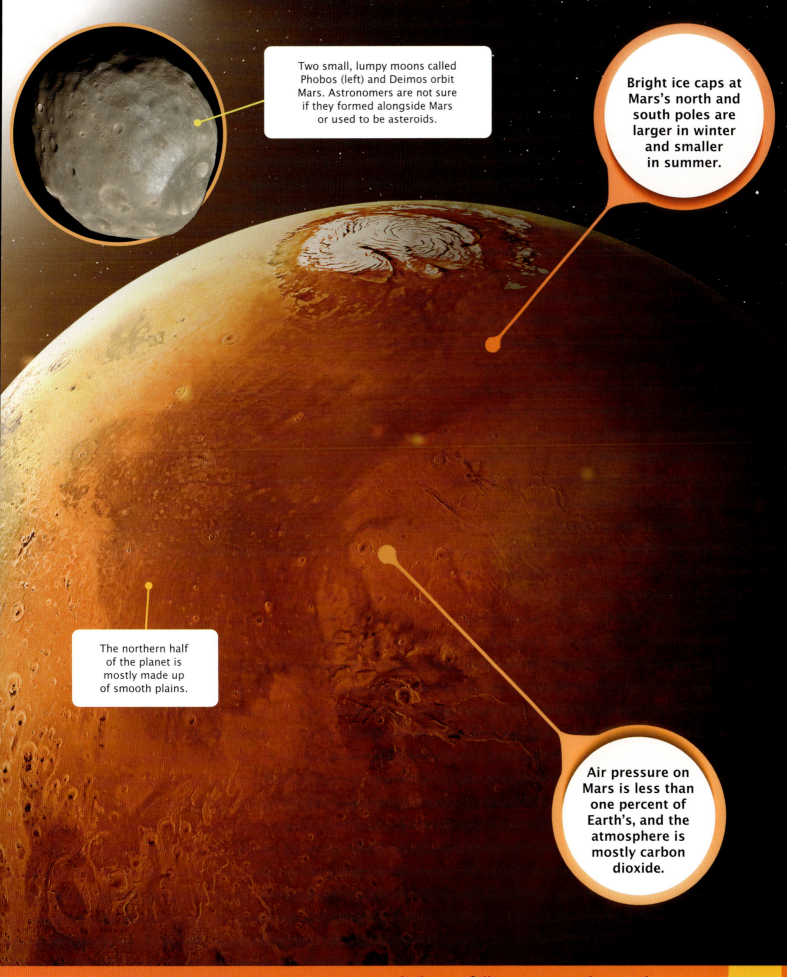

Two small, lumpy moons called Phobos (left) and Deimos orbit Mars. Astronomers are not sure if they formed alongside Mars or used to be asteroids.

Bright ice caps at Mars's north and south poles are larger in winter and smaller in summer.

The northern half of the planet is mostly made up of smooth plains.

Air pressure on Mars is less than one percent of Earth's, and the atmosphere is mostly carbon dioxide.

DID YOU KNOW? The Martian moon Phobos is falling in a spiral toward the planet. It will smash into it about 50 million years from now.

The Asteroid Belt

Between the orbits of Mars and Jupiter lies a wide region of space where most of the Solar System's asteroids orbit. Astronomers think there could be a few hundred millon of these rocky and icy worlds, but they are so spread out that it is easy to pass through the belt.

Staying Small

The belt is a region where Jupiter's strong gravity stops small objects grouping together to form bigger ones, so no planet could ever form here. When asteroids do crash into each other, they break into smaller objects. The orbits of these objects spread out to form asteroid "families."

This artist's impression (picture) shows the asteroids much more tightly packed than they are in reality.

Ceres's smooth landscape suggests an icy crust.

Ceres

The largest object in the belt, Ceres, is only one third the diameter of Earth's Moon. It is a dwarf plant, large enough for its gravity to pull it into a ball, but not large enough to clear the surrounding area. Experts think there could be a layer of salty water beneath the solid crust. The bright patches in the middle of craters may be caused by this water rising to the surface.

DWARF PLANET PROFILE

Name: Ceres
Diameter: 945 km (587 miles)
Length of day: 0.38 Earth days
Length of year: 4.6 Earth years
Mass: 0.00015 Earths

ASTEROID BELT

52

Many asteroids contain huge amounts of metal. In the future, robot missions may be sent to mine them.

Vesta is the second biggest asteroid, with a huge crater at its south pole.

Most asteroids are too small for gravity to have pulled them into a spherical (ball-like) shape.

DID YOU KNOW? Jupiter's gravity kicks asteroids out of some parts of the asteroid belt, sometimes into orbits that come closer to Earth.

Jupiter

Named after the ruler of the Roman gods, Jupiter is the largest planet in our Solar System. This gas giant is the fifth planet, separated from the four inner, rocky planets by the Asteroid Belt. Ninety percent of Jupiter's atmosphere is hydrogen gas. Most of the rest is helium.

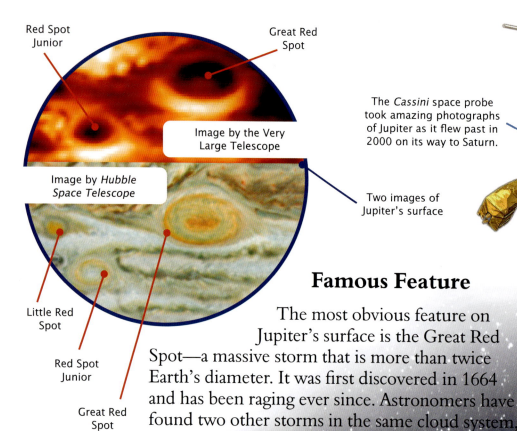

Red Spot Junior
Great Red Spot
Image by the Very Large Telescope
Image by *Hubble Space Telescope*
Little Red Spot
Red Spot Junior
Great Red Spot

The *Cassini* space probe took amazing photographs of Jupiter as it flew past in 2000 on its way to Saturn.

Two images of Jupiter's surface

Ganymede is the largest moon in the Solar System.

Famous Feature

The most obvious feature on Jupiter's surface is the Great Red Spot—a massive storm that is more than twice Earth's diameter. It was first discovered in 1664 and has been raging ever since. Astronomers have found two other storms in the same cloud system, nicknamed Red Spot Junior and Little Red Spot.

Moons and Rings

Jupiter has 95 moons. The four largest—Io, Europa, Ganymede, and Callisto—can be seen from Earth. They are called the Galilean moons, because the Italian astronomer Galileo Galilei was one of the first to describe them. Jupiter is also orbited by thin, dark rings of dust.

PLANET PROFILE

Diameter: 143,000 km (88,800 miles)
Length of day: 9 h 56 m
Length of year: 11.86 Earth years
Number of moons: 95

JUPITER

White bands of cloud are called zones.

Red-brown bands are called belts.

DID YOU KNOW? Jupiter is two-and-a-half times bigger than the other Solar System planets put together.

Saturn, Uranus, and Neptune

The three giant planets of the outer solar system are all smaller than Jupiter. Saturn is quite similar to Jupiter, but Uranus and Neptune are "ice giants"—beneath their blue-green atmospheres they are mostly a mix of slushy chemicals including water.

Rings

All four giant planets are surrounded by ring systems, but Saturn's are by far the most impressive. They are made up of trillions of icy particles in orbit above the planet's equator. They often crash into each other, which keeps them in orbit.

Saturn's rings are thousands of miles across, but they are very thin.

This is Titan, the largest of Saturn's 146 moons.

SATURN PROFILE

Diameter: 116,500 km (72,400 miles)
Length of day: 10 h 33 m
Length of year: 29.46 Earth years
Number of moons: 146

DID YOU KNOW? Some astronomers think that Uranus and Neptune might have swapped orbits early in the Solar System's history.

Uranus has 13 rings and 28 known moons.

World on its Side

Most of the Solar System's planets are a little tilted in their orbits around the Sun, but only Uranus is completely knocked over on one side. This makes it look like the planet "rolls" along its orbit. It gives Uranus extreme seasons—at the poles, winter is one long night lasting almost 40 years, followed by a summer of about the same length.

URANUS

Saturn's weather bands are like Jupiter's, but the planet's clouds are surrounded by a creamy haze (fog).

NEPTUNE

Storms on Neptune look like dark spots. High clouds seem white.

57

Stars and the Galaxy

Our Sun is just one of 200 billion stars in a vast, slowly spinning spiral galaxy called the Milky Way. The Sun is a very average star and only appears bright because it is nearby. Other stars are so far away that their light takes many years to reach Earth.

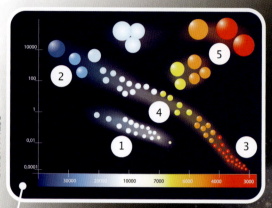

Types of Star

A star's brightness in the sky depends on its distance from Earth and how much light energy it is producing. Stars shine from nuclear fusion reactions (see page 17), during which hydrogen atoms fuse into helium. Stars vary from lower-energy dwarfs, 50,000 times fainter than the Sun, to giants 30 million times brighter.

This graph shows the kinds of star at different temperatures and brightnesses. Red stars are cooler and blue ones are hotter.

KEY TO STAR TYPES
1. WHITE DWARFS
2. BLUE GIANTS
3. RED DWARFS
4. SUNLIKE STARS
5. RED SUPERGIANTS

How Stars Die

When a star runs out of nuclear fuel in its core, it goes through a series of changes as it dies. First it grows in size and brightens, becoming a red giant. All but the heaviest stars then burn off their outer layers, leaving behind just a core called a white dwarf.

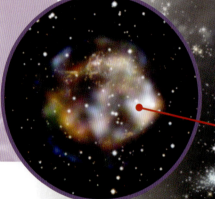

The most massive stars die in an explosion called a supernova that can briefly outshine an entire galaxy. It leaves behind an expanding bubble of superhot gas.

GALAXY PROFILE

Name: Milky Way
Diameter: 120,000 light-years
Mass: Approx 1.2 trillion Suns
Number of stars: Approx 200 billion
Distance to core: 27,000 light-years
Description: Spiral galaxy with four spiral arms and a central bar of stars.

The Milky Way is about 120,000 light-years across. Our Solar System orbits its core every 240 million years.

At the heart of the Milky Way, billions of red and yellow stars orbit a huge black hole.

Stars form from collapsing clouds of gas. They begin their lives in clusters of hot blue and white stars.

The Milky Way is a huge flattened disc of gas, dust, and stars. New stars are born in spiral regions that wind their way out from the galaxy's core.

DID YOU KNOW? Astronomers measure the distance to stars in light-years—how far light travels in a year. One light-year is 9.5 trillion km (5.9 trillion miles).

Black Holes

The strangest objects in the Universe, black holes, are formed by the death of the largest stars of all. With gravity so strong that not even light can escape, they pull anything that passes too close to its doom. A blast of radiation is the only sign the object was ever there.

Birth of a Black Hole

When the core of a dying giant star collapses, if it has more than twice the mass of the Sun, it carries on collapsing until the core has shrunk to a tiny size. A huge amount of mass is packed into that core. The more mass an object has, the stronger the pull of its gravity. As its gravity grows strong enough to prevent light from escaping, it forms a black hole.

A computer image shows two black holes joining together.

A black hole itself is almost invisible. However, as it feeds it creates a disk of superhot material that releases X-rays as it spirals inwards.

SPACECRAFT PROFILE

Name: *Chandra X-ray Observatory*
Launched: 1999
Mirror diameter: 1.2 m (3.9 ft)
Weight: 4,790 kg (10,560 lb)
Description: NASA's main X-ray observatory, which has discovered many new black holes

DID YOU KNOW? According to English physicist Stephen Hawking, black holes slowly lose energy and disappear over billions of years.

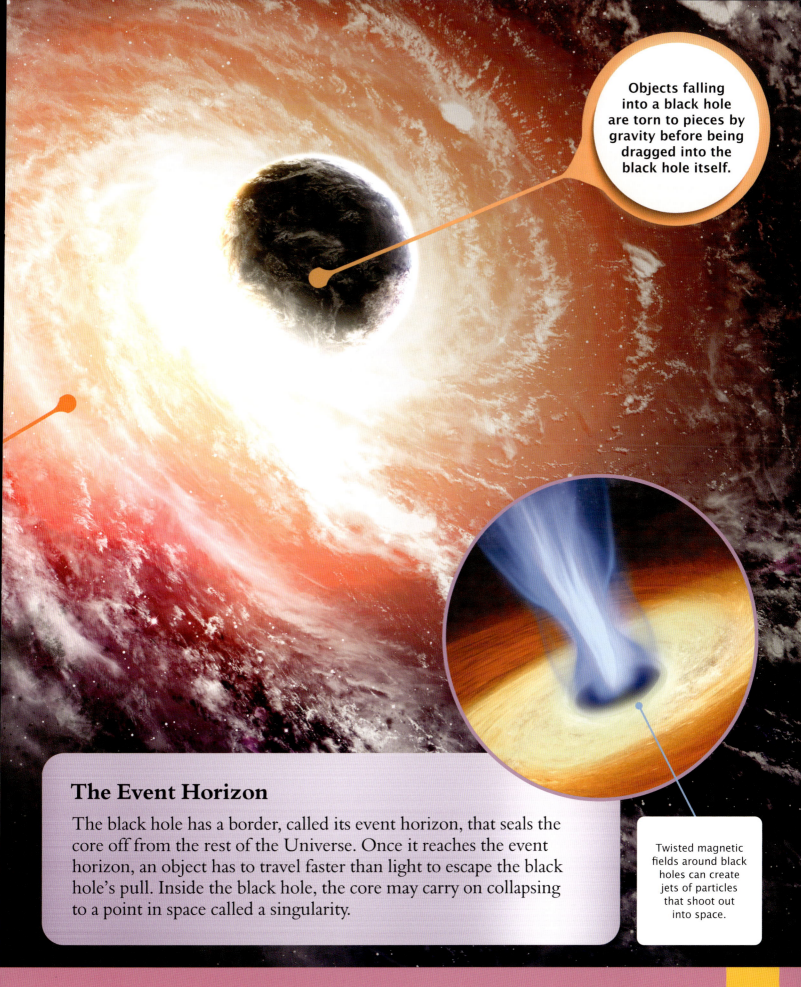

Objects falling into a black hole are torn to pieces by gravity before being dragged into the black hole itself.

The Event Horizon

The black hole has a border, called its event horizon, that seals the core off from the rest of the Universe. Once it reaches the event horizon, an object has to travel faster than light to escape the black hole's pull. Inside the black hole, the core may carry on collapsing to a point in space called a singularity.

Twisted magnetic fields around black holes can create jets of particles that shoot out into space.

Exoplanets

An exoplanet is a planet outside our Solar System. Since 1992, when the first exoplanet was discovered, astronomers have discovered more than 4,000, orbiting over 3,000 stars. They have also found signs of many more being born. These worlds are often very different from Earth, either too hot, too cold, or too waterless for life to exist. However, one day, astronomers may discover an exoplanet where life could, possibly, exist.

Planets form in nebulae (dust clouds) that are rich in dust made from heavier elements, such as that in the Orion Nebula.

How Planets are Born

As stars leave their birth nebulae, they are often surrounded by a flattened disk called a proplyd. Over time, the material in this disk starts to clump together until some clumps have enough gravity to pull in more gas and dust from their surroundings. Once this has happened, they quickly grow into protoplanets, which crash and form planets.

The *Hubble Space Telescope* discovered that many newborn stars in the Orion Nebula are surrounded by proplyds.

DID YOU KNOW? The closest star to Earth, a faint red dwarf called Proxima Centauri, is orbited by an Earth-like planet that could be suitable for life.

Planet hunters have found a lot of "hot Jupiters"—giant exoplanets orbiting very near their stars.

Planet Hunting

Astronomers use two main methods to look for planets. One way is to look for the tiny wobbles in a star's movement that are caused by an orbiting planet pulling it in different directions. Another is to watch for tiny dips in a star's brightness that happen when a planet is passing in front of it. With both methods it is easier to find giant planets, similar to Jupiter, rather than smaller ones.

This image of a planetary system called HR8799 was taken by the Keck Observatory.

NEBULA PROFILE

Name: Orion Nebula
Catalogue number: Messier 42
Distance: 1,340 light-years
Constellation: Orion
Size: Approx 25 light-years wide
Description: The heart of a huge star-forming region that spreads across Orion

The Universe

The Universe is (probably) everything that exists—a vast and perhaps endless expanse of space and time. Our Milky Way is just one of more than 100 billion galaxies. Powerful telescopes let us see millions of these galaxies spread out across space.

Spiral galaxies appear blue and white because of the young, bright stars in their discs.

Measuring the Universe

Astronomers can work out how far away other galaxies are by looking for stars called variables. These stars change their brightness over time and some follow a repeating cycle. We can compare the variable's true brightness with how bright it appears to work out its distance—usually many millions of light-years. Another method is to look for exploding stars, or supernovae, in distant galaxies and see how bright they get.

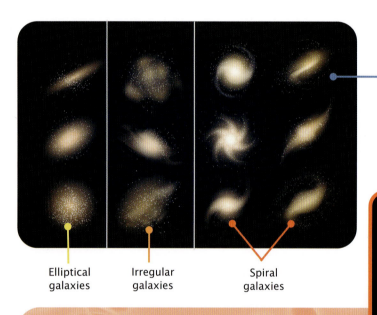

Galaxies have many shapes. Most of them are spirals like our Milky Way, ball-shaped ones called ellipticals, or shapeless clouds called irregulars.

Elliptical galaxies

Irregular galaxies

Spiral galaxies

Cosmic Expansion

When astronomers first worked out the true distance to nearby galaxies, they noticed a pattern—the farther away a galaxy is, the faster it is moving away from us. This is because space itself is expanding, carrying galaxies away from each other like the raisins in a rising fruit cake.

Astronomers discovered the motion of stars and galaxies by measuring the "red shift" in their light. An object moving away from Earth has its light stretched to longer, redder wavelengths, while one moving toward us appears "blue shifted."

DID YOU KNOW? Looking across space is the same as looking back in time—the light we detect from the most distant galaxies has been on its way to us for 13.4 billion years.

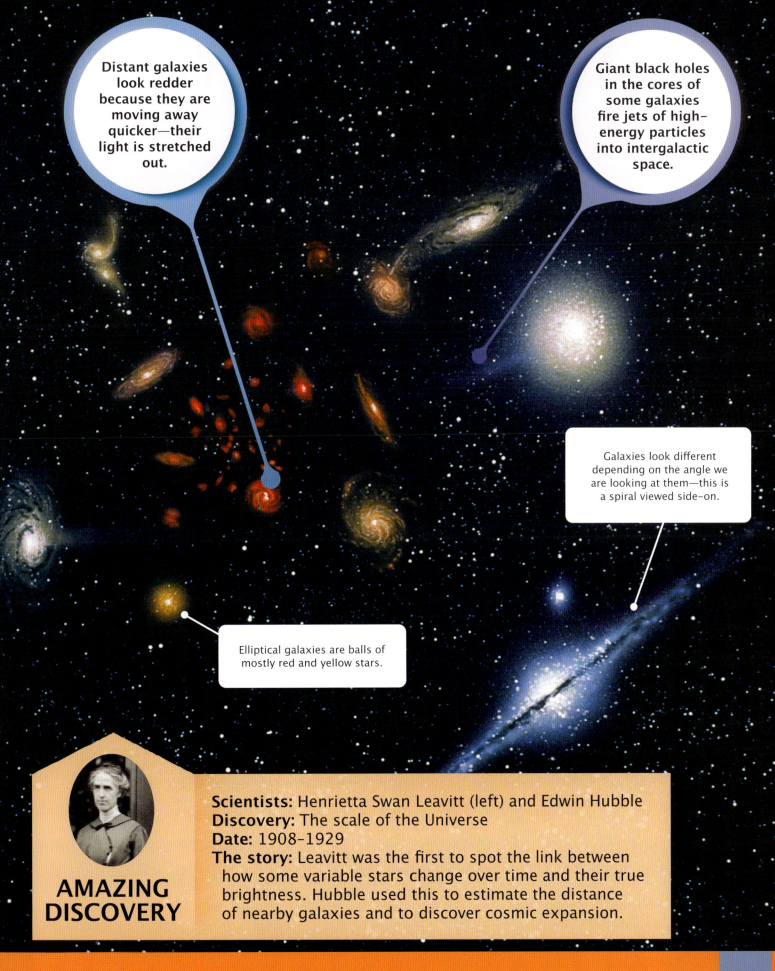

Distant galaxies look redder because they are moving away quicker—their light is stretched out.

Giant black holes in the cores of some galaxies fire jets of high-energy particles into intergalactic space.

Galaxies look different depending on the angle we are looking at them—this is a spiral viewed side-on.

Elliptical galaxies are balls of mostly red and yellow stars.

AMAZING DISCOVERY

Scientists: Henrietta Swan Leavitt (left) and Edwin Hubble
Discovery: The scale of the Universe
Date: 1908–1929
The story: Leavitt was the first to spot the link between how some variable stars change over time and their true brightness. Hubble used this to estimate the distance of nearby galaxies and to discover cosmic expansion.

The Big Bang and Beyond

Matter, energy, space, and time were all created in the Big Bang explosion 13.8 billion years ago.

The Universe was born out of a huge explosion that took place about 13.8 billion years ago. This Big Bang released huge amounts of energy that made all the matter in the Universe. It even created space and time.

Evidence for the Big Bang

The discovery that all galaxies are moving apart shows that they must have been much closer together in the distant past, when the Universe would have been much denser and hotter. We can even see the faint afterglow of the Big Bang—waves of cosmic microwave background radiation (CMBR).

The CMBR is a faint glow of radio waves that comes from all over the sky. Brighter and darker areas show the seeds of galaxy clusters in the early Universe.

Will the Universe Ever End?

The Universe has three possible futures. Gravity from all the matter within it could slow its expansion and pull everything back to a Big Crunch. Another idea is that a mysterious force called dark energy could push everything apart in a Big Rip. Finally, space might just keep on expanding.

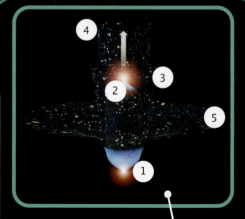

The Universe began with the Big Bang (1). It may end in an explosive Big Crunch (2) or keep expanding (3). This illustration also shows what would happen if the Universe had no dark energy (4) or if it had so much (5) that it would eventually tear itself apart in a Big Rip.

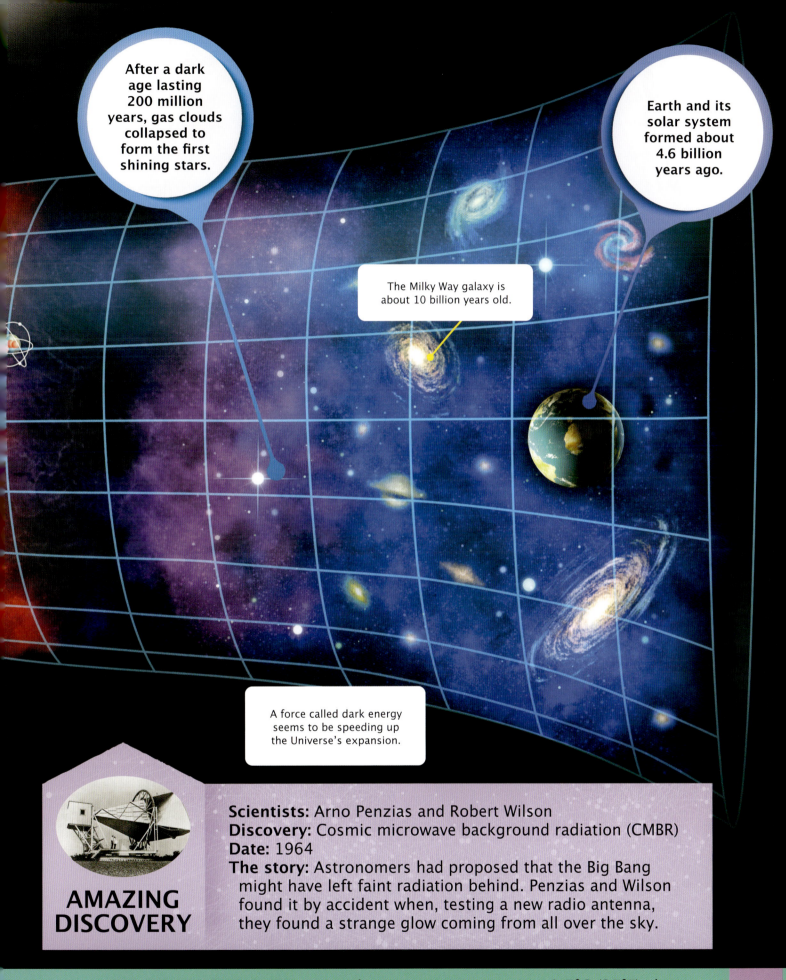

After a dark age lasting 200 million years, gas clouds collapsed to form the first shining stars.

Earth and its solar system formed about 4.6 billion years ago.

The Milky Way galaxy is about 10 billion years old.

A force called dark energy seems to be speeding up the Universe's expansion.

AMAZING DISCOVERY

Scientists: Arno Penzias and Robert Wilson
Discovery: Cosmic microwave background radiation (CMBR)
Date: 1964
The story: Astronomers had proposed that the Big Bang might have left faint radiation behind. Penzias and Wilson found it by accident when, testing a new radio antenna, they found a strange glow coming from all over the sky.

DID YOU KNOW? CMBR warms the entire Universe to just 2.7°C (37°F) above the coldest possible temperature, –273.15°C (–459.67°F) or absolute zero.

Telescopes

Telescopes are the most important tools astronomers use to look at objects in space. They gather up much more light than our human eyes so we can see fainter objects, and they create a magnified (blown-up) image so we can see much smaller details.

Two Designs

Telescopes come in two types. Refractors use two or more lenses at either end of a long tube to create a magnified image. Reflectors use a mirror to reflect light to a lens and can have a more compact design. The job of the first lens or mirror is to collect light from a large area and bend or reflect it so that it passes through the smaller eyepiece lens.

The Yerkes Observatory refractor is the world's largest successful lens-based telescope.

Birth of the Telescope

The first telescopes were made by Dutch lensmakers around 1608, but the invention was made famous by Italian astronomer Galileo Galilei, who built his own telescope a few months later. He used it to make important discoveries, studying moons around Jupiter, craters on the Moon, and star clouds in the Milky Way.

Galilei's studies made him believe that the planets move around the Sun, as Nicolaus Copernicus had suggested in 1510.

DID YOU KNOW? Galilei's first telescope, constructed in 1609, could magnify only by three times.

TELESCOPE PROFILE

Name: Yerkes refractor
Built: 1897
Lens diameter: 102 cm (40 in)
Length: 19.2 m (63 ft)
Weight: 23.5 tonnes (26 tons)
Location: Williams Bay, Wisconsin, U.S.A.

A shutter opens to allow the telescope to see out into space.

An observatory dome protects the telescope from the weather.

A refracting telescope uses a big lens to bend light to a focus and a smaller eyepiece to make a magnified image.

A reflecting telescope uses two curved mirrors to collect and focus light before passing it to a magnifying eyepiece.

A stand holds the telescope's weight so it can swivel with a gentle push.

69

Rockets

Rising into space on a jet of flames, rockets need an explosive chemical reaction (the burning of rocket fuel) to push them through Earth's atmosphere. Rockets are noisy, wasteful, and expensive, but they are still the best way of reaching orbit around Earth.

Stage by Stage

Most rockets are made up of many "stages," each with their own fuel tanks and rocket engines. These stages may be stacked on top of each other or sit side by side. Only the top stage reaches orbit with its cargo—the burnt-out lower stages fall back to Earth and are usually destroyed.

> A rocket stage is mostly made of fuel tanks and engines. Only a small cargo on the top reaches space.

> Booster stages help raise the speed of the top stage and cargo before falling back to Earth.

NASA's Space Launch System carries the *Orion* spacecraft into orbit.

The *V–2* was a rocket with explosive cargo, used as a weapon during World War II. Most modern rockets are based on the *V–2*.

SPACECRAFT PROFILE

Name: *Saturn V*
Launch dates: 1967–1973
Total launches: 13
Height: 110.6 m (363 ft)
Diameter: 10.1 m (33 ft)
Weight: 2.29 million kg (5.04 million lb)

DID YOU KNOW? The *Saturn V* rocket that took astronauts to the Moon in 1969 was the world's biggest rocket for more than 50 years.

Action and Reaction

Rockets rely on a rule that the English scientist Isaac Newton worked out in 1687: "For every action, there is an equal and opposite reaction." This means that the force of exploding gases coming from a rocket engine is always the same as the reaction: the force pushing the engine itself in the opposite direction. The rocket pushes against itself, not the air around it, so it can work even in space where there is no air.

The first stage has four rocket engines.

Isaac Newton discovered the principle of the rocket.

International Space Station

> The *ISS*'s solar panels can produce up to 110 kW of power.

The *International Space Station* (*ISS*) is the ninth space station that humans have built. It is the first one where space agencies from different countries have worked together—16 nations are part of the project. The *ISS* is the largest and most expensive spacecraft ever built.

Panel Power

The *ISS* has eight pairs of solar panels. Solar cells in the panels change energy from the Sun into electricity. A system of trusses (joining corridors) connects the different modules (sections). They hold electrical lines, cooling lines for machines, and mobile transporter rails. The solar panels and robotic arms fix to the trusses, too.

ZVEZDA DOCKING PORT

SOLAR PANEL

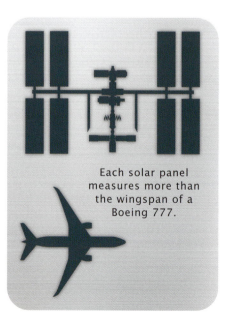

Each solar panel measures more than the wingspan of a Boeing 777.

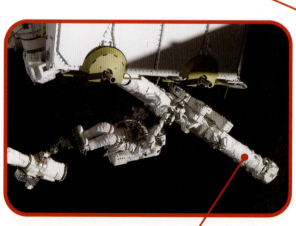

DID YOU KNOW? Canadarm 2, the *ISS*'s main robotic arm, is 16.7 m (55 ft) long and can lift weights up to 116 tonnes (127.8 tons).

Life on the Station

The *ISS* has three laboratories: the Columbus laboratory, the Kibo laboratory, and the U.S. Destiny laboratory. Every day, *ISS* crew carry out science experiments in the labs, and scientists on Earth also take part. There are research projects into making new materials and growing special crystals.

KIBO LABORATORY

U.S. DESTINY LABORATORY

COLUMBUS LABORATORY

CANADARM 2

NASA astronaut Karen Nyberg works in the U.S. Destiny laboratory.

The first *ISS* module launched into orbit was the Russian-built Zarya in 1998.

SPACECRAFT PROFILE

Name: International Space Station
Launch date: 1998
Width: 109 m (358 ft)
Length: 88 m (289 ft)
Weight: 419.6 tonnes (462.5 tons)
Orbiting speed: 8 km/s (17,895.5 mph)
Crew size: 3–7 people

Satellites

Satellites are robot spacecraft put in orbit around Earth to do many different jobs. Some watch the weather or photograph our planet to learn more about it. Others help us communicate or find our way around the world. The world's first satellite, *Sputnik 1*, was put into orbit by the Soviet Union in 1957. Around 5,000 satellites are in orbit today.

Different Orbits

Satellites are put into an orbit that is best for the job they have to do. Some sit happily in a low Earth orbit (LEO) that puts them just beyond the atmosphere. Others enter much higher geostationary (fixed) orbit above the equator, where they stay above a single point on Earth's surface. Satellites that try to study the whole of Earth's surface are put in tilted orbits that loop above and below the Earth's poles as the planet rotates beneath them.

Communications satellites often use geostationary orbits.

Cameras take images of Europe and Africa every 15 minutes.

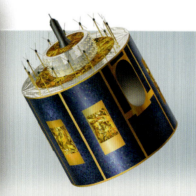

SPACECRAFT PROFILE

Name: *Meteosat 10*
Launch date: July 5, 2012
Diameter: 3.2 m (10.5 ft)
Height: 2.4 m (7.9 ft)
Orbit: 35,786 km (22,236 miles)
Orbital period: 23 h 56 m (matching Earth's rotation)

DID YOU KNOW? The higher a satellite orbits, the longer it takes to go around the Earth.

The drum-shaped satellite spins 100 times per second.

Space Helpers

The curved shape of the Earth makes it impossible to send radio signals (which travel in straight lines) very far. Communication satellites solve this problem. Orbiting high above Earth, they can be seen from places on Earth that are far away from each other. This means signals can be bounced from one place to another along two straight-line paths.

The European-built *Meteosat* satellites are designed to watch weather on Earth from an orbit high above the equator.

NASA's Tracking and Data Relay satellites are designed for communication with orbiting spacecraft.

Sputnik 1 consisted of an 84-kg (185-lb) metal ball that held a simple radio beacon that could send and receive radio signals.

75

Space Probes

Humans have not made it farther into space than the Moon, but we have been able to explore much of the Solar System using space probes. These robot explorers have visited all the major planets and many smaller worlds, too.

Voyager 2 is one of a pair of spacecraft that flew past the giant planets of the outer Solar System in the 1970s and 1980s.

Specialist Robots

Probes are designed to carry out one kind of mission. Some probes are orbiters that will become satellites of other planets. Others may carry out high-speed flyby missons and collect information as they fly past. Some probes are built to land on the surface of planets or moons and even drive across their surface.

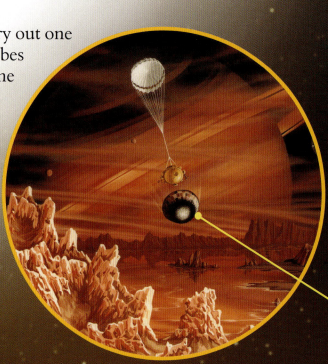

The *Huygens* lander was designed to parachute into the atmosphere of Saturn's moon, Titan.

SPACECRAFT PROFILE

Name: *Voyager 2*
Launch date: August 20, 1977
Weight: 825.5 kg (1,820 lb)
Electrical power: 470 W
Current speed: 55,000 km/h (34,000 mph)
Targets: Jupiter, Saturn, Uranus, and Neptune

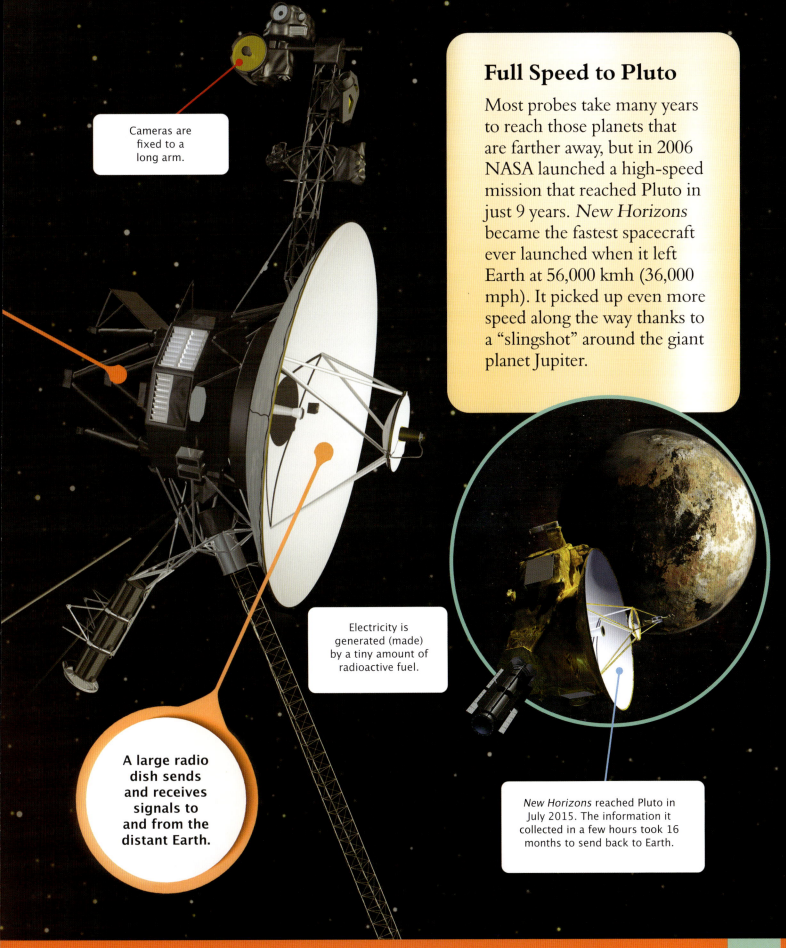

Cameras are fixed to a long arm.

Full Speed to Pluto

Most probes take many years to reach those planets that are farther away, but in 2006 NASA launched a high-speed mission that reached Pluto in just 9 years. *New Horizons* became the fastest spacecraft ever launched when it left Earth at 56,000 kmh (36,000 mph). It picked up even more speed along the way thanks to a "slingshot" around the giant planet Jupiter.

Electricity is generated (made) by a tiny amount of radioactive fuel.

A large radio dish sends and receives signals to and from the distant Earth.

New Horizons reached Pluto in July 2015. The information it collected in a few hours took 16 months to send back to Earth.

DID YOU KNOW? In 2018, *Voyager 2* left the Solar System, entering interstellar space. In 40,000 years it should pass by the star Ross 248.

CHAPTER 4: TECHNOLOGY
Simple Machines

Ramps, wedges, levers, wheels and axles, screws, and pulleys are all simple machines that people have used since ancient times. Ramps and wedges might not seem like machines, but they are. Machines are devices that use the laws of physics to make tasks easier.

Making Work Easier

Doing any physical task involves work—in other words, applying a force to an object that moves it. The amount of work for a particular job is always the same, but a machine makes it easier. The machine multiplies the amount of force we apply, or it increases the distance over which the force acts.

Even before the invention of the axle, the people who built Stonehenge may have used basic wheels—sledges on rolling logs—to move massive stones.

Simple to Modern

Ancient inventors found many ingenious ways to power their simple machines. They used the weight of falling water, the movement of tides, and the force of wind. Modern machines date from the Industrial Revolution. In 1712, Thomas Newcomen built the first successful steam engine, which used the force of expanding or condensing steam to power machines.

This 1834 engraving shows a textile factory with steam-powered printing machines. Steam was used in industry until the early 1900s, when electricity began to take over.

The farther away the swings are from the axle, the faster they move.

The swings are attached to a wheel. The wheel turns when force is applied to the central axle.

A wheel will not work without an axle—a central rod or cylinder that it can turn around. The wheel and axle work together to help things move. The force can be applied to the wheel or the axle.

A motor moves the axle. The circle turned by the wheel is much larger than the circle turned by the axle.

AMAZING DISCOVERY

Scientist: Archimedes
Discovery: Machines of war
Date: 213 BCE
The story: Greek mathematician Archimedes built pulley systems, cranes, catapults, and other machines to help defend his home city against invading Roman ships in 213 BCE. He also wrote the first proper explanations of the science behind such machines.

DID YOU KNOW? An axe's wedge-shaped head is a simple machine: Force applied to the thick end is concentrated in the thin edge, so it has enough pressure to chop.

Engines, Motors, and Generators

Engines are machines that use one form of energy (such as heat or electricity) to produce another—motion (or kinetic) energy that can do work. Steam, gasoline (petrol), and diesel engines all burn fuels to create this energy. Electric motors rely on electricity and magnetism.

Electric Motors

An electric motor works because of the relationship between permanent magnets and an electromagnet. A spinning rotor sits in a drum lined with fixed magnets called stators. Alternating current passes through coiled wires around the rotor. It produces a changing magnetic field that pushes the coil away from the stators.

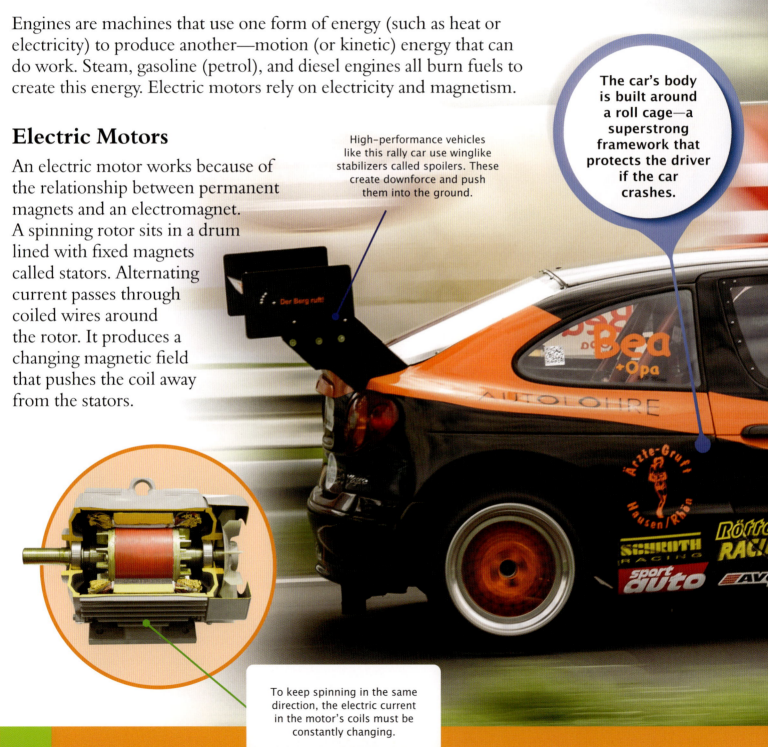

High-performance vehicles like this rally car use winglike stabilizers called spoilers. These create downforce and push them into the ground.

The car's body is built around a roll cage—a superstrong framework that protects the driver if the car crashes.

To keep spinning in the same direction, the electric current in the motor's coils must be constantly changing.

80

AMAZING DISCOVERY

Scientist: Ányos Jedlik
Discovery: Spinning electric motor
Date: 1828
The story: Hungarian scientist Jedlik came up with the key to a working electric motor. He worked out that changing the direction of current flowing inside an an electric coil would keep it spinning in a ring of magnets.

Generating Turbines

Turbines are one of the most common ways of producing electricity. They work like an electric motor in reverse. Motion energy spins a wire-wrapped rotor in a magnetic field and makes current flow in the rotor wires. The motion energy can come from expanding steam, water falling from a dam, ocean waves, or gusts of wind.

This cutaway shows the insides of a wind turbine, which makes "green" or renewable electricity. The motion energy comes from the wind turning the blades.

A combustion engine turns chemical energy (the combustion, or burning, of fuel) into mechanical power.

Most car engines burn gasoline/petrol (ignited by an electric spark) or diesel fuel (ignited by compressed hot air).

DID YOU KNOW? The world's tiniest electric motor is just one-36,000th of the width of a human hair. It was built from a single molecule in 2011.

81

Electronics

Electronics are built into our televisions, smartphones, games consoles, laptops, and e-books. Everyday appliances such as washing machines and dishwashers rely on them, too. Electronic devices control and adjust the flow of small numbers of electrons in an electric current. They can use the electric current to represent some kind of signal or information.

Electronic Components

The first electronic devices were amplifiers that could boost weak currents to useful levels. These amplifiers were like valves and made current flow in only one direction. The same technology made radios and computers possible. Today's valves, called diodes and triodes, are incredibly small. They are made using materials called semiconductors.

A CD player's lens directs intense laser light created by a special diode onto the reflecting surface of a CD.

Tiny pits cover the disc. These dots or dashes represent digital information such as games, music, or pictures.

Adding other elements to these thin wafers of silicon will turn them into semiconductors. A semiconductor creates a barrier that lets current flow in only one direction.

AMAZING DISCOVERY

Scientists: John Ambrose Fleming and William Shockley
Discovery: Valves and transistors
Date: 1904, 1947
The story: In 1904, Fleming invented a lightbulb-like device called the valve diode, which caused a strong current to flow one way when a weak current was received. In 1947, Shockley used semiconductor materials to build tiny transistors that did the same thing.

DID YOU KNOW? A string of eight bits can represent any number from 0 to 255. 64 bits can represent any number up to 9,223,372,036,854,775,807.

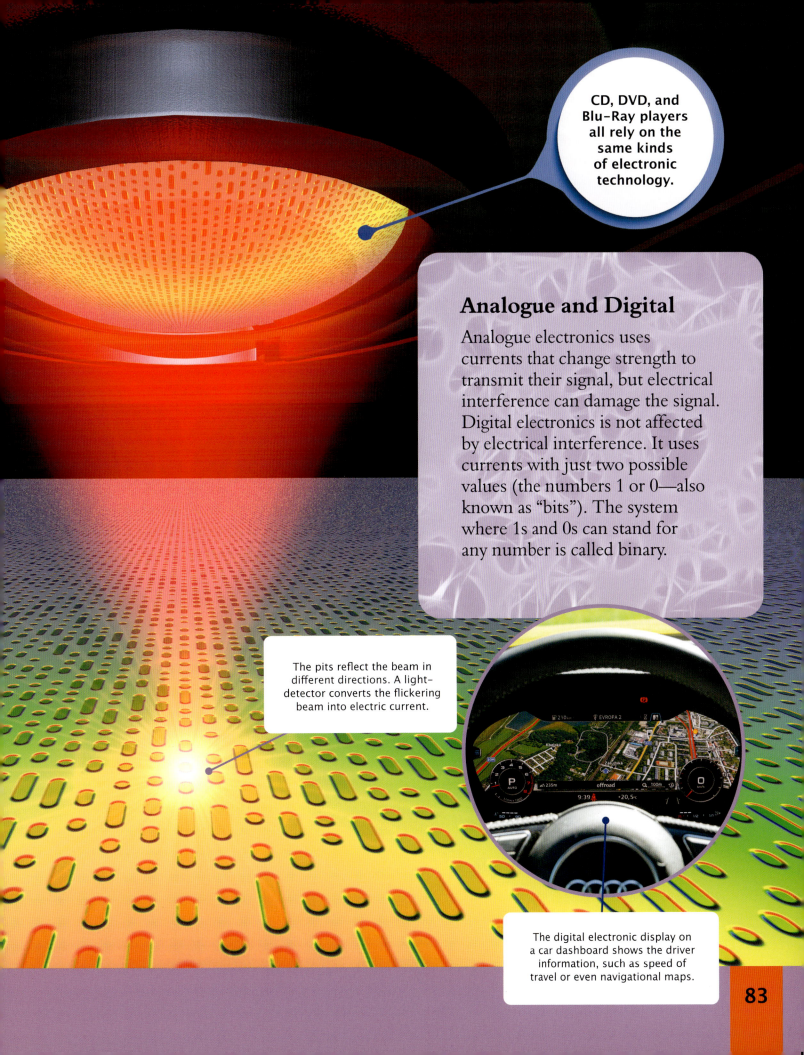

CD, DVD, and Blu-Ray players all rely on the same kinds of electronic technology.

Analogue and Digital

Analogue electronics uses currents that change strength to transmit their signal, but electrical interference can damage the signal. Digital electronics is not affected by electrical interference. It uses currents with just two possible values (the numbers 1 or 0—also known as "bits"). The system where 1s and 0s can stand for any number is called binary.

The pits reflect the beam in different directions. A light-detector converts the flickering beam into electric current.

The digital electronic display on a car dashboard shows the driver information, such as speed of travel or even navigational maps.

Computers

At its most basic, a computer is a device that does simple calculations very quickly, even for very large numbers, and identifies patterns in the numbers. By adding clever design and programming to this basic mathematical ability, we now have computers that can carry out a mind-boggling variety of different tasks.

The Brain

The computer's central processing unit (CPU) "reads" information stored in the computer's memory, performs calculations, and then "writes" results back to other parts of the memory. Electronic components called logic gates let the CPU do mathematics and make decisions based on binary numbers (strings of 1s and 0s).

Although computers are great for games, they can also make difficult and repetitive tasks much easier.

Built between 1943 and 1946, room-sized ENIAC was one of the first digital computers. It could carry out 5,000 instructions a second.

AMAZING DISCOVERY

Scientists: Charles Babbage and Ada Lovelace
Discovery: The analytical engine
Date: 1837, 1843
The story: In 1837, long before electronics, English inventor Babbage designed a universal computing machine using brass wheels. It was never built, but mathematician Lovelace worked out the commands needed to run it, making her the first computer programmer. She published her findings in 1843.

DID YOU KNOW? Modern phones can process trillions instructions per second.

Computer Memory

Computers store information they need fast access to on memory chips. Basic operating instructions are written on permanent Read-Only Memory (ROM) chips. Less urgent data, such as applications or the user's files, is saved on a slower magnetic hard disk and then moved to faster Random Access Memory (RAM) chips when it is needed.

Special computer circuits can create sounds from digital files.

A computer's motherboard connects all of its various components, including the CPU, ROM and RAM memory chips, and hard disk drive.

Special graphics processors (GPUs) create realistic moving images on the screen.

A mouse lets the computer user highlight and manipulate items on the screen.

85

Connected World

Our phones, televisions, Internet, and many other modern technologies rely on computers and other machines being able to talk to each other over huge distances. They communicate by sending their signals through networks of wires or cables or by beaming them through the air in electromagnetic radio waves.

Sending Signals

We send analogue signals in two forms. We can use electric current, changing or modulating its strength to transmit the signal, or we can use radio waves and change their shape. Either way, a receiver decodes the patterns to work out the signal. Today, however, most signals are sent digitally. The information is converted into streams of binary numbers, and sent between machines as 1s and 0s.

HYLAS-1, a communications satellite, circles the Earth in the same time it takes Earth to spin on its axis. Its orbit is 35,800 km (22,245 miles) above the equator.

HYLAS-1

Satellites such as *HYLAS-1* are solar-powered—they generate their electricity from sunlight.

A phone mast can beam out hundreds of calls at the same time. The signals are digital so they cannot get mixed up like the "crossed wires" of the past.

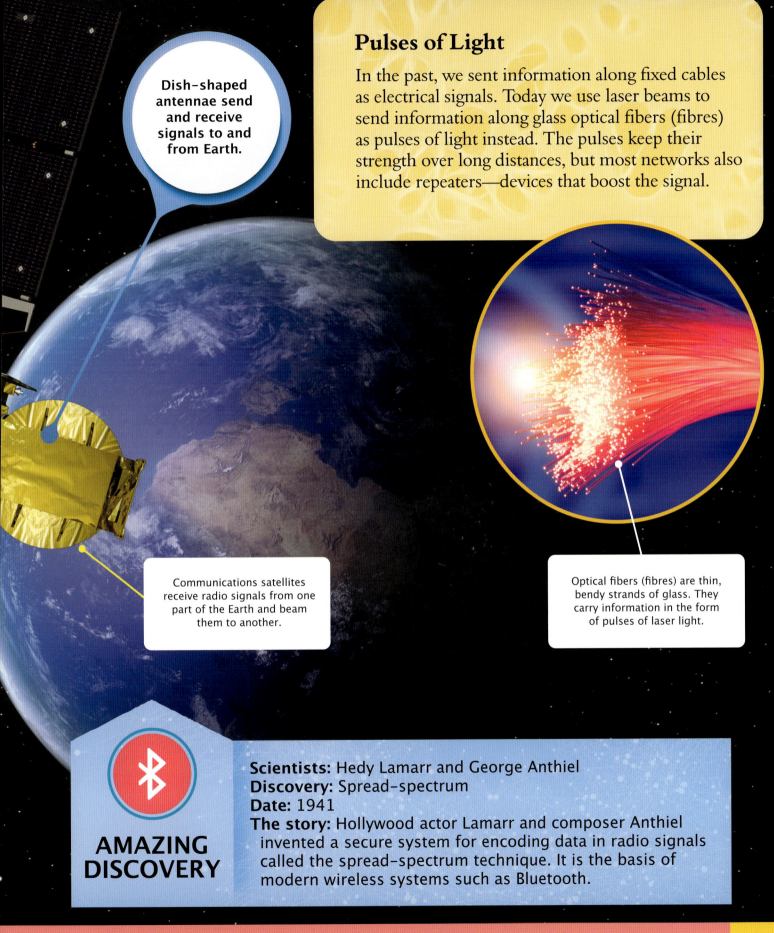

Dish-shaped antennae send and receive signals to and from Earth.

Pulses of Light

In the past, we sent information along fixed cables as electrical signals. Today we use laser beams to send information along glass optical fibers (fibres) as pulses of light instead. The pulses keep their strength over long distances, but most networks also include repeaters—devices that boost the signal.

Communications satellites receive radio signals from one part of the Earth and beam them to another.

Optical fibers (fibres) are thin, bendy strands of glass. They carry information in the form of pulses of laser light.

AMAZING DISCOVERY

Scientists: Hedy Lamarr and George Anthiel
Discovery: Spread-spectrum
Date: 1941
The story: Hollywood actor Lamarr and composer Anthiel invented a secure system for encoding data in radio signals called the spread-spectrum technique. It is the basis of modern wireless systems such as Bluetooth.

DID YOU KNOW? Signals have been successfully sent more than 10,000 km (6,214 miles) along optical fibers (fibres) without using repeaters to boost them.

Flying Machines

Humans have always dreamed of taking to the air. In the 1780s the French Montgolfier brothers became the first to achieve this with their hot-air balloons. However, powered and steerable flight became possible only in the 20th century.

Like a Bird

Powered aircraft have birdlike wings that generate an upward force called lift. The wing's shape creates a difference in the air pressure above and below that pushes it upward. Aircraft wings cannot flap like a bird's, so they must move much faster through the air to keep the plane off the ground.

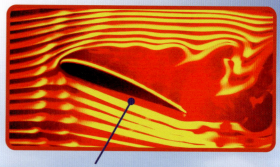

This image of a wing being tested in a wind tunnel shows how air is forced faster over the upper surface. Adjusting the shape and angle of the wing affects the amount of lift.

Up, Up, and Away

Helicopters produce lift with their rotor blades—spinning wings that cut through the air without the entire aircraft needing to move. The fast-moving tail blade generates a sideways force that stops the machine from spinning with its main rotor.

Helicopters can take off and land vertically. The pilot adjusts the angle of each spinning blade to alter the amount of lift it produces, and tilts the entire rotor to push the helicopter forward.

The fuselage (aircraft body) of metal alloys and other materials is both strong and light.

The bullet-shaped nose reduces drag, helping the aircraft cut through the air at high speed.

Jet engines use spinning blades to compress air before using it to burn fuel. Hot exhaust gases blown out of the engines push the aircraft forward.

Flaps on the wings adjust their shape to alter how much lift they create.

AMAZING DISCOVERY

Scientists: Orville and Wilbur Wright
Discovery: Aircraft controls
Date: 1903–1905
The story: The American Wright brothers invented controls that let them control the precise angle of an aircraft in the air and the shape of its wings. This helped them to make the first powered, controlled flight in 1903.

DID YOU KNOW? Ukraine's Antonov An-225 was the world's biggest aircraft, with a wingspan of 88.4 m (262.5 ft). It carried up to 250 tonnes (550,000 lb) of cargo.

Nuclear Energy

Compared to its size, the forces at work inside an atom's central nucleus are enormous. Nuclear power plants tap into this huge energy source. They use a process called nuclear fission that makes some heavy, unstable atoms split into smaller, more stable forms.

Nuclear Fission

Fission happens all the time in nature. Nuclei of elements such as uranium are naturally unstable or "radioactive." They disintegrate at random, releasing small bursts of energy. Nuclear power harnesses this process by creating a chain reaction. Each disintegration instantly triggers several more. Power stations often use uranium isotope 235. An isotope is a rare form of an element.

The US National Ignition Facility (NIF) houses the world's largest, most energetic laser. It hopes to copy the nuclear fusion going on in the Sun to provide an unlimited, cheap source of electricity.

Nuclear power plants use the energy they release to turn water into steam. The steam drives electricity-producing turbines and then escapes through huge cooling towers.

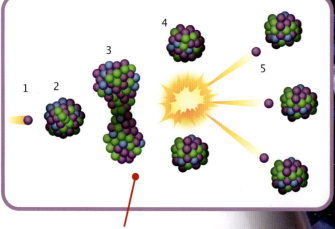

In a fission chain reaction, a neutron particle (1) strikes an unstable atom (2), making it split apart (3). The fission process leaves behind smaller nuclei (4) and more neutrons (5), so the nuclear reaction can start all over again.

Future Fusion?

Fusion reactions release energy by joining lightweight nuclei instead of breaking apart heavy ones. Unlike fission, fusion does not involve rare heavy elements and doesn't leave behind long-lasting pollution. It sounds like a recipe for cheap, clean energy, but the problem is that fusion only takes place at temperatures like those in the core of the Sun.

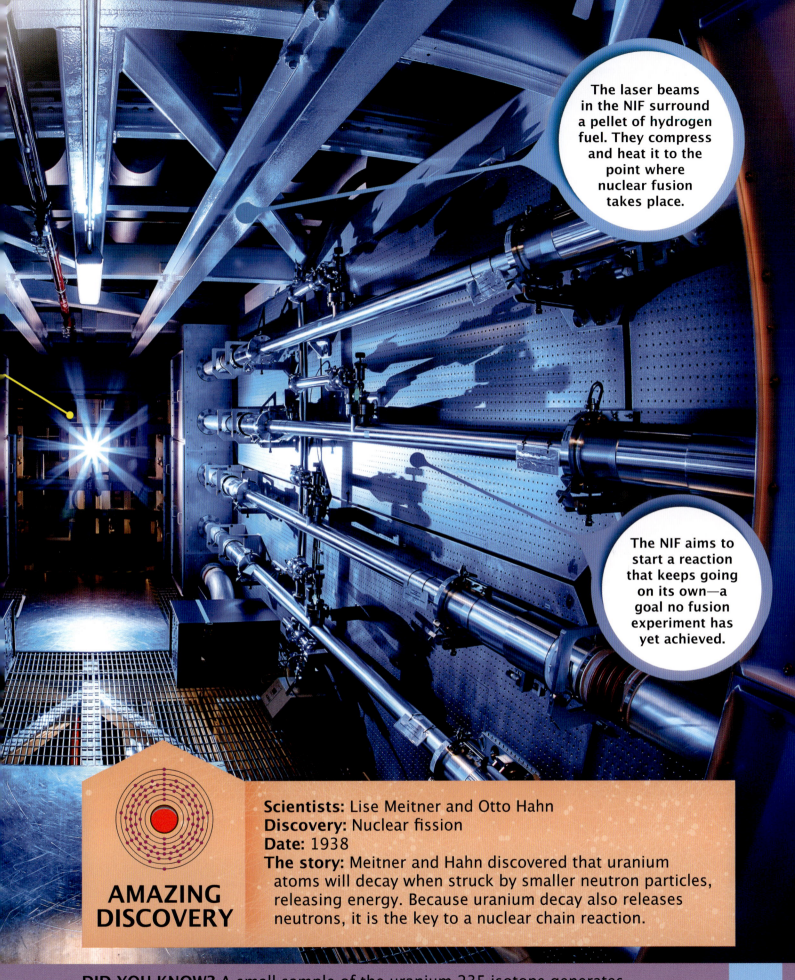

The laser beams in the NIF surround a pellet of hydrogen fuel. They compress and heat it to the point where nuclear fusion takes place.

The NIF aims to start a reaction that keeps going on its own—a goal no fusion experiment has yet achieved.

AMAZING DISCOVERY

Scientists: Lise Meitner and Otto Hahn
Discovery: Nuclear fission
Date: 1938
The story: Meitner and Hahn discovered that uranium atoms will decay when struck by smaller neutron particles, releasing energy. Because uranium decay also releases neutrons, it is the key to a nuclear chain reaction.

DID YOU KNOW? A small sample of the uranium 235 isotope generates 3.7 million times more energy than the same amount of coal.

Nanotechnology

Imagine machines made up of individual atoms, able to copy themselves, assemble objects, and even repair our bodies or fight disease at a molecular level. This is the idea behind nanotechnology—and while this new science has not yet delivered all these dreams, it is already starting to affect our everyday lives.

Teeny-Tiny Tech

Nanotechnology involves building on the scale of nanometres (billionths of 1 m/3.3 ft) or less. Nanomaterials are substances with engineered atomic-scale structures that give them useful properties. We already use them to make self-cleaning glass, dirt-repellent paints and sprays, and superfine filters for purifying water and trapping viruses.

Carbon nanotubes can be used in touch-screen devices, such as tablets, and high-strength bullet-proof vests.

Building with Atoms

Nanoengineers can also build structures out of individual atoms. They use a machine called an atomic force microscope to "see" the separate atoms on a material—and they can even pick them up and move them around! This technology could eventually let us build complex computers atom by atom.

Scanning tunneling microscopes are the best way of mapping and building with single atoms.

AMAZING DISCOVERY

Scientists: Richard Smalley, Robert Curl, and Harold Kroto
Discovery: Fullerenes
Date: 1985
The story: Smalley, Curl, and Kroto led a team of chemists who discovered a ball of carbon atoms that they called buckminsterfullerene. This was the first hint that carbon could create strong rings and tubes for use in nanotechnology.

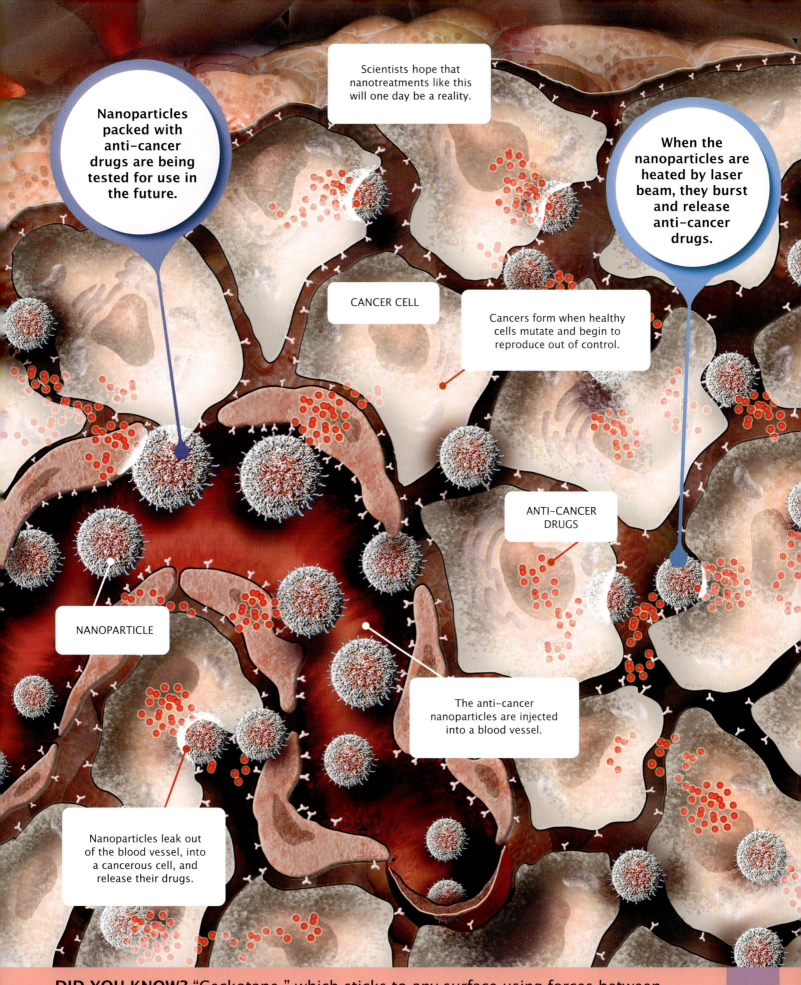

CHAPTER 5: PLANET EARTH

Inside the Earth

Our planet is a huge ball of rock 12,742 km (7,918 miles) across. It might seem solid all the way through, but not far beneath the surface is a deep layer called the mantle, which is a mix of semi-molten and solid rock. Deeper still, Earth's core is a swirling ball of molten and solid metal.

Layers Within Layers

Earth's crust floats on the upper, semi-molten part of the mantle and is cracked into giant plates. Rocks churn and grind past each other in the mantle, carrying heat from the core to the surface. The superhot core is made of iron and nickel, and it's mostly molten but solid at its heart.

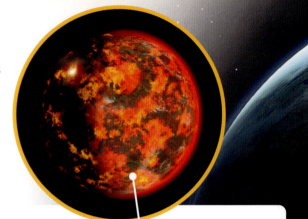

Earth was born about 4.6 billion years ago out of material left over from making the Sun. At first, even the surface was hot, molten rock. Our planet has been slowly cooling down ever since.

Earth's Magnetic Field

The liquid part of Earth's metal core produces huge electric currents as it swirls, and these create a magnetic field. It is as if our planet is a giant magnet, with magnetic north and south poles close to the axis of its spin. This magnetic field forms a bubble around the Earth, which we call the magnetosphere.

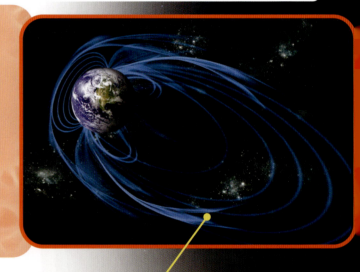

The magnetosphere repels dangerous particles from the Sun. Harmless, lower-energy solar particles fall into the atmosphere over the magnetic poles to create aurorae (see page 44).

AMAZING DISCOVERY

Scientist: Andrija Mohorovicic
Discovery: Earth's internal layers
Date: 1909
The story: Scientist Mohorovicic observed that earthquake shockwaves change their speed depending on their depth below the surface. He realized this was because they passed through different rock types and temperatures.

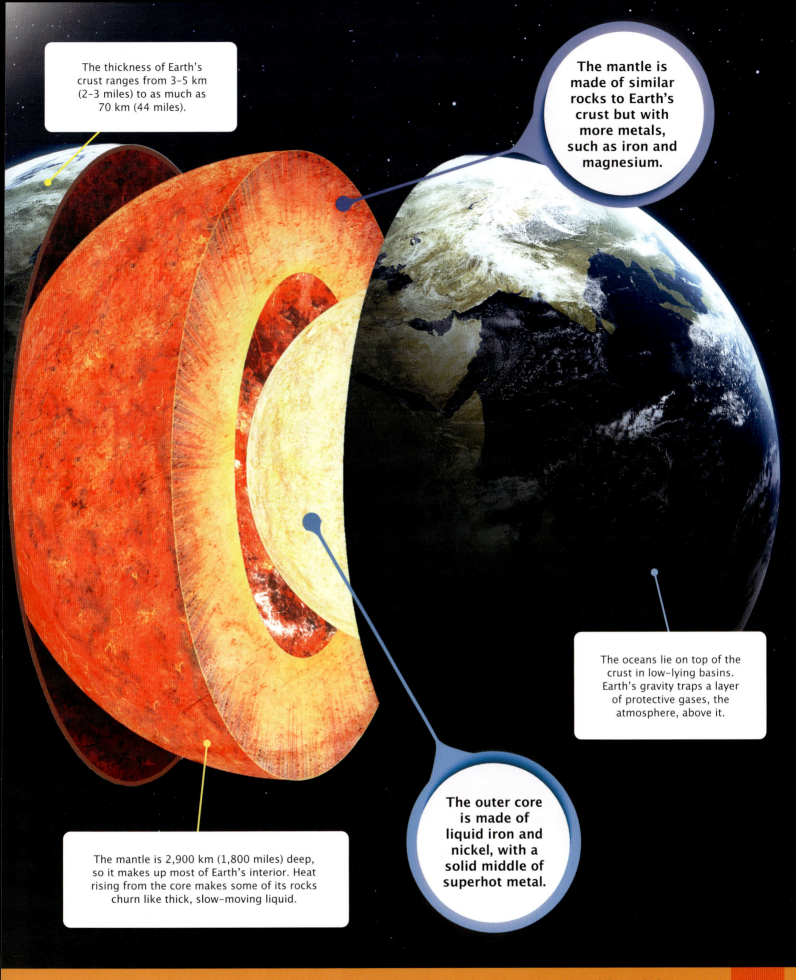

The thickness of Earth's crust ranges from 3–5 km (2–3 miles) to as much as 70 km (44 miles).

The mantle is made of similar rocks to Earth's crust but with more metals, such as iron and magnesium.

The oceans lie on top of the crust in low-lying basins. Earth's gravity traps a layer of protective gases, the atmosphere, above it.

The outer core is made of liquid iron and nickel, with a solid middle of superhot metal.

The mantle is 2,900 km (1,800 miles) deep, so it makes up most of Earth's interior. Heat rising from the core makes some of its rocks churn like thick, slow-moving liquid.

DID YOU KNOW? Geologists estimate that the boundary between Earth's solid inner and liquid outer cores is 6,000°C (10,832°F)—hotter than the surface of the Sun.

Rocks and Minerals

Most of Earth's elements are naturally locked up in complex chemical molecules. These form solid substances called minerals, which can have beautiful crystal structures. Most rocks are made up from a mix of different minerals. Some elements, such as gold, prefer not to bond with others, so they can be found naturally in pure form.

Elements in the Earth

The rocks that make up Earth's thin outer crust mostly contain just a few fairly light elements. Heavy elements, including precious metals, tend to sink down toward Earth's core. The main elements in the rocky crust are oxygen (47 percent), silicon (28 percent), aluminum/aluminium (8 percent), iron (5 percent), and calcium (3.5 percent).

Mineral molecules bond together to form crystals. This agate (a form of silicon dioxide) includes crystals on a range of different scales, some too small to see.

Most useful elements are found as chemical compounds in mineral form. Once they have been mined, we use chemical processes to extract the elements.

Gold does not form minerals. These miners are extracting it in its pure form from "veins" in the rock.

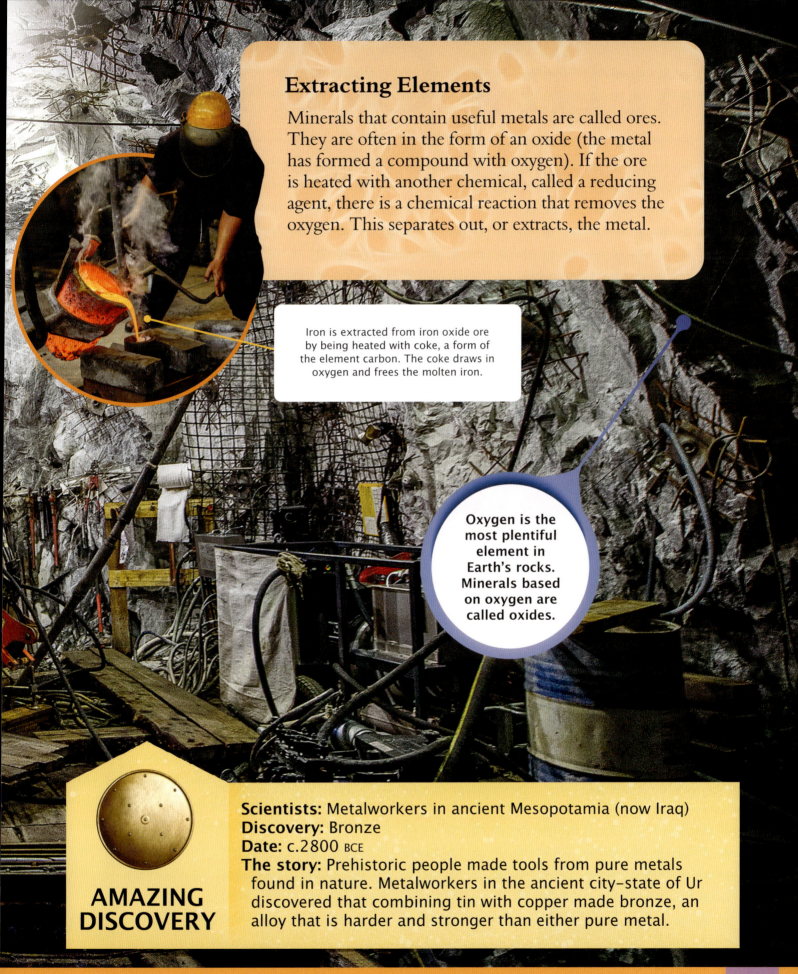

Extracting Elements

Minerals that contain useful metals are called ores. They are often in the form of an oxide (the metal has formed a compound with oxygen). If the ore is heated with another chemical, called a reducing agent, there is a chemical reaction that removes the oxygen. This separates out, or extracts, the metal.

Iron is extracted from iron oxide ore by being heated with coke, a form of the element carbon. The coke draws in oxygen and frees the molten iron.

Oxygen is the most plentiful element in Earth's rocks. Minerals based on oxygen are called oxides.

AMAZING DISCOVERY

Scientists: Metalworkers in ancient Mesopotamia (now Iraq)
Discovery: Bronze
Date: c.2800 BCE
The story: Prehistoric people made tools from pure metals found in nature. Metalworkers in the ancient city-state of Ur discovered that combining tin with copper made bronze, an alloy that is harder and stronger than either pure metal.

DID YOU KNOW? At least 30 possible new minerals are discovered every year, but many are different shades of minerals that are already named.

Earth's Crust

Earth's crust is part of what makes our planet unique. It is broken into seven major plates (and many smaller ones) that move around on top of the slowly churning mantle. Over millions of years these plates rearrange Earth's continents and oceans in a process that is called plate tectonics.

Floating Continents

The crust floats on top of the mantle because it is made of lighter rocks. Where the crust is highest (on continents or at high mountain ranges), it also stretches down the deepest—rather like an iceberg. Continental crust can be up to 70 km (44 miles) thick.

Where plates in the crust pull apart, thin new crust is produced by volcanic eruptions from the mantle.

Places such as China's Striped Mountains show how sedimentary rock forms in strata, or layers.

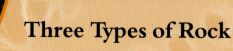

Three Types of Rock

Igneous rocks, such as basalt, form from cooled magma, either underground or where it's erupted as lava from a volcano. Sedimentary rocks, such as sandstone, are made when ground-down particles of rock settle and compress. Metamorphic rocks are created when another kind of rock is put under great heat or pressure, changing the minerals it contains—heated limestone becomes marble, for example.

Some mountains are made from igneous rocks that solidified from molten lava.

Even the highest mountains are steadily worn away over time by heat, cold, wind, and rain.

Some mountains contain rocks that formed on the seabed millions of years ago.

AMAZING DISCOVERY

Scientist: James Hutton
Discovery: Cycles in Earth's history
Date: 1785
The story: Scottish geologist Hutton showed how the three main types of rock relate to each other because of repeated cycles of settling, lifting up, and wearing away, stretching back over hundreds of millions of years.

DID YOU KNOW? Most tectonic plates move around 2.5 cm (1 in) per year, but the South Pacific Nazca plate is racing along more than twice as fast.

Volcanoes and Earthquakes

Powerful forces are unleashed in places where the plates of Earth's crust come together. Huge masses of rock crumple against or grind past each other and trigger devastating earthquakes. Where crust is driven down into the mantle, molten rock escapes through chains of volcanoes.

Violent eruptions happen when trapped gas bursts from pockets of magma beneath Earth's surface.

Plate Boundaries

If plates meet head-on, what happens next depends on the types of crust involved. Thin ocean crust will be pushed under thick continental crust, and as it melts in the mantle it will release heat that creates volcanoes. Where two continental plates meet, they buckle to create towering mountain ranges.

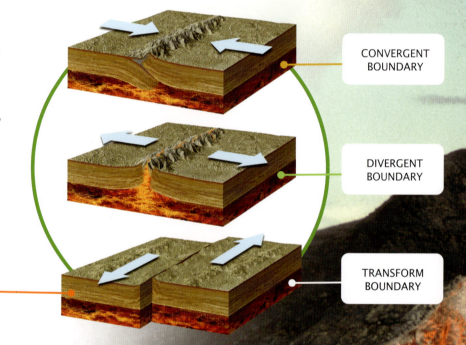

CONVERGENT BOUNDARY

DIVERGENT BOUNDARY

TRANSFORM BOUNDARY

Plates collide at convergent boundaries, pull apart (often beneath the oceans) at divergent boundaries, and grind past each other at transform boundaries.

AMAZING DISCOVERY

Scientist: Alfred Wegener
Discovery: Tectonic drift
Date: 1912
The story: Meteorologist Wegener noticed how the edges of widely separated landmasses fit together like a jigsaw puzzle. He suggested that continents move slowly around on Earth's crust, but his idea began to be accepted only in the 1950s.

100

Volcanoes form where tectonic movements heat and melt underground rock to form molten magma. When magma erupts at the surface, it is called lava.

Earthquakes

When Earth's crust suddenly shifts, it triggers waves of disturbance called earthquakes. This can happen when tectonic plates collide or when they grind sideways past each other. The waves spread through the crust and also down through the Earth. Sometimes the vibrations can be detected on the other side of the world.

Many of our biggest cities, such as Mexico City, are built in earthquake zones. Unfortunately scientists cannot yet predict exactly where or when a disastrous quake will strike.

Volcanoes and earthquakes happen at plate boundaries and also above random "hot spots" in Earth's mantle.

Liquid lava from volcanoes cools down rapidly. It solidifies into new igneous rocks.

DID YOU KNOW? The 1883 eruption of Krakatoa volcano in Indonesia was the loudest sound in recorded history. People heard the explosion 5,000 km (3,100 miles) away!

Mountains

A mountain is a large peak of rock that rises above the surrounding land. Some mountains stand alone, but most are part of mountain ranges, where a series of mountains are in a line or curve. There are also mountains and mountain ranges beneath the sea: Some islands are actually the tops of mountains.

> At 8,848 m (29,029 ft) tall, Mount Everest is the world's highest mountain.

Fold and Fault-Block Mountains

There are three types of mountains: fold mountains, fault-block mountains, and volcanoes (see page 100). All mountains take millions of years to form. Fold and fault-block mountains are made by the movement of Earth's plates.

MOUNTAIN BUILDING

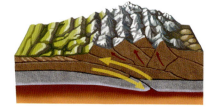

FOLD MOUNTAINS
Fold mountains form at convergent plate boundaries. As the plates move toward each other, rock is pushed and folded upward like a rumpled tablecloth.

FAULT-BLOCK MOUNTAINS
Fault-block mountains form where the rock is broken into chunks by plate movement. Some chunks are forced upward, sometimes on a tilt, and others are forced down.

LONGEST MOUNTAIN RANGE ON EACH CONTINENT

- **Africa:** Southern Great Escarpment, 5,000 km (3,100 miles)
- **South America:** Andes, 7,240 km (4,500 miles)
- **North America:** Rocky Mountains, 4,800 km (3,000 miles)
- **Australia:** Great Dividing Range, 3,500 km (2,175 miles)
- **Asia:** Himalayas, 2,400 km (1,500 miles)
- **Europe:** Scandinavian Mountains, 1,700 km (1,100 miles)
- **Antarctica:** Transantarctic Mountains, 3,540 km (2,200 miles)

Scandinavian Mountains

The Sierra Nevada

The Sierra Nevada range, in the western United States, are fault-block mountains. About 5 million years ago, a block of crust started to lift and tilt as a smaller plate moved beneath the North American plate. The lifting and tilting continues today, sometimes causing earthquakes in the region.

Along the eastern edge of the Sierra Nevada mountains, we can see the nearly straight edge of the uptilted block of crust.

The Himalaya mountains, in Asia, are fold mountains. The range started to form about 50 million years ago as the Indian plate slid under the Eurasian plate.

Climbers come from all over the world to test their skills on one of the range's 50 mountains that are over 7,200 m (23,600 ft) tall.

DID YOU KNOW? The longest mountain range of all is beneath the Atlantic Ocean: the Mid-Ocean Ridge is about 16,000 km (10,000 miles) long.

Crystals

If it has enough room, a mineral will grow into a regular, geometrical shape called a crystal. This is because its molecules stick together in a particular repeating pattern.

The Cave of Crystals in Mexico contains some of the largest natural crystals ever found.

Common Crystal

Quartz is one of the most common crystals. It can be clear or, if it contains trace minerals or impurities, take other forms—amethyst is purple quartz, citrine is yellow, and rose quartz is milky pink, for example. The basic quartz molecule has four oxygen atoms and one silicon atom. So long as nothing else gets in the way, quartz molecules grow to form six-sided prisms.

As these clear quartz crystals formed, they trapped the needle-shaped crystals of another mineral, rutile.

MAJOR MINERAL GROUPS

Silicates: Silicon and oxygen, plus other elements
Oxides: Oxygen plus one or more metal elements
Sulfates: Sulfur and oxygen, plus other elements
Sulfides: Sulfur plus a metal element
Carbonates: Carbon and oxygen, plus other elements
Native elements: Only one element
Halides: Fluorine, chlorine, bromine, or iodine, plus a metal element

Sylvite, a halide

104

It probably took at least half a million years for these crystals to form. They started to grow when gypsum on the cave floor was heated by magma in a chamber 3–5 km (2–3 miles) below.

Crystal Systems

VESUVIANITE

CUBIC A 6-, 8-, or 12-sided prism on a square base

PYRITE

TETRAGONAL A rectangular prism on a square base

SULFUR

HEXAGONAL/TRIGONAL Two crystal systems (of 6- or 3-sided shapes) that form one crystal family

TITANIUM QUARTZ

ORTHORHOMBIC A flattened rectangular prism shape

MONOCLINIC A rectangular prism on a parallelogram base

CHALCANTHITE

EPIDOTE

TRICLINIC The most irregular crystal shape with the least symmetry

Water originally filled this cave but was pumped out by miners working above. Today the cave is reflooded, because exposure to air was damaging the crystals.

Geologists exploring the cave wore protective suits because it was so hot—up to 58°C (136°F)—and humid.

DID YOU KNOW? The largest crystal discovered in the Cave of Crystals was 12 m (39 ft) long, 4 m (13 ft) wide, and weighed 50 tonnes (55 tons).

Metals

Metals are solids that are usually hard and shiny. They melt when they are heated and are malleable (can be hammered into new shapes). Some metals, such as silver, copper, platinum, zinc, iron, and mercury are "native element minerals"—minerals that are made of a single element.

Metal Properties

Metals and alloys (mixes of two or more metals) sometimes occur as nuggets, grains, or veins in rock. More often, metals are found in ores, chemically bonded to other elements. Being hard, shiny, and easy to shape makes metals ideal for tools, machines, construction materials, coins, and art. Most metals allow heat and electricity to travel through them easily, so they are also used for wiring, electronics, and cooking equipment.

Bolivia's Cerro Rico ("rich mountain"), near the city of Potosí, has one of the world's largest silver and tin mines.

Miners blast at the underground rock with explosives, then load the resulting rubble onto mine train carts. These carry the silver ore to the surface.

If these gold crystals had unlimited space and were not in a narrow vein, the crystals would be cubic.

Transporting platinum ore, South Africa

METAL PRODUCTION
Plus the nation that produces the largest share of each

Gold: 3,200 tonnes (3,500 tons)—China, 13 percent
Copper: 5.3 million tonnes (5.8 million tons)—Chile, 27 percent
Silver: 6,108 tonnes (6,733 tons)—Mexico, 16 percent
Tin: 125,000 tonnes (137,800 tons)—China, 42 percent
Platinum: 110,000 tonnes (121,000 tons)—South Africa, 68 percent

DID YOU KNOW? Metals make up one-quarter of the weight of Earth's crust, with the most common being aluminum (aluminium), iron, and calcium.

It is rare to find a pure silver nugget. Silver is usually found in ores such as argentite (silver and sulfur), galena (silver and lead), or chlorargyrite (silver and chlorine).

The only light in the 1-m (3.3-ft) wide tunnel comes from the miners' headlamps.

Using Metals

People learned to extract copper 10,000 years ago. By 3,000 years ago we were adding tin to make bronze, an alloy that was stronger than copper or tin. We could extract and work iron—a process that requires much higher temperatures—from around 1,200 years ago.

This electromagnetic crane is separating out iron from other scrap so it can be reused. Only a few metals are magnetic—iron, nickel, cobalt, and some alloys.

Fossils

The rocks of our planet are like a history book. Paleontologists study fossils—ancient animals and plants preserved in rock—to find out about the past. Archeologists specialize in the story of humankind. They dig up human remains and artifacts.

Preserved in Rock

If plant or animal remains sink down into sediment or are trapped in volcanic lava or ash, their hard parts fossilize (turn to rock.) The process can take millions of years. Ancient objects are found preserved in the ground, too—from tools to treasure troves and from buildings to boats.

These are the fossilized remains of an extinct animal called a trilobite. The oceans were home to trilobites from 520 to 250 million years ago (mya).

Most of the rock at Atapuerca is sedimentary chert, sandstone, and limestone. There is also quartzite, a metamorphic rock.

FAMOUS FOSSIL BEDS

Auca Mahuevo, Argentina: Titanosaur nesting site, 83–79 mya
La Brea Tar Pits, USA: Ice Age animals, 20,000–10,000 ya
Liaoning, China: Feathered dinosaurs, 133–120 mya
Olduvai Gorge, Tanzania: Early humans, from 1.9 mya
Riversleigh, Australia: Megafauna, from 25 mya

Smilodon skull, La Brea, USA

This dig is at Atapuerca, northern Spain. Early humans lived here from nearly 1 million years ago to the present.

These archeologists are working in the biggest cave at Atapuerca. They have found animal skulls, Stone Age tools, and bones from our ancestor *Homo heidelbergensis*.

Top Marks

Fossil remains do not have to be bodies and bones. They can be traces left behind. Footprints and animal tracks, root holes and burrows … all of these can harden into rock and leave a record of past life.

A theropod made these footprints in the Cretaceous Period. Theropods were mostly meat-eating dinosaurs.

DID YOU KNOW? The oldest fossil footprints of human ancestors found are in Tanzania and date back 3.7 million years.

Fossil Fuels

Coal, petroleum (oil), and natural gas are cheap, reliable, and provide more than two-thirds of the world's energy. However, combusting (burning) them is a major cause of global warming because it gives off carbon dioxide. Although carbon dioxide is naturally present in the atmosphere, excess carbon dioxide traps too much of the Sun's heat, leading to a rise in temperatures.

Forming Fuel

Fossil fuels are the remains of plants and animals. The story of coal begins in prehistoric, swampy forests. Mud or acidic water broke down fallen tree trunks, creating peat bogs. Over millions of years, sediment buried the peat, pressing it to make seams of coal. Petroleum (oil) and natural gas formed in a similar way from the bodies of animals and plants that sank into sediment on the seabed.

The natural form of petroleum (oil) is crude oil. Before we can use it, it has to be processed in a refinery, such as this one at Wakayama, Japan.

Over long distances, boats or trains transport coal, while pipes carry petroleum (oil) and natural gas. Large trucks move fossil fuels over short distances.

From lightest to heaviest, the refined oil produces bottled gas and fuel for cars, aircraft, trucks, heating, and power stations.

Sticky bitumen (tar) is left behind after the oil has been refined into different fuels. We use tar to waterproof roads and roofs.

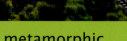

DID YOU KNOW? Anthracite is the best-quality coal. It is a metamorphic rock, formed when sedimentary coal comes under huge heat and pressure.

Precious Peat

Peat bogs are "carbon sinks"—they absorb harmful carbon dioxide from the atmosphere. These wetlands are also a unique habitat for rare plants and animals. Unfortunately, many bogs have been drained for grazing or harvested for their peat.

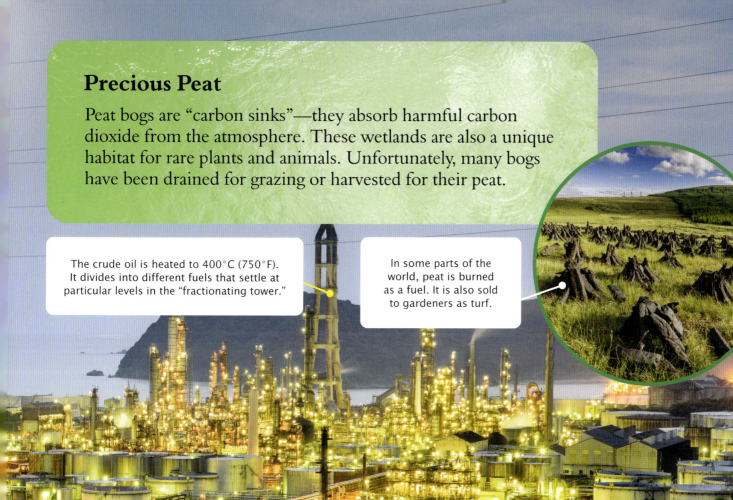

The crude oil is heated to 400°C (750°F). It divides into different fuels that settle at particular levels in the "fractionating tower."

In some parts of the world, peat is burned as a fuel. It is also sold to gardeners as turf.

This unit stores liquefied petroleum gas (LPG), or bottled gas.

Yeosu, South Korea

LARGEST REFINERIES
Daily processing capacity
One barrel = 159 l (42 US gallons)

1,240,000 barrels: Jamnagar Refinery, Gujarat, India
940,000 barrels: Paraguaná Refinery, Falcón, Venezuela
850,000 barrels: SK Energy Refinery, Ulsan, South Korea
817,000 barrels: Ruwais Refinery, Ruwais, UAE
730,000 barrels: Yeosu Refinery, South Korea

111

CHAPTER 6: WEATHER, CLIMATE, AND HABITAT

The Atmosphere

Earth is surrounded by a thin but vital layer of gas called the atmosphere. It provides the air we breathe, creates a protective blanket that keeps out the worst extremes of hot and cold, and gives us a complex system of ever-changing weather.

Atmospheric Gases

Without an atmosphere absorbing and trapping the Sun's heat, our planet would be unbearably hot in the day and icy-cold at night. The main gases in the atmosphere are nitrogen and oxygen. Oceans, rocks, and life absorb and produce different gases, creating a delicate balance. There is a layer of ozone in the stratosphere, about 25 km (16 miles) up. Ozone is a kind of oxygen with three atoms instead of the usual two. The ozone layer absorbs harmful ultraviolet (UV) radiation from the Sun.

Space particles collide with atoms of gases in the atmosphere, give them energy, and make them glow.

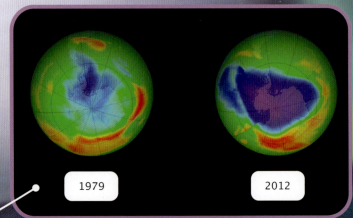

1979   2012

These satellite images show that a "hole" has opened up in the ozone layer because of pollution. Green, yellow, and red areas have higher ozone levels; blue and purple have the least.

AMAZING DISCOVERY

Scientist: George Hadley
Discovery: Atmospheric circulation and winds
Date: 1735
The story: Amateur meteorologist (weather scientist) Hadley was the first person to realize that wind patterns were due to the Earth spinning on its axis and the way air rises in hot areas and sinks in colder ones.

Aurorae, also known as the northern and southern lights, happen close to the poles. Earth's magnetic field attracts tiny particles from space.

Oxygen atoms glow green at low altitudes and red at high ones. Nitrogen produces blue or purple.

Most aurorae are in the thermosphere. They happen 80–640 km (50–400 miles) above the ground.

Balancing the Climate

Carbon dioxide (CO_2) is called a greenhouse gas because it traps heat like the glass of a greenhouse. The CO_2 in our atmosphere keeps our planet warm. However, burning fossil fuels such as coal and oil create more CO_2 than there used to be. This is heating the planet at a faster rate and changing our climate.

The atmosphere is divided into layers that stretch out into space. It gets thinner the higher we go.

1. TROPOSPHERE up to 12 km (7.5 miles)
2. STRATOSPHERE 12–50 km (7.5–31 miles)
3. MESOSPHERE 50–80 km (31–50 miles)
4. THERMOSPHERE 80–700 km (50–435 miles)
5. EXOSPHERE 700–10,000 km (435–6,214 miles)

DID YOU KNOW? At the outer edge of the exosphere, 10,000 km (6,214 miles) above Earth's surface, lightweight gas particles are constantly blown away into space.

Seasons

It takes just over 365 days for Earth to travel around the Sun. During that time, which we call a year, we go through a cycle of seasons. There is a reason for the seasons! Earth is tilted on its axis (an imaginary line through its middle from pole to pole). When places tilt toward the Sun, they receive more heat.

Four Seasons

Most places have four seasons—spring, summer, fall (autumn), and winter. When our hemisphere (half of the Earth) tilts toward the Sun, we have summer. When it tilts away, we have winter. June is summer in the north and winter in the south.

In fall (autumn) the leaves of deciduous trees lose their green pigment, chlorophyll. They turn shades of red, orange, and yellow.

Deciduous trees drop their leaves before winter. The leaves are not tough enough to survive the winter cold.

In March, the northern hemisphere has spring, the season between winter and summer; the southern hemisphere has fall (autumn).

In September, the southern hemisphere has spring; the northern hemisphere has fall (autumn), the season between summer and winter.

THREE SPRING EQUINOX FESTIVALS

Nowruz: Also called Persian New Year. People clean their houses, buy new clothes, and go on picnics.
Return of the Sun Serpent: At the Mayan temple in Chichen Itza, Mexico, sunlight and shadow create the illusion of a "snake" slithering down the steps.
Songkran: This Thai festival is traditionally held on April 13 every year. People celebrate with water fights!

Songkran

The fall (autumn) equinox is on 21, 22, 23, or 24 September in the northern half of the world and 19, 20, or 21 March in the southern half.

Two Seasons

In the area around the equator, called the tropics, the amount of sunlight and heat does not change much through the year. There are only two types of season—wet and dry. Temperatures are around 25°C (77°F) in the wet season and 20°C (68°F) in the dry.

In southern Asia, farmers plant rice at the start of the rainy season. Some still use water buffalo to prepare the fields.

DID YOU KNOW? Twice a year, in March and September, the Sun shines directly on the equator. These are called the equinoxes.

Day and Night

As well as orbiting the Sun, Earth spins on its axis (an imaginary line like a spinning top's spindle). It rotates once roughly every 24 hours. At any moment, half of our planet is facing toward the Sun (experiencing daytime) and half is facing away (experiencing night).

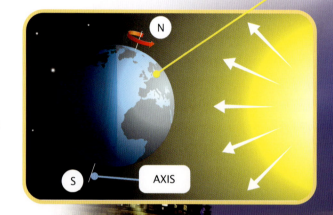

Earth spins counterclockwise on its axis, giving us night and day.

Shortest and Longest

The northern hemisphere has the most sunlight on June 21 (its summer solstice) and the least on December 21 (its winter solstice). It is the opposite in the southern hemisphere. The shortest day (winter solstice) is June 21 and the longest day (summer solstice) is December 21.

What's the Time?

Before clocks, people told the time by the Sun. Midday was when the Sun is highest in the sky. Today we split the world into time zones. Each north-to-south strip has an agreed standard time.

The World Clock in Berlin shows the local time in 148 major cities from around the world. A country's local time is measured in hours behind or ahead of Coordinated Universal Time or UTC. The International Date Line is 12 hours behind UTC. We gain a day if we cross it from west to East—Tuesday becomes Monday again.

DID YOU KNOW? One in every four years is a leap year with an extra day (February 29). Leap years keep our calendar in sync with our orbit around the Sun.

DAY AND NIGHT FACTS

Earth's rotational speed: 1,670 kmh (1,038 mph) at the equator
Midnight sun: At the poles, the Sun never sets on the longest day—that is June for the north and December for the south.
Polar night: At the poles, the Sun never rises on the shortest day—that is June for the south and December for the north.

Midnight sun in Norway

The night sky in the city is never really dark. There are too many artificial lights.

Except for where there are clouds, the daytime sky looks blue. This is because of the way the atmosphere scatters the light from the Sun.

Wherever we are in the world, the Sun always appears to "rise" in the east and set in the west. In reality, it is Earth that is moving.

This image is two photographs merged together to show Trafalgar Square, London, UK, at night and during the day.

117

Earth's Water

Earth is the only planet in our Solar System with the right surface temperature for water to exist as liquid, solid ice, and gas (water vapor). The water cycle changes water between these forms, moves it around, and shapes our planet.

Erosion

Water is an irresistible force. Rivers and slow-moving bodies of ice called glaciers wear away and erode Earth's rocks. Seas beat at cliffs. Over thousands of years, water shapes the landscape and transports ground-down particles, or sediment, into low-lying areas. Water is an even more powerful erosive force than wind or extreme hot or cold.

Water naturally flows downhill. Rainfall over land finds its way to the oceans through rivers, lakes, and underground springs.

The Grand Canyon in Arizona is an 1,800-m (1.1-mile) deep valley. It has been carved out by the winding Colorado River over the past 6 million years or more.

Islands of the Maldives in the Indian Ocean

AREAS OF THE OCEANS

Pacific Ocean: 168,723,000 sq km (65,144,000 sq miles
Atlantic Ocean: 85,133,000 sq km (32,870,000 sq miles)
Indian Ocean: 70,560,000 sq km (27,243,000 sq miles)
Southern Ocean: 21,960,000 sq km (8,479,000 sq miles)
Arctic Ocean: 15,558,000 sq km (6,007,000 sq miles)

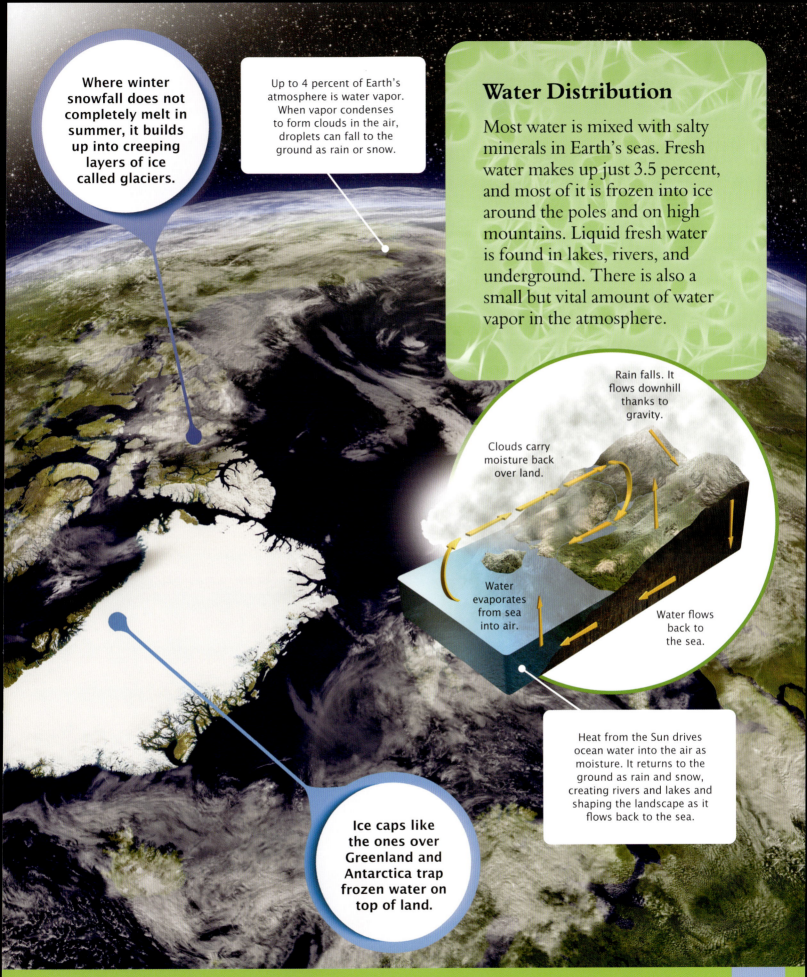

Where winter snowfall does not completely melt in summer, it builds up into creeping layers of ice called glaciers.

Up to 4 percent of Earth's atmosphere is water vapor. When vapor condenses to form clouds in the air, droplets can fall to the ground as rain or snow.

Water Distribution

Most water is mixed with salty minerals in Earth's seas. Fresh water makes up just 3.5 percent, and most of it is frozen into ice around the poles and on high mountains. Liquid fresh water is found in lakes, rivers, and underground. There is also a small but vital amount of water vapor in the atmosphere.

Rain falls. It flows downhill thanks to gravity.

Clouds carry moisture back over land.

Water evaporates from sea into air.

Water flows back to the sea.

Heat from the Sun drives ocean water into the air as moisture. It returns to the ground as rain and snow, creating rivers and lakes and shaping the landscape as it flows back to the sea.

Ice caps like the ones over Greenland and Antarctica trap frozen water on top of land.

DID YOU KNOW? If all of Earth's water was collected into a ball, it would be about 1,385 km (860 miles) across—just 0.1 percent of our planet's entire volume.

Weather Systems

All weather is driven by the uneven way that the Sun heats the atmosphere, land, and oceans. This causes air masses to move about. A big mass of air that has a steady temperature will bring steady weather. Global winds, ocean currents (streams of moving water), the cold air around mountain ranges, and other geographical features on the ground all affect the weather.

Weather Fronts

A warm front is the point where a warm air mass meets a colder air mass and moves up and over the colder air. A cold front is where a colder air mass advances into and pushes up a warm air mass.

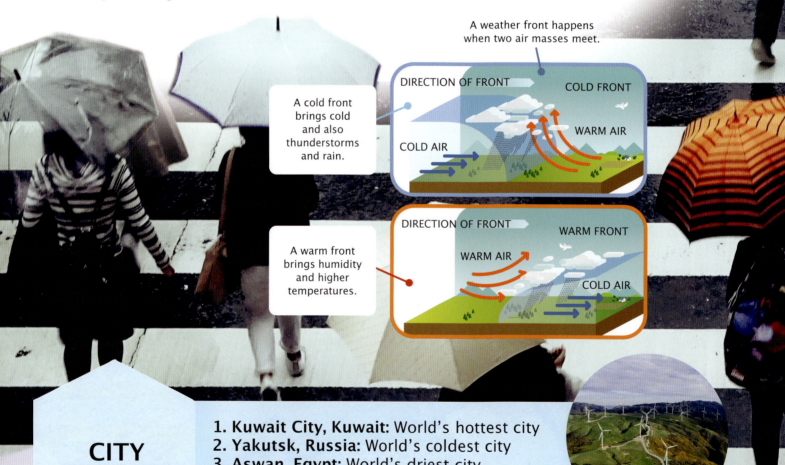

A weather front happens when two air masses meet.

A cold front brings cold and also thunderstorms and rain.

A warm front brings humidity and higher temperatures.

CITY WEATHER EXTREMES

1. **Kuwait City, Kuwait:** World's hottest city
2. **Yakutsk, Russia:** World's coldest city
3. **Aswan, Egypt:** World's driest city
4. **Buenaventura, Colombia:** World's wettest city
5. **Wellington, New Zealand:** World's windiest city

Wind farm outside Wellington, New Zealand

DID YOU KNOW? Other planets with atmospheres have winds: Neptune has the highest wind speeds of 2,092 km/h (1,300 mph).

Weather forecasting helps us prepare for whatever weather is to come.

Wind

Wind is the movement of air. Wind happens when there is a difference in temperature in the Earth's atmosphere. Warm air is lighter than cool air, so it rises higher above the Earth. Cool air rushes into the space where the warm air once was.

Most countries around the world have rain of some kind at some time during the year, even deserts.

NORTH POLE

EQUATOR

SOUTH POLE

Wind is also created by the spin of the Earth and the difference in temperature between the equator and polar areas. Global winds carry warm air around the Earth.

Storms and Precipitation

When water freezes in clouds it forms tiny flat six-sided crystals. These crystals join together to make snowflakes. No two snowflakes look the same.

Rain, snow, and hail are all forms of precipitation. When the air cools, moisture in the air forms into tiny, floating droplets, which we call clouds. The droplets collect into bigger drops until they are too heavy to stay aloft—then they fall as rain. In cold weather, the moisture turns into crystals and forms snow or hail instead.

Thunder and Lightning

During a thunderstorm you will hear thunder and see lightning and (usually) heavy rain. Thunderstorms develop in tall, dark cumulonimbus clouds. Ice and water particles bump into each other inside the cloud, building up an electric charge. When the negative charge in the cloud connects to a positive charge on the ground or elsewhere in the cloud, we see an electrical spark—lightning! Thunder is caused by the lightning and can be a loud crack or a low rumble.

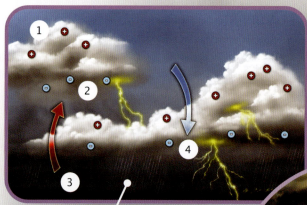

Inside a thundercloud, frozen raindrops collide with each other, creating an electric charge. (1) Positive charges (protons) collect at the top of the cloud and (2) negative charges (electrons) collect at the bottom, nearer to the ground.

(3) Opposites attract, so when a positive charge builds up on the ground, (4) it connects to a negative charge reaching down from the cloud and lightning strikes.

Lightning makes a hole in the air called a channel. Thunder is the sound of the hole collapsing when the lightning has gone.

PRECIPITATION RECORDS

Heaviest rainfall: 156 cm (61 in) in a day, Cherrapunji, India, 1995
Largest hailstone: 18 cm (7 in) across, Nebraska, USA, 2003
Heaviest snowfall: 256 cm (101 in) in a day, Capracotta, Italy, 2015

World's largest hailstone

DID YOU KNOW? You can hear thunder up to 24 km (15 miles) away and you can see lightning up to 161 km (100 miles) away!

During a blizzard visibility is greatly reduced so you cannot see very far ahead.

Types of Clouds

Different cloud types form in different weather conditions. Some clouds form close to the ground; others high in the sky. We can predict the weather by looking at cloud shapes and how high in the sky they are.

A blizzard is a long-lasting heavy snow storm with very strong winds. Blizzards happen when warm air rises over very cold or freezing air near the ground.

1. Altocumulus is a mid-level cloud.
2. Nimbostratus clouds can bring rain.
3. Cumulonimbus clouds bring heavy rain and storms.
4. Fluffy cumulus clouds form at low levels.

Tornadoes

Tornadoes form when certain types of weather collide. When warm and humid air near the ground meets colder air above, it punches through the cold layer and storm clouds develop. Winds blowing through the clouds twist the rising air currents, forming a whirlwind. The whirlwind spins faster and faster until it becomes a fierce tornado.

Danger Ahead!

As the tornado swirls across the land, it picks up any objects in its path and can carry them a long distance. Most tornadoes happen in the United States, in the Great Plains, in an area known as Tornado Alley.

A very strong tornado can pick up cars and houses and destroy everything in its path.

Tornadoes connect the clouds and the ground. They are also called twisters or cyclones.

Tornadoes are measured using the Fujita Scale or F-Scale. The scale ranges from F0 to F5, the strongest and most destructive type of tornadoes.

DEADLIEST TORNADOES

Daulatpur-Saturia Tornado: Around 1,300 killed, Bangladesh, 1989
Tri-State Tornado: 695 killed, Missouri, Illinois, and Indiana, USA, 1925
Dhaka Tornado: 681 killed, Bangladesh, 1973
East Pakistan Tornado: 660 killed, Bangladesh, 1969

Map of the Tri-State tornado

DID YOU KNOW? The fastest winds on Earth occur inside tornadoes, where wind speeds can reach 402 km/h (250 mph).

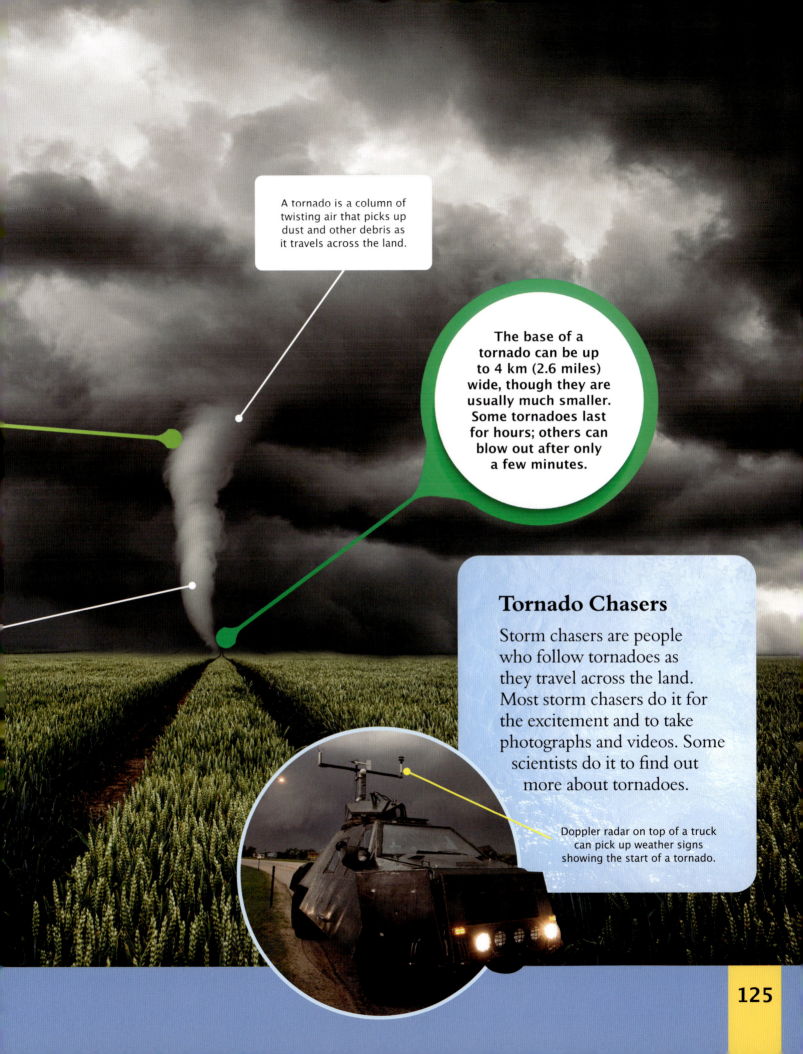

A tornado is a column of twisting air that picks up dust and other debris as it travels across the land.

The base of a tornado can be up to 4 km (2.6 miles) wide, though they are usually much smaller. Some tornadoes last for hours; others can blow out after only a few minutes.

Tornado Chasers

Storm chasers are people who follow tornadoes as they travel across the land. Most storm chasers do it for the excitement and to take photographs and videos. Some scientists do it to find out more about tornadoes.

Doppler radar on top of a truck can pick up weather signs showing the start of a tornado.

Hurricanes

Hurricanes are powerful, swirling storms also known as tropical cyclones or typhoons. They begin out at sea and can travel across the water to reach land, where they cause devastation. Strong winds and dark clouds rotate on the outside of a hurricane. The middle, called the eye of the storm, is usually calm and cloudless.

Hurricane Havoc

Hurricane winds can reach up to 252 km/h (157 mph) as the warm air spirals around the storm system. A hurricane can also raise the sea level beneath it, causing floods that threaten lives, destroy houses, and damage crops.

When a hurricane strikes, homes are evacuated and people gather in a place of safety. Many are left homeless.

Most hurricanes form in late summer when sea temperatures are at their highest.

The Beaufort Scale measures the force of wind based on speed and the effect it has on its surroundings. There are 13 levels.

0	1	2	3	4	5	6
Speed: less than 1 km/h (1 mph). Calm. Smoke rises vertically.	Speed: 1–5 km/h (1–3 mph). Light air. Smoke drifts in the direction of the wind.	Speed: 6–11 km/h (4–7 mph). Light breeze. Wind felt on face; leaves rustle.	Speed: 12–19 km/h (8–12 mph). Gentle breeze. Leaves and small twigs constantly moving.	Speed: 20–28 km/h (13–18 mph). Moderate breeze. Raises dust and loose paper; small branches moved.	Speed: 29–38 km/h (19–24 mph). Fresh breeze. Small trees with leaves begin to sway. Small crested waves on inland water.	Speed: 38–49 km/h (25–31 mph). Strong breeze. Large branches moved. Umbrellas used with difficulty.

WORST TROPICAL CYCLONES

Deadliest: Bhola Cyclone, Bangladesh, 1970, over 500,000 dead
Costliest: Hurricane Katrina, USA, 2005, over $125 billion in damage and 1,800 dead
Highest wind gusts: Cyclone Olivia, Australia, 1996, 405 km/h (255 mph)

Satellite image

How Hurricanes Form

Hurricanes form over warm water when different weather systems come together (1). They all rotate and swirl into one giant spiral (2). Warm, moist air rises on the edges of the storm. (3) Dry air sinks through the eye of the storm.

1 2 3

Inward-flowing winds, low pressure at the core of the storm, and rain are all features of a hurricane.

Huge cumulonimbus clouds tower up into the atmosphere, causing heavy rain and lightning.

7	8	9	10	11	12
Speed: 50–61 km/h (32–38 mph). Near gale. Whole trees moved. Difficulty walking against the wind.	Speed: 62–74 km/h (39–46 mph). Gale. Twigs break off trees. Difficult to walk.	Speed: 75–88 km/h (47–54 mph). Strong gale. Chimney pots and roof slates might be damaged.	Speed: 89–102 km/h (55–63 mph). Storm. Trees uprooted. Serious damage to buildings.	Speed: 103–117 km/h (64–72 mph). Violent storm. Widespread damage.	Speed: 118 plus km/h (73 plus mph). Hurricane. Devastation.

127

Climate Zones

> The brown bear is found in the boreal forests of northern North America and Eurasia. In winter, its fur is very thick and long, up to 12 cm (5 in).

Climate is the general weather in a place over time, such as the temperature and how much rain falls. The three basic climates are tropical (near the equator), polar (around the poles), and temperate (everything in between). A biome is a group of habitats that share a similar climate.

A Rough Guide

Differences in temperature, light, and rainfall across the seasons create different biomes. Boreal forests are found south of the Arctic, while rain forests are typical in tropical climates. Biomes do not have clear borders but slowly change from one to another.

- TEMPERATE BROADLEAF FOREST
- CONIFEROUS FOREST
- TEMPERATE GRASSLAND
- MEDITERRANEAN
- TROPICAL RAIN FOREST
- DESERT
- MOUNTAIN
- TUNDRA
- POLAR

On this map, the world's land is divided into nine biomes that share similar climates. Each biome can be subdivided into even more precise biomes.

WORLD'S LARGEST CORAL REEFS

1. **Great Barrier Reef:** 2,500 km (1,550 miles)
2. **Red Sea Reef:** 1,900 km (1,180 miles)
3. **New Caledonia Barrier Reef:** 1,500 km (930 miles)
4. **Mesoamerican Barrier Reef:** 940 km (585 miles)
5. **Florida Reef:** 580 km (360 miles)

Copperband butterflyfish

Underwater Biomes

Rivers, lakes, ponds, streams, and many wetlands are all freshwater biomes. Marine, or saltwater, biomes range from estuaries, coastal areas, and coral reefs to the different depths of the pelagic zone (open ocean). Each biome has its own conditions.

Most trees in boreal forests are conifers. Instead of flat leaves, they have thin needles that help to save water. Their branches slope downward so snow can fall off.

Shallow-water coral reefs, like this one in the Red Sea, teem with life.

Brown bear cubs stay with their mother for around two and a half years. After that, they must fend for themselves.

Tough bracken ferns die back in winter but survive and cover the forest floor in summer.

DID YOU KNOW? The Russian boreal forests, or "taiga," are rich in insects during the breeding season, so many birds nest here, including wood warblers.

Deserts

Desert winds blow the sand into ripples, ridges, and dunes. The Sahara's sand is a distinctive reddish-gold shade.

With an average of less than 250 mm (10 in) of rain a year, deserts are the driest places on Earth. Those closer to the equator, such as the Sahara, are hot year-round. Further from the equator, deserts can be cold part or all of the time. Instead of sand, some are bare rock, stripped of all soil.

Desert Animals

A desert looks lifeless, but insects, small reptiles, and mammals are active at night, hiding from the daytime heat in burrows. Special features let them benefit from any moisture—the fogstand beetle collects water on its back from early morning fogs.

A few traders still use camels to transport goods across the Sahara. However, most rely on trucks or planes.

The Arabian oryx is a desert antelope that can go for weeks without water. It can also sense rainfall from far away. Its white coat reflects the sunlight.

WORLD'S LARGEST DESERTS

1. **Antarctica:** 14.25 million sq km (5.5 million sq miles)
2. **Arctic:** 14 million sq km (5.4 million sq miles)
3. **Sahara Desert:** 9 million sq km (3.5 million sq miles)
4. **Arabian Desert:** 2.6 million sq km (1 million sq miles)
5. **Gobi Desert:** 1.3 million sq km (500,000 sq miles)

Antarctica

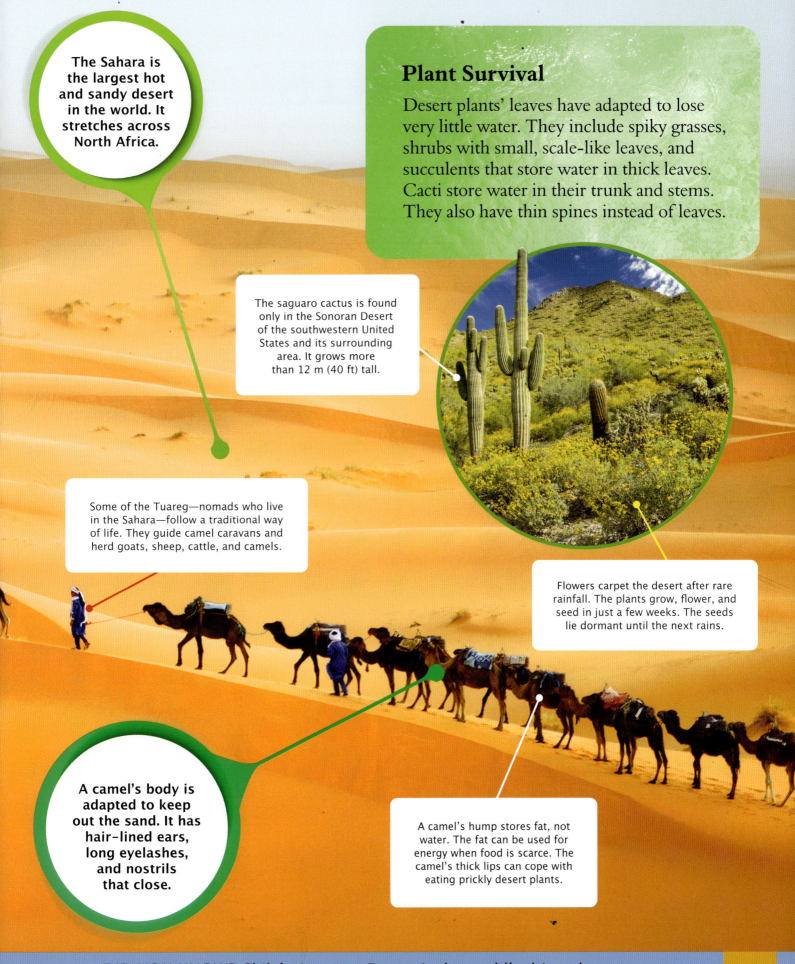

The Sahara is the largest hot and sandy desert in the world. It stretches across North Africa.

Plant Survival

Desert plants' leaves have adapted to lose very little water. They include spiky grasses, shrubs with small, scale-like leaves, and succulents that store water in thick leaves. Cacti store water in their trunk and stems. They also have thin spines instead of leaves.

The saguaro cactus is found only in the Sonoran Desert of the southwestern United States and its surrounding area. It grows more than 12 m (40 ft) tall.

Some of the Tuareg—nomads who live in the Sahara—follow a traditional way of life. They guide camel caravans and herd goats, sheep, cattle, and camels.

Flowers carpet the desert after rare rainfall. The plants grow, flower, and seed in just a few weeks. The seeds lie dormant until the next rains.

A camel's body is adapted to keep out the sand. It has hair-lined ears, long eyelashes, and nostrils that close.

A camel's hump stores fat, not water. The fat can be used for energy when food is scarce. The camel's thick lips can cope with eating prickly desert plants.

DID YOU KNOW? Chile's Atacama Desert is the world's driest desert. Some parts of it have had no rain since weather stations were set up there.

Grasslands

Grasslands are found around the world, from the cold north to the hot tropics. Warm, tropical grasslands include the African and Australian savannahs. Temperate grasslands are cooler and wetter, such as the American prairies, the veld in South Africa, and the South American pampas.

Grassland Animals

A wide variety of animals live in grasslands. Wild sheep clamber about in mountain grasslands while giraffes, zebra, and antelope graze on the African savannah. Huge areas of grassland are now being cleared for crops and animal farming.

In the pampas, giant anteaters sniff out termite nests. They tear them open with their sharp claws and use their long, sticky tongue to scoop out the insects.

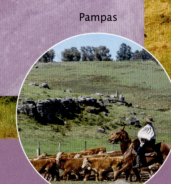

Pampas

WORLD'S LARGEST GRASSLANDS

1. **Savannah, Africa:** 12.9 million sq km (5 million sq miles)
2. **Prairie, North America:** 3.6 million sq km (1.4 million sq miles)
3. **Pampas, South America:** 760,000 sq km (295,000 sq miles)
4. **Steppe, Central Eurasia:** stretches 8,000 km (5,000 miles) from the Danube River to the Pacific

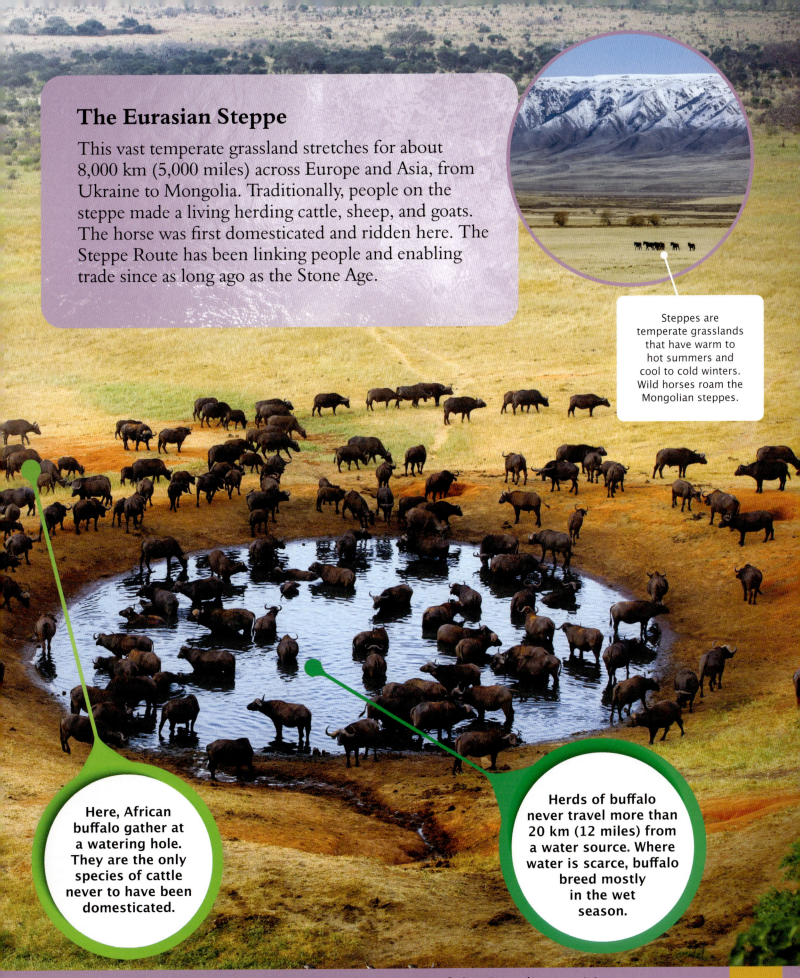

The Eurasian Steppe

This vast temperate grassland stretches for about 8,000 km (5,000 miles) across Europe and Asia, from Ukraine to Mongolia. Traditionally, people on the steppe made a living herding cattle, sheep, and goats. The horse was first domesticated and ridden here. The Steppe Route has been linking people and enabling trade since as long ago as the Stone Age.

Steppes are temperate grasslands that have warm to hot summers and cool to cold winters. Wild horses roam the Mongolian steppes.

Here, African buffalo gather at a watering hole. They are the only species of cattle never to have been domesticated.

Herds of buffalo never travel more than 20 km (12 miles) from a water source. Where water is scarce, buffalo breed mostly in the wet season.

DID YOU KNOW? More than 70 percent of the Canadian prairies has been converted to other uses, such as agriculture and industry.

Forests

Rain forests grow near the equator, where it is hot and humid year round. Temperate forests grow in areas to the north and south, which are cooler and have seasons. Boreal forests grow in the subarctic region and are also called snow forests. Eight out of ten land species—plant and animal—live in forests.

Forest Trees

Broadleaved trees have flat, wide leaves and their seeds are inside fruits. In warm regions, many broadleaved trees keep their leaves year-round. In cooler regions, most broadleaved trees drop their leaves in fall (autumn). Conifer trees grow in places with cold winters and have thin, sharp needles instead of broad leaves. These help to retain water and can survive snow. Their seeds are inside hard, woody cones, which close when wet and open when dry.

Howler monkeys make a shrieking noise that can be heard 3–5 km (2–3 miles) across the forest.

Fast-moving forest fires destroy habitat and leave people and animals homeless. Small fires can be healthy for some forests by clearing away dead and diseased growth and allowing sunlight through.

Mountain Forests

Tropical mountain forests are home to a wide range of animals, from gorillas in Central Africa to jaguars in South America. In freezing, snowy areas or mountainous regions, trees cannot grow above a certain height, called the tree line, as it is too cold and windy for them to survive.

A cougar perches on a lookout point in the South American forest. Its sharp claws retract to help it climb trees and hunt.

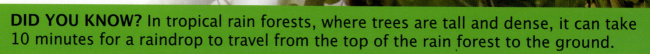

DID YOU KNOW? In tropical rain forests, where trees are tall and dense, it can take 10 minutes for a raindrop to travel from the top of the rain forest to the ground.

Monkeys, sloths, and other species use the trees to move around. Many spend all their time in the trees and hardly ever touch the ground.

New World monkeys use their long tails as another limb to hang onto branches as they swing through the forest.

WORLD'S LARGEST RAIN FORESTS

1. **Amazon, South America:** 5.5 million sq km (2.1 million sq miles)
2. **Congo Basin, Africa:** 2 million sq km (772,000 sq miles)
3. **New Guinea, Southeast Asia:** 700,000 sq km (270,000 sq miles)
4. **Valdivian, South America:** 248,000 sq km (95,000 sq miles)

The Asian elephant lives in Southeast Asian forests.

Polar Regions

With biting winds, low temperatures, and lengthy winters, life is tough at the poles. The Arctic Circle includes the Arctic Ocean, ringed by northerly North America, Europe, and Asia. The Antarctic Circle contains most of Antarctica and the southerly waters of the Southern Ocean.

Year-Round Ice

Sea ice floats on the Arctic Ocean for most of the year. Arctic land is tundra with permafrost (permanently frozen ground). Antarctica is mostly covered by a permanent ice sheet.

Temperatures in Antarctica can plummet as low as −89°C (−129°F)

Trees cannot root in the permafrost. Only small, scrubby plants survive in the tundra. They bloom briefly during the short summer.

ARCTIC ANIMALS IN DANGER

Eskimo curlew: Critically endangered (possibly extinct)
Snowy owl: Vulnerable—100,000 left
Polar bear: Vulnerable—maximum 31,000 left
Walrus: Vulnerable—fewer than 225,000 left
Reindeer (caribou): Vulnerable—around 2 million left
Greenland shark: Vulnerable—population unknown

Walrus

Herd Instincts

Reindeer or caribou travel in herds across the Arctic tundra. Each herd can consist of hundreds of individuals. As the summer starts, they begin one of the world's largest animal migrations. Some herds travel north for 1,610–2,575 km (1,000–1,600 miles) to give birth and find more abundant food.

Caribou have two layers of fur to keep them warm. Their hair contains air pockets that act as extra insulation against the cold.

These gentoo penguins are the most northerly of the four Antarctic species. The other three are chinstrap, Adélie, and emperor penguins.

Gentoos are the fastest-swimming penguins. They zip through the icy water at 36 km/h (22 mph), catching krill and other crustaceans.

DID YOU KNOW? The Arctic is home to about 4 million people from more than 40 ethnic groups, including Inuit, Sami, and Nenets (Samoyeds).

Wetlands

Wetlands are habitats where water saturates the ground to form shallow pools or stretches of water. Found in every continent except Antarctica, they support a variety of wildlife. Wetlands include mangrove forests, swamps, bogs, marshes, fens—and peatlands, making up almost half of the world's wetlands.

Clean and Fresh

Wetlands help to control flooding. They also attract many different species of animals. However, wetland areas face serious threats from farming, building, and contamination. Some wetlands have been created deliberately to treat water contaminated by industry.

In the Florida wetlands, alligators warm up in the sun. They are ectothermic so they rely on external sources of heat to control their body temperature.

Land Meets Sea

Sandy beaches, rock pools, mangrove forests, and coastal cliffs are habitats that are found where land meets the sea. Tidal wetlands are areas that are periodically flooded at high tides.

1. A crab scuttles along a damp, sandy beach.
2. When the tide is out, rock pools reveal amazing starfish.
3. Puffins raise their chicks on cliff edges close to the sea where they hunt for food.

Some male herons use the trails on their caps to attract females during the mating season. They can make the trail stand upright on top of their head.

The Cocoi heron lives in the South American wetlands. It feeds on fish, frogs, and water insects and makes its nest in bushes or reedbeds.

Aquatic plants grow on or near water. They provide cover for fish, produce oxygen, and provide food for wildlife.

WETLANDS OF THE WORLD

Largest wetland: Pantanal (Brazil, Bolivia, and Paraguay)—up to 195,000 sq km (75,000 sq miles)
Largest mangrove forest: Sundarbans (Bangladesh and India)—14,000 sq km (5,400 sq miles)
Largest reed bed: Lower Danube and Danube Delta (Bulgaria, Moldova, Romania, Serbia, and Ukraine)—5,180 sq km (2,000 sq miles)

Sundarbans

DID YOU KNOW? Wild rice, Chinese water chestnuts, water spinach, watercress, and Indian lotus are all aquatic plants harvested for food.

Farmland

A lot of natural habitats around the world, such as forests and grasslands, are disappearing to make way for farmland because demand for food is growing as the world's population increases. Arable farmers grow crops such as wheat and tend orchards for fruit. Other farmers raise herds of cows, sheep, and other animals.

Growing Crops

Rice is a grain that is the main food source for over half the world's population. Most of the world's rice is grown in Asia. Maize (or corn) is grown in every continent except Antarctica and is eaten as both a cereal and a vegetable. It is processed to make cooking oil and is used in lots of other foods, such as potato chips and ice cream.

Cows are raised for their meat and their milk. Milk from cows, goats, and other livestock is used to make foods such as cheese, ice cream, curd, and yogurt.

Pesticides

Arable farms provide habitats for birds, small mammals, and insects. However, pesticides threaten this biodiversity—what kills insect pests may also kill the animals that eat them. Chemical fertilizers also threaten wildlife. Running off the soil into waterways, they endanger aquatic creatures.

Barns owls hunt small mammals in arable fields. Other birds nest and raise their young in the hedgerows that border fields.

WORLD'S BIGGEST CROPS

1. **Sugarcane:** 1.8 billion tonnes (2 billion tons)
2. **Maize (Corn):** 1.07 billion tonnes (1.8 billion tons)
3. **Wheat:** 760 million tonnes (840 million tons)
4. **Rice:** 700 million tonnes (772 million tons)
5. **Potatoes:** 380 million tonnes (420 million tons)

Harvesting maize in the USA

Rice is a type of grass and needs a lot of clean, fresh water to grow. Rice fields are also called paddy fields.

Rice is usually grown in a flat field. Rice grown on a terrace like this cannot be harvested by machine, so a large human workforce is required.

These women are preparing to plant rice seedlings in paddy fields in Vietnam.

DID YOU KNOW? Processed maize (corn) is used for many non-food items, such as glue, paint, dye, fireworks, soap, shoe polish, and aspirin.

Climate Change

Climate change is nothing new! In the last 650,000 years, the Earth has had seven periods of cooling where glaciers advanced—and then retreated as the temperature rose. The difference now is that human activity is driving the change, with devastating effects on the other species that share our planet. Since 1880, Earth's average surface temperature has risen by 1°C (2°F).

Human Activity

One key cause of climate change is the burning of fossil fuels such as coal, gas, and oil. This releases carbon dioxide (CO_2) into the air, which traps heat from the Sun, warming the Earth—the so-called Greenhouse Effect.

Trees absorb CO_2 and are vital to keep the planet healthy. Yet huge areas of forests, such as this one in Borneo, are cut down to make way for crop and cattle farms.

Rising Sea Levels

Experts predict sea levels will rise 0.3 m–2.5 m (1 ft–8.2 ft) during the next century due to global warming. This is partly because water expands as its temperature rises. Melting glaciers and polar ice are also adding extra water into the oceans.

If sea levels continue to rise, many of the 1,192 low-lying coral islands that make up the Maldives in southern Asia will be underwater some time this century.

CLIMATE CHANGE IN FIGURES

32 percent: Increase in CO_2 emissions between 1760 and 2021

2016: The year Bhutan became the first country to produce less CO_2 than its plant life absorbs

87 percent: The proportion of CO_2 produced by human activity that is caused by burning fossil fuels (coal, oil, and natural gas)

Bhutan

Arctic sea ice is currently shrinking by 13 percent each decade.

The Arctic is warming nearly twice as fast as the rest of the world. Polar bears and seals need the Arctic ice to survive.

Polar bears depend on sea ice. Melting ice forces them to travel farther to reach the seals that are their prey.

DID YOU KNOW? The Glacier National Park in Montana, USA, had over 150 glaciers in 1850. In 2021, it was down to 25 as a result of global warming.

Chapter 7: Life on Earth

Kingdoms of Life

Our planet is home to at least 9 million species of living things. They range from tiny bacteria to blue whales and humans to giant redwood trees. Biologists group together species that share characteristics to create a "tree of life." They organize living things into five kingdoms: animals, plants, fungi, prokaryotes (bacteria and blue-green algae), and protoctists (such as amoebas).

Bacteria use chemical reactions and cell division to survive and copy themselves. The first living organism did this, too.

One Big Family

All living things are descended from a single common ancestor—a simple organism that lived about 4 billion years ago. This organism's descendants found different ways to survive. They branched out to produce the millions of species on Earth today, as well as countless others along the way.

What is a Species?

Living things belong in the same species if they can breed with each other and produce offspring that can also breed. It is not always possible to test this, but scientists can look for shared genes or body features instead.

Dogs come in an amazing variety of shapes and sizes, but they are a single species. Because their genes are almost identical, different breeds can mate and have puppies.

Coral reefs, like this one off the island of Fiji in the South Pacific, are home to tens of thousands of species.

AMAZING DISCOVERY

Scientist: Carl Linnaeus
Discovery: The tree of life
Date: 1735
The story: Swedish scientist Linnaeus invented a two-name system for classifying every living thing by its genus and species (e.g., *Homo sapiens* for modern humans). This was the first step toward grouping species in a tree of life.

Scientists collect each group of closely related species together into a genus. Related genera are grouped into families, families into orders, orders into classes, classes into phyla, and phyla into kingdoms.

Three-quarters of all living organisms are found on land.

The green sea turtle, *Chelonia mydas*, belongs to a larger family of sea turtles called the Cheloniidae.

DID YOU KNOW? Scientists estimate that about 99 percent of all the species that have ever lived are now extinct.

145

Story of DNA

Every living thing has its own set of instructions that tells it how to create the chemicals vital to life—and how to put them together. These instructions, called genes, are found inside a long, twisty molecule called DNA (short for deoxyribonucleic acid).

Pairs and Patterns

The DNA molecule looks like a spiral ladder. The ladder's "rungs" are made of pairs of chemicals called bases. The order of the base pairs spells out a code that can be used to build proteins and other chemicals.

The DNA molecule forms a long, winding ladder shape that is called a double helix.

ADENINE
THYMINE
GUANINE
CYTOSINE

BASE PAIR

The ladder rungs are made of pairs of chemicals—either adenine and thyamine or guanine and cytosine.

DID YOU KNOW? The longest human chromosome, known as chromosome 1, contains more than 249 million base pairs.

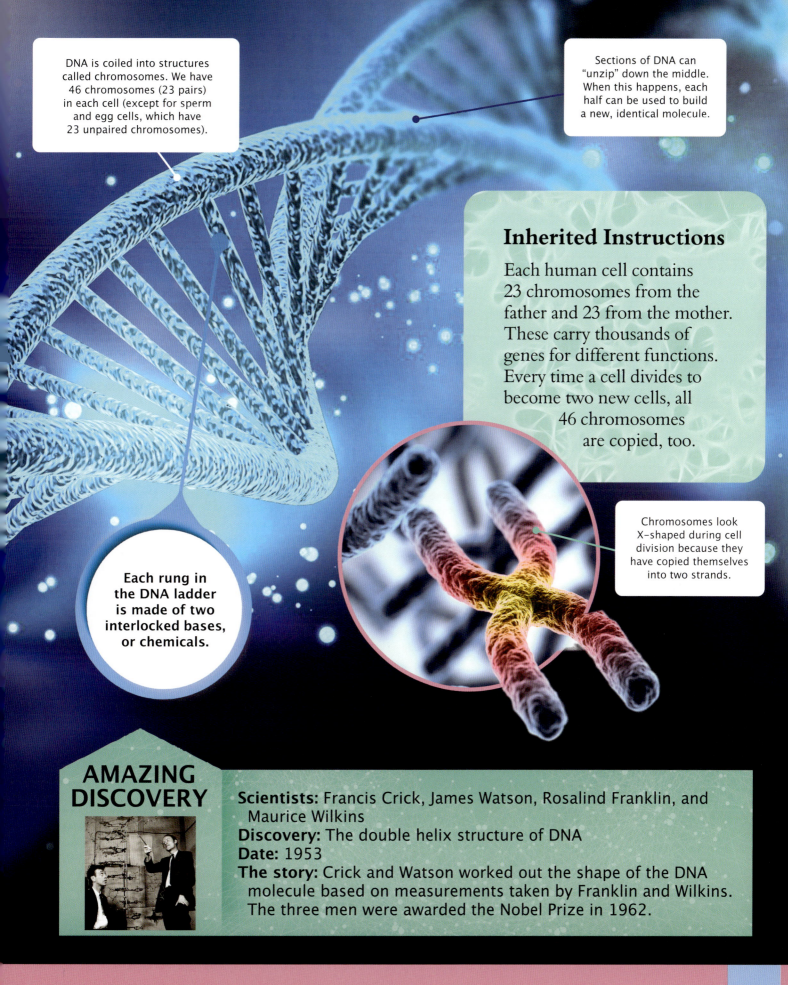

DNA is coiled into structures called chromosomes. We have 46 chromosomes (23 pairs) in each cell (except for sperm and egg cells, which have 23 unpaired chromosomes).

Sections of DNA can "unzip" down the middle. When this happens, each half can be used to build a new, identical molecule.

Inherited Instructions

Each human cell contains 23 chromosomes from the father and 23 from the mother. These carry thousands of genes for different functions. Every time a cell divides to become two new cells, all 46 chromosomes are copied, too.

Chromosomes look X-shaped during cell division because they have copied themselves into two strands.

Each rung in the DNA ladder is made of two interlocked bases, or chemicals.

AMAZING DISCOVERY

Scientists: Francis Crick, James Watson, Rosalind Franklin, and Maurice Wilkins
Discovery: The double helix structure of DNA
Date: 1953
The story: Crick and Watson worked out the shape of the DNA molecule based on measurements taken by Franklin and Wilkins. The three men were awarded the Nobel Prize in 1962.

Cell Machinery

All living organisms are made up of tiny building blocks called cells. Most cells are microscopic, but they are very complicated. They can convert food into energy, make useful chemicals, and reproduce themselves. The simplest life forms are just one cell; the most complex contain millions.

Two Types of Cell

There are two main types of cell. Bacteria and single-celled organisms have prokaryotic cells—simple cells that do not have a separate nucleus to contain their DNA. Larger organisms have eukaryotic cells. These contain separate chemical machines called organelles that carry out different functions.

ANIMAL CELL ORGANELLES

- The golgi store substances for later or get them ready to leave the cell.
- Cell membrane
- Mitochondrion fuels the cell by releasing energy from sugars, starch, proteins, and fats.
- Ribosomes decode DNA and build proteins.
- Endoplasmic reticulum makes and stores proteins.
- Peroxisome breaks down toxins, proteins, and fatty acids.
- Centriole helps the cell divide.
- Lyosome breaks down waste.

Prokaryotic cells may have whiplike tails called flagella that help them move around. This *E. coli* bacterium has flagella sticking out in all directions.

AMAZING DISCOVERY

Scientist: Robert Hooke
Discovery: The cell
Date: 1665
The story: English scientist Hooke built some of the first high-powered microscopes. He realized that many body tissues were made up of tiny self-contained units that he named "cells" after the hexagonal structures in honeycomb.

In all eukaryotic cells the nucleus holds most of the genetic material, or DNA.

Making Copies

Cells can reproduce in one of two ways. Mitosis is a process that creates perfect copies. It is used during body growth and to replace damaged or dead cells. Meiosis creates special cells with 23 unpaired chromosomes. The process of meiosis creates our reproductive cells (sperm in males or eggs in females).

MITOSIS
DNA IS COPIED
CELL DIVIDES ONCE
TWO CELLS WITH ALL THE DNA (46 CHROMOSOMES)

MEIOSIS
DNA IS COPIED
CELL DIVIDES TWICE
FOUR CELLS WITH HALF THE DNA (23 CHROMOSOMES)

Mitosis creates two copies of the cell's DNA, then the cell splits to create two exact copies. In meiosis, two copies of the DNA are also made, but the cell divides twice to produce four cells that each contain half the original amount of DNA.

Cell walls let substances in and out. In animal cells like this, the wall is a thin membrane. Plant cell walls are thicker and more rigid.

A jellylike fluid called cytoplasm is inside the cell. The organelles float in it.

DID YOU KNOW? Animal cells are usually between 0.001 mm (0.00004 in) and 0.1 mm (0.004 in) in size.

Plants

There are nearly 400,000 plant species on Earth. Plants are living things that can make their own food. During this process they produce oxygen, the gas that all animals, including humans, must breathe to stay alive.

Food from Sunlight

Plants take in carbon dioxide from the air through their leaves and water from the soil through their roots. Then they use the energy in sunlight to transform these ingredients into sugars. This process, called photosynthesis, is a chemical reaction. It takes place in the leaves, helped by a green chemical called chlorophyll.

Sequoia trees can live up to 3,000 years. Some other plants live less than a year.

This cross-section of a leaf shows the transport vessels in the middle. These carry water to the leaf and sugary glucose away from it.

Plant Reproduction

Seedless plants, such as liverworts, mosses, and ferns, reproduce by releasing spores. If a spore lands in a suitable place, it produces sex cells and, after fertilization, a new plant can grow. Seed plants produce seeds when male sex cells fertilize female ones. A seed contains a complete embryo plant along with a supply of food.

Pollen contains male sex cells. These must reach other flowers to fertilize their female sex cells. Pollen can be carried by insects and birds that visit the flower to feed on nectar.

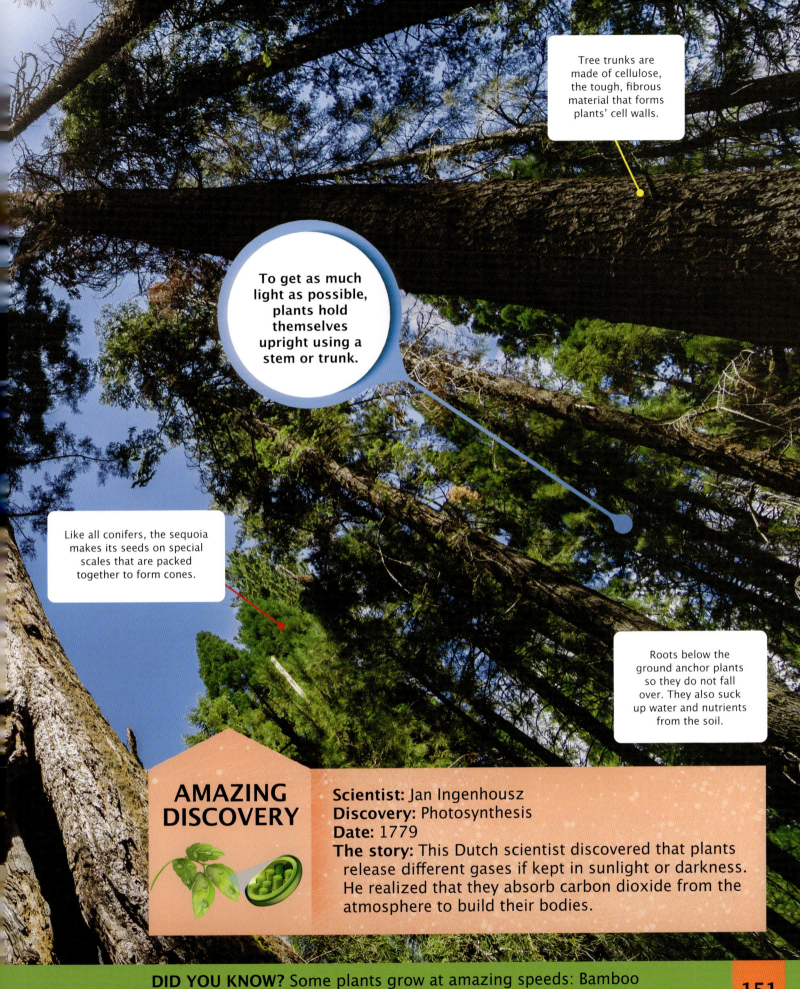

Tree trunks are made of cellulose, the tough, fibrous material that forms plants' cell walls.

To get as much light as possible, plants hold themselves upright using a stem or trunk.

Like all conifers, the sequoia makes its seeds on special scales that are packed together to form cones.

Roots below the ground anchor plants so they do not fall over. They also suck up water and nutrients from the soil.

AMAZING DISCOVERY

Scientist: Jan Ingenhousz
Discovery: Photosynthesis
Date: 1779
The story: This Dutch scientist discovered that plants release different gases if kept in sunlight or darkness. He realized that they absorb carbon dioxide from the atmosphere to build their bodies.

DID YOU KNOW? Some plants grow at amazing speeds: Bamboo can shoot up by as much as 91 cm (35 in) in a single day.

Animals

Animals are living things that get their energy from food, water, oxygen, and the Sun. Unlike plants, they can usually move around in search of food. To harvest energy from their food, animals need to breathe in oxygen.

Animal Types

Fish, amphibians, reptiles, birds, and mammals all have a backbone and skeleton to support their body. They are called vertebrates and make up less than 10 percent of animals. The rest are invertebrates, which do not have a skeleton. They include arthropods, such as insects and spiders, which have a tough outer casing called an exoskeleton, and soft-bodied mollusks.

Crustaceans

Centipedes and millipedes

Insects

Spiders

ARTHROPODS

Annelids

Mollusks

Roundworms

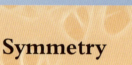
PSEUDOCOELOMATES

ACOELOMATES

Flatworms

Sponges

Symmetry

Most animals have a body plan that is symmetrical—the same on both sides. Features such as limbs and some organs are copied in mirror image. The gut, used to process food, leads from one end of the body to the other.

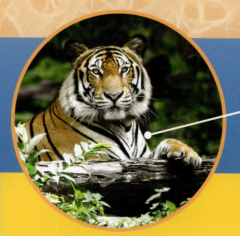

Symmetry appears in the very first few cells of a developing animal embryo. It often appears in adult features, such as this tiger's beautiful fur.

152

AMAZING DISCOVERY

Scientist: Jennifer Clack
Discovery: *Acanthostega*
Date: 1987
The story: When Clack found a skeleton of *Acanthostega* in Greenland—"Boris"—she realized it was a key step in the evolution of tetrapods (land vertebrates). Boris lived 360 million years ago and had a fishlike body with four legs. She later found tracks of another early tetrapod.

This simple tree shows the different groups in the animal kingdom and how they relate to each other.

The huge diversity of animals that exist today all evolved from simple one-celled organisms called protists.

DID YOU KNOW? Arthropods account for 80 percent of all known animal species. Most are small but the Japanese spider crab has a legspan up to 3.5 m (11 ft).

Web of Life

Living things are connected and dependent on each other through a complex web of relationships known as an ecosystem. These relationships keep the numbers of different species in balance. Species can come under threat if anything upsets this balance, such as changes to the environment.

Everything is Connected

Plants generate the oxygen that animals need. They are also food for plant-eating animals (herbivores). In turn, meat-eating animals (carnivores) hunt herbivores. All living animals release the carbon dioxide that plants need for photosynthesis. When a plant or animal dies, bacteria, fungi, and other organisms help to recycle its nutrients back into the soil.

The way living things depend on each other for food is called a food chain. A predator such as a big cat is right at the top of the food chain, because no other animal hunts it.

Plants are called producers because they make their own food. Animals are called consumers because they eat plants and other animals.

Mushrooms are fungi. There are around 5.1 million species of fungus.

AMAZING DISCOVERY

Scientists: James Lovelock and Lynn Margulis
Discovery: Gaia theory
Date: 1972–1979
The story: Chemist Lovelock and microbiologist Margulis showed how living things can affect Earth's atmosphere, oceans, and even rocks. Their Gaia theory argues that our entire planet is a single vast ecosystem.

A tree can be a home to mosses, ivy, and other plants, as well as providing animals with food, oxygen, and shelter.

Most of the fungus is made up of underground threads called hyphae. They feed on nutrients in the soil.

Introduced Species

Within any ecosystem, numbers of different species may go up and down, but they usually return to a balance point. If a new species is introduced into an ecosystem, however, it can have a devastating effect. It competes with the existing species for food, water, space, and breeding sites—and it might spread disease, too.

Away from its native Amazon basin and the bugs that feed on it there, the water hyacinth is an invader. It is fast growing and crowds out other aquatic plants.

DID YOU KNOW? The dodo, a giant flightless bird from Mauritius, died out within 80 years of humans and their rats, pigs, dogs, and cats landing on its island home.

Darwin's Theory

Why are some species of living thing so similar to each other and others so different? Does one species change, or evolve, into another over time? These questions puzzled scientists for centuries—until British naturalist Charles Darwin came up with his theory of evolution by natural selection.

Darwin was inspired by the many new species that explorers were discovering. He also wanted to explain the existence of fossils that were many millions of years old.

Voyage of the *Beagle*

Darwin's theory was driven by his studies aboard the survey ship HMS *Beagle* in the 1830s. In Patagonia he found fossils of giant extinct mammals, such as *Megatherium*. Visiting the isolated Galápagos Islands, Darwin observed finches, marine iguanas, and tortoises that had adapted to different island homes.

Darwin's Finches

There are about 15 finch species across the Galápagos, and they show evolution in action. A single ancestor species became stranded on the volcanic islands some time after their formation. Over time, their descendants spread across the islands and their beaks adapted to suit the main food on each island.

John Gould, the *Beagle*'s natural history artist, sketched the finches in the Galápagos. Their beaks had evolved to suit particular foods. Nut-eaters had large, short bills for cracking shells. Insect-catchers had longer, pointier bills.

This is one of five giant tortoise species on Isabela Island, the most recently formed of the Galápagos Islands.

Each species has a unique shell shape. The tortoises also come in a range of sizes.

Giant tortoises live on seven of the Galápagos Islands. There are more than ten different species.

AMAZING DISCOVERY

Scientists: Charles Darwin (left), Alfred Russel Wallace
Discovery: The origin of species
Date: 1859
The story: Darwin spent 20 years after the *Beagle* developing his ideas about evolution and natural selection. He published his theory only after receiving a letter from Wallace, who had come up with a similar theory while exploring South America and Asia.

DID YOU KNOW? French scientist Jean-Baptiste Lamarck was the first to suggest species arise through a process of evolution in 1800—but he could not explain how.

Evolution at Work

Evolution explains how living things slowly change over many generations and new species arise. Each individual has a slightly different mix of genetic instructions from its parents. Genes that give it a better chance of survival are more likely to be passed on to the next generation. Over time, individuals with a particular advantage outbreed and replace those without it.

Selection Pressures

Natural selection drives evolution. It is about how individuals adapt to different pressures from the environment. These can include availability of food, competition for mates, threats from predators, diseases, or a changing climate. The fittest usually survive and breed, passing on the genes that helped them cope with the conditions.

Each year, vast herds of wildebeest and zebra migrate across the Serengeti to better grazing. Only the fittest survive.

The journey is tough. It weeds out any individuals that tire easily or are prone to disease.

Megatherium was a giant ground sloth that died out 10,000 years ago. It could not face the selection pressure from changes in its habitat. Today the only sloths are small tree-dwellers.

The most dangerous moment of the migration is when the animals must cross the crocodile-infested Mara River.

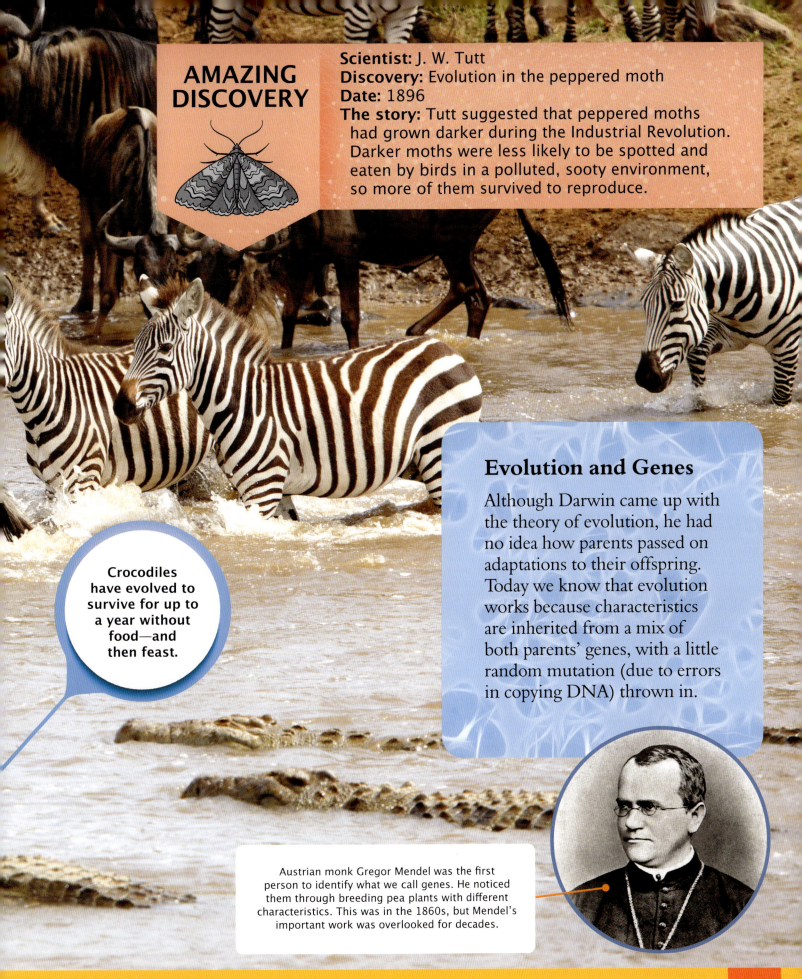

AMAZING DISCOVERY

Scientist: J. W. Tutt
Discovery: Evolution in the peppered moth
Date: 1896
The story: Tutt suggested that peppered moths had grown darker during the Industrial Revolution. Darker moths were less likely to be spotted and eaten by birds in a polluted, sooty environment, so more of them survived to reproduce.

Crocodiles have evolved to survive for up to a year without food—and then feast.

Evolution and Genes

Although Darwin came up with the theory of evolution, he had no idea how parents passed on adaptations to their offspring. Today we know that evolution works because characteristics are inherited from a mix of both parents' genes, with a little random mutation (due to errors in copying DNA) thrown in.

Austrian monk Gregor Mendel was the first person to identify what we call genes. He noticed them through breeding pea plants with different characteristics. This was in the 1860s, but Mendel's important work was overlooked for decades.

DID YOU KNOW? Biologists study evolution at high speed using the *Drosophila* fruit fly—a species that can produce a new generation every ten days!

History of Life

Life has existed on Earth for about 4 billion years. For most of that time, known as the Precambrian, it was just simple, single-celled organisms. From around 540 million years ago (mya), there has been more complex life, and it has passed through distinct phases.

Divisions of Time

The story of complex life on Earth is usually broken into three stages—the Palaeozoic, Mesozoic, and Cenozoic eras (meaning ancient, middle, and recent life). Each era is divided into geological periods lasting tens of millions of years. Geologists identify these periods from the types of rock and the presence of particular fossils.

Anomalocaris was an ancestor of arthropods. It lived in the oceans 510 mya, during the Cambrian period.

Fossils of trilobites only come from the six periods that form the Palaeozoic. They appeared in the first of these periods, the Cambrian, and went extinct in the last, the Permian.

Mass Extinctions

Throughout history, major changes in life on Earth began with natural disasters, such as impacts from space, volcanic eruptions, or climate change. These disasters wipe out many of the previously dominant animals, leaving the way open for new ones to take their place.

About 66 mya, the effects of a huge asteroid impact drove the dinosaurs to extinction. Since then, mammals have become the main large land animals.

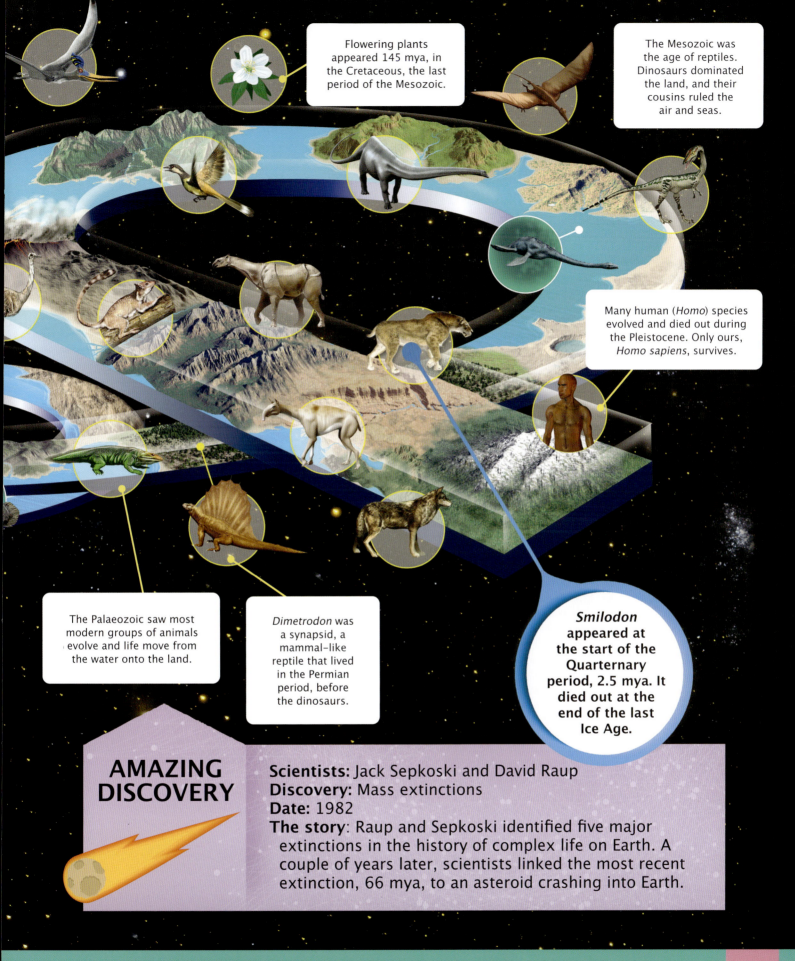

Cats

Cats are carnivores with soft fur, a short snout, and sharp claws. The first cats appeared around 30 million years ago. Today wild cats live everywhere except Australia and the Antarctic. There are 41 wild cat species. Four—the lion, tiger, jaguar, and leopard—are in their own family: the big cats.

Forward-facing eyes let this Bengal tiger judge distance accurately. Most cats are nocturnal hunters and see well in the dark.

Getting a Grip

Cats use their sharp claws to grab prey. In most species the claws retract into the paw when they are not being used. However, the cheetah's claws are always out. They grip the ground and stop the cat from slipping when it runs.

The cheetah is the world's fastest mammal. In short bursts it can sprint at 105 km/h (65 mph).

Hearing is a tiger's most important sense. The cat can swivel each ear independently to pick up faraway sounds from all directions.

Long, sensitive whiskers can detect small air movements. This is useful for finding prey at night.

Stripes camouflage tigers in forests and grasslands. Tigers spend an hour every day licking their fur. This removes loose hairs and keeps the coat clean and warm.

The large, sharp canine teeth kill prey. Behind these, the carnassial teeth are used for cutting through flesh.

Family Life

Lions are the only cats that hunt and live in groups. All other species are loners that come together only to breed. Most cats live in forests or grasslands, but some have adapted to other environments. Sand cats live in deserts, hunting birds and lizards and surviving on very little water.

Lions live in family groups called prides. A typical pride includes related lionesses, their cubs, and a couple of adult males.

BENGAL TIGER
PANTHERA TIGRIS
"CAT TIGER"
MAMMAL

Habitat: Forests, swamps, grasslands; S Asia
Length: Male 3 m (9.8 ft); female 2.6 m (8.5 ft)
Weight: Male 250 kg (550 lb); female 160 kg (350 lb)
Diet: Mammals—e.g. deer, wild pigs
Lifespan: Up to 18 years
Wild population: 2,000–2,500; Endangered

DID YOU KNOW? The largest cat on record was a Siberian tiger that weighed 384 kg (845 lb)—about the same as 90 pet cats!

Foxes

Foxes are the smallest members of the dog family. They have triangular faces, pointed ears, and bushy tails. Intelligent and adaptable, foxes live everywhere except Antarctica. They have a range of calls, barks, and yelps to communicate fear, warnings, threats, and playfulness.

The highly adaptable red fox lives in cities, woods, mountains, and deserts. It is a hunter and a scavenger.

In cold weather, a red fox covers its body with its long, bushy tail for extra warmth.

Compared to other dogs, foxes are short and stocky. A red fox can jump as far as 2 m (6.5 ft). It is a strong swimmer, too.

RED FOX
VULPES VULPES
"FOX FOX"
MAMMAL

Habitat: Forests, farmland, cities, grasslands; Almost worldwide
Length: Male 1.5 m (4.7 ft); female 1.2 m (4 ft)
Weight: Male 12 kg (27 lb); female 9.5 kg (21 lb)
Diet: Mammals, birds, insects, reptiles, fruit, garbage
Wild population: Unknown; Least Concern

DID YOU KNOW? Most foxes have 42 teeth, but the bat-eared fox has 48. Its teeth are extremely pointy and help it crunch up termites and other minibeasts.

The red fox uses its senses of hearing and smell to pinpoint the position of prey animals.

Unlike most dogs, a fox cannot bare its teeth.

Skilled Survivor

The 12 "true foxes" include red foxes, Arctic foxes, and kit foxes. The red fox is the most widespread carnivore. It eats anything from invertebrates and small mammals to grasses and kitchen waste. Foxes bury stashes of food in times of plenty and then return to them when they are hungry.

The Arctic fox has adapted to live in the cold north. Its winter coat is white to blend in with the snow.

Desert Dweller

The smallest wild dog is the fennec fox, which lives in the driest parts of North Africa. It stays cool by losing excess body heat through its huge ears. The ears also funnel sounds so that the fox can locate prey at night and underground. Prey provides most of the fox's moisture.

The fennec fox is the smallest wild dog. Standing only 20 cm (8 in) tall, it is about the same size as a pet kitten.

165

Bears

There are eight species of bear. They live in Asia, Europe, and the Americas. Most are omnivores that feed on plants and insects and live in forest habitats. They only eat meat if they find carrion or a slow-moving, weak animal. Polar bears are the exception: These speedy hunters are carnivores.

The Bear's Year

Polar bears are active all year round, but other bears in the far north—grizzlies and black bears—hibernate in winter. In warmer places, there is plenty of food all year. Species such as Indian sloth bears do not need to hibernate.

When salmon swim upriver to breed in late summer, grizzlies have a fishy feast! It helps them put on weight needed for hibernation.

Underneath the dense, waterproof fur is a thick layer of fatty blubber to protect the polar bear from the cold.

Bears are usually loners, but mothers look after their cubs for two years or more. The cubs grow quickly because their mother's milk is about one-third fat.

POLAR BEAR
URSUS MARITIMUS
"SEA BEAR"
MAMMAL

Habitat: Tundra, ice floes, oceans; Arctic
Length: Male 2.8 m (9.2 ft); female 2.4 m (7.2 ft)
Weight: Male 600 kg (1,320 lb); female 260 kg (570 lb)
Diet: Seals, carrion, fish
Lifespan: Up to 25 years
Wild population: 30,000; Vulnerable

All bears have amazingly sensitive noses. They can smell food up to 50 km (30 miles) away.

Picky Pandas
Most bears eat many kinds of food, but pandas are choosy. Ninety-nine percent of their diet is bamboo. Pandas live in the mountains of China. They are threatened by habitat loss and only around 1,500 are left in the wild.

The bear's pale, creamy coat helps to camouflage it against the snow.

Most mammals are digitigrade—they walk on their toes. Bears (and humans) are plantigrade—they stand on the soles of their feet.

Pandas spend most of their waking hours eating. They eat about 600 bamboo stems a day.

DID YOU KNOW? The smallest bear is the sun bear. It grows no bigger than a 10-year-old child, but its tongue is an amazing 25 cm (10 in) long!

Seals

The zoological name for seals and their relatives is pinnipeds, which means "fin foot." Their webbed back feet provide the power for swimming, while the front legs are used for walking—clumsily!—on land. Seals, sea lions, and walruses all live in cool water and avoid tropical seas.

In their Element

Underwater, seals pursue prey at speeds up to 27 km/h (17 mph), thanks to their streamlined bodies. However, like all marine mammals, they must surface to breathe. Elephant seals hold their breath longest—their dives last 100 minutes or more.

Large eyes can see well in the low light levels underwater.

The common seal is a true or earless seal. It does not have external ear flaps.

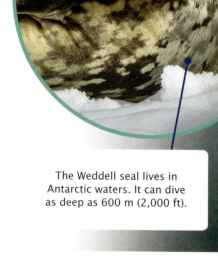

The Weddell seal lives in Antarctic waters. It can dive as deep as 600 m (2,000 ft).

The nostrils completely close when the seal is diving. The animal has a good sense of smell on land.

Whiskers sense tiny movements in the water, helping the seal locate prey when it is too dark to see.

DID YOU KNOW? The Saimaa ringed seal is the rarest pinniped. It is found in only one lake in Finland, and the total population is just 320.

A thick layer of blubber beneath the skin insulates the seal (keeps it warm) and aids buoyancy.

Pinnipeds in Danger

The pinnipeds are made up of three families: true or earless seals, eared seals (sea lions and fur seals), and walruses. Almost a third are at risk, threatened mainly by climate change and pollution. In the past, many fur seals were hunted close to extinction for their fur.

In the past, walruses have been hunted for their ivory tusks. Today, the trade in ivory is illegal.

COMMON SEAL
PHOCA VITULINA
"CALF-LIKE SEAL"
MAMMAL

Habitat: North Sea, Baltic, N Atlantic, N Pacific
Length: Male 1.8 m (5.9 ft); female 1.6 m (5.2 ft)
Weight: Male 120 kg (265 lb); female 90 kg (200 lb)
Diet: Seals, carrion, fish
Lifespan: Up to 20 years
Wild population: 350,000; Least Concern

Whales and Dolphins

Dolphins and whales are cetaceans—highly intelligent mammals that mate, feed, and give birth in all the world's oceans. Cetaceans are split into two groups: baleen whales, which eat invertebrates, and toothed whales, such as dolphins, which consume much bigger prey.

A pod of short-beaked common dolphins work together to attack a baitball of blue jack mackerel.

This is a baby humpback whale. Baby whales drink the equivalent of one-and-a-third bathtubfuls of mother's milk a day!

Filter Feeders

Blue whales, humpbacks, and other baleen whales are filter feeders. These huge animals have sieve-like plates inside their mouths to filter plankton, krill, or other foods from the water.

COMMON DOLPHIN
DELPHINUS DELPHIS
"DOLPHIN DOLPHIN"
MAMMAL

Habitat: Atlantic, Pacific, Indian Ocean, Mediterranean Sea
Length: Male 2.2 m (7.2 ft); female 2.1 m (6.9 ft)
Weight: Male 120 kg (265 lb); female 105 kg (230 lb)
Diet: Fish, squid, octopus
Lifespan: Around 20 years
Wild population: Unknown: Least Concern

DID YOU KNOW? Blue whales are the largest animals that have ever lived on Earth. Adults can be 27 m (89 ft) long and weigh more than 145 tonnes (160 tons).

Dolphins travel in pods of up to 1,000. They live mainly in warm waters, hunting fish and squid.

The dolphins herded the fish into a ball shape. It is easy to pick off individuals from the edge of the ball.

Finding Food

Dolphins and other toothed whales use echolocation to navigate and find prey. They produce clicks that travel through the water and then bounce back to them off objects. Cetaceans also use noises to communicate with each other. Humpbacks are known for their long, complex songs.

The orca is the largest species of dolphin. It mostly hunts seals, but it also eats squid, sea birds, fish, and even turtles.

Bats

There are around 1,100 living species of bats, making up about one-fifth of all mammal species. They live worldwide except in the frozen Arctic and Antarctic. Bats are the only mammals that have evolved true powered flight. Other "flying" mammals, such as the flying squirrel, can only glide.

Batty Diets

Seventy percent of bats feed on insects. One brown bat ate 1,000 mosquitoes in an hour! Bats have adapted to hunt other sources of meat, such as birds, frogs, lizards, fish, or other bats. Vampire bats are famous for drinking blood from cows, horses, or sheep. The largest bats, called megabats or flying foxes, feed on fruit.

The spectral vampire bat is the world's largest carnivorous bat. It feeds on small birds and reptiles.

The greater bulldog bat is a fishing bat. It uses its feet to snatch fish or insects from lakes or rivers.

Bat Senses

Bats have keen eyesight and a good sense of smell. However, most bats find food using echolocation. They send out high-frequency sound waves, then listen to how the waves bounce back off objects. From this, the bats can work out an object's exact position, size, and shape.

By hanging upside-down, bats can drop into the air and then fly. It takes less energy than taking off upward like a bird.

DID YOU KNOW? The world's biggest bat is the giant golden-crowned flying fox from the Philippines. It weighs 1.2 kg (2.6 lb) and has a 1.7-m (5.6-ft) wingspan.

LYLE'S FLYING FOX
PTEROPUS LYLEI
MAMMAL

Habitat: Forests, farmland, cities; SE Asia
Length: 22 cm (8.7 in)
Wingspan: 90 cm (35 in)
Weight: 390 g (0.9 lb)
Diet: Ripe fruit, nectar
Lifespan: Up to 20 years
Wild population: Unknown; Decreasing

Flying foxes live in tropical forests. They do not have echolocation. They use eyesight and smell to find flowers and fruit to eat.

The wings are thin skin stretched over thin bones. Sleeping bats wrap their wings around themselves for warmth.

173

Elephants

Elephants evolved 50 million years ago. The three species alive today are African bush and forest elephants and Asian elephants. They live in family groups of up to 12 females and their calves, led by an older female called the matriarch. Adult male elephants live alone or in male-only herds.

African or Asian?

The African bush elephant is the world's largest land animal. One male weighed 11,000 kg (24,000 lb). Asian elephants are smaller and have smaller ears than African elephants. Their backs are flat or humped; African elephants' backs have a dip in the middle.

Elephant babies take longer to develop inside their mother than any other land mammal. The mother elephant is pregnant for 22 months.

The front teeth, or tusks, dig up roots and strip bark from trees. Inside the mouth, four huge molars grind up plant food.

The ears are used as fans to cool the elephant on hot days. Each elephant can be identified by the shape and size of its ears.

ASIAN ELEPHANT

ELEPHAS MAXIMUS
"LARGEST OX"
MAMMAL

Habitat: Forests, scrub; S Asia
Length: Male 3 m (9.8 ft); female 2.7 m (8.9 ft)
Weight: Male 4,500 kg (9,920 lb); female 2,750 kg (6,060 lb)
Diet: Leaves, twigs, bark
Lifespan: Up to 60 years
Wild population: 40,000; Endangered

Trunk Talk

The elephant's trunk is an extension of its nose and top lip. It is incredibly sensitive and versatile. It can carry food and water into the mouth, squirt water, or spray dust. It is also used to touch and stroke.

Elephants suck up dust and then blow it over their back and shoulders. It acts as a sunscreen and keeps away insects.

The tail is 1.3 m (4 ft) long and tipped with long, thick hair. It can be flicked like a fly swatter to drive away insects.

The trunk is so complicated that it takes a calf a year to master using it! It can grasp, suck, touch, and smell.

DID YOU KNOW? An elephant's trunk has more than 40,000 muscles. The whole human body contains fewer than 1,000 muscles!

Giraffes

The giraffe is the world's tallest animal, standing up to 5.7 m (18.7 ft) high. This hoofed mammal lives in female family groups on the African savannah, feeding on twigs and leaves from the treetops. There are nine subspecies, which are distinguished by the patterns of their coats.

Large eyes and great height give the giraffe excellent vision.

Both male and female giraffes have short horns covered in bristly hairs. The males butt these when they spar for dominance.

Like our fingerprints, no two giraffes have exactly the same markings.

Standing Tall

Giraffe calves can stand and walk within an hour of being born. They spend their lives standing up and even sleep on their feet. Giraffes gallop at up to 48 km/h (30 mph) and look graceful—unless they are drinking. Their legs are shorter than their neck, so they bend down very awkwardly!

A drinking giraffe is very vulnerable. It takes a while to stand up straight again.

The giraffe can use its 46 cm/18 in-long tongue to grip a plant while its teeth strip off the leaves.

Zebra or Giraffe?

The okapi is a close cousin of the giraffe, but it lacks the long neck and has a zebra's stripes. Hunted for its unusual and beautiful skin, as well as for meat, the okapi is endangered today. Its forest home is also threatened by illegal mining and logging.

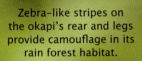

Zebra-like stripes on the okapi's rear and legs provide camouflage in its rain forest habitat.

GIRAFFE
GIRAFFA CAMELOPARDALIS
"FAST-WALKING CAMEL LEOPARD"
MAMMAL

Habitat: Savannah, forests; E and S Africa
Length: Male 5.5 m (18 ft); female 4.8 m (15.7 ft)
Weight: Male 1,200 kg (2,650 lb); female 830 kg (1,830 lb)
Diet: Leaves, twigs, bark
Lifespan: Up to 25 years
Wild population: Unknown; Vulnerable

DID YOU KNOW? Giraffes and humans have the same number of bones in their neck—seven. Each giraffe vertebra can be 25 cm (10 in) long.

Apes

The orangutan is the only ape that lives alone instead of in groups. However, a young orangutan stays with its mother for the first eight years of life.

Apes are primates that do not have tails. There are two groups. The great apes are humans, Central Africa's chimpanzees and gorillas, and the orangutan of Borneo and Sumatra. The lesser apes are the 18 gibbon species, which are smaller than their great ape cousins.

Intelligent Beasts

The great apes are large, intelligent animals. They have very advanced brains, great memories, and are good at solving problems. Chimpanzees are the most frequent tool users. They use sticks as "fishing rods" to collect termites from termite mounds. They also shape sticks into "spears" for hunting small primates. Chimps are the only apes that regularly eat meat. The protein helps fuel their big brains.

A chimpanzee slurps up termites from its "fishing" stick. It even frays the end of the stick so it will pick up more insects.

Under Threat

All the non-human great apes are endangered, and gorillas and orangutans are critically endangered. They have been affected by habitat destruction, hunting, and disease, and have also been removed from the wild for the illegal pet trade.

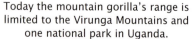

Today the mountain gorilla's range is limited to the Virunga Mountains and one national park in Uganda.

An orangutan's face is bare, though males have fleshy cheek pads. The rest of the body is covered in straggly orange hair.

Sensitive lips test fruits for ripeness. The orangutan also makes lip-smacking sounds to communicate.

BORNEAN ORANGUTAN

PONGO PYGMAEUS
"LITTLE PERSON OF THE FOREST"
MAMMAL

Habitat: Rain forests; Borneo
Length: Male 1.4 m (4.6 ft); female 1.2 m (4 ft)
Weight: Male 85 kg (190 lb); female 37 kg (82 lb)
Diet: Fruit, shoots, leaves
Lifespan: Up to 45 years
Wild population: 55,000; Critically Endangered

DID YOU KNOW? Orangutans' powerful arms are one-and-a-half times longer than their legs. A male's armspan can be 2 m (7 ft) from fingertip to fingertip.

Marsupials

Kangaroos, koalas, and their relatives are marsupials, or pouched mammals. Most mammal babies develop inside their mother's body, and many can walk or even run shortly after birth. Marsupial babies are born tiny, underdeveloped, and helpless. They crawl into their mother's pouch to carry on growing there.

Australian Life

There are a few marsupial species, such as the opossums, in North and South America. However, most live in Australia and New Guinea. They include kangaroos, koalas, wombats, wallabies, quokkas, and Tasmanian devils. Pouched mammals were the only kind of mammal in Australia until early settlers brought non-native dogs, mice, and rabbits.

The large nose sniffs out fresh eucalyptus leaves and scent markings left by other koalas.

The red kangaroo is the largest marsupial. This young male will grow almost as tall as a human, be able to leap 9 m (29.5 ft), and run at 70 km/h (44 mph).

The mother's pouch holds the baby koala, which is called a joey.

KOALA
PHASCOLARCTOS CINEREUS
"ASHY POUCHED BEAR" MAMMAL

Habitat: Forests, scrub; E Australia
Length: Male 75 cm (30 in); female 70 cm (28 in)
Weight: Male 9 kg (20 lb); female 7 kg (15 lb)
Diet: Eucalyptus leaves
Lifespan: Up to 20 years
Wild population: 75,000; Vulnerable

All Sorts of Diet

Kangaroos and wallabies eat any grass or leaves, while koalas feed mainly on eucalyptus. Insect-eating marsupials, such as bilbies, bandicoots, and numbats, have pointed snouts for extracting minibeasts from bark or soil. The Tasmanian devil is the largest carnivorous marsupial.

The Tasmanian devil is the size of a small dog, but it can capture prey as large as a medium kangaroo.

Extremely thick, waterproof fur protects the koala against hot and cold temperatures.

DID YOU KNOW? The female Virginia opossum has the shortest pregnancy of any mammal—just 12 days.

Vultures

Vultures are the vacuum cleaners of the natural world. They eat carrion (dead bodies). Without vultures, the decaying bodies of dead animals would spread disease. Rotting meat contains deadly microbes, but vultures have extremely strong stomach acid that kills these.

The powerful beak can rip through skin and flesh and pull off chunks of meat.

The bald head and neck will not get clogged up with blood while feasting—feathers would!

Seek and Find

Although vultures are meat-eaters, they rarely kill prey. They prefer to scavenge. They glide high on warm air currents, seeking out carrion with their excellent senses of smell and sight. They watch each other carefully—if one drops to earth, the others quickly follow.

A large carcass can attract as many as 100 vultures from eight different species. The biggest birds feed first, because they have the strength to tear open the body.

KING VULTURE

SARCORAMPHUS PAPA
"FLESH BEAK FATHER" BIRD

Habitat: Forests, grasslands, swamps; C & S America
Length: 75 cm (2.5 ft)
Wingspan: 1.8 m (5.9 ft)
Weight: 4 kg (8.8 lb)
Diet: Carrion
Lifespan: Up to 25 years
Wild population: Unknown; Least Concern

DID YOU KNOW? The Ruppell's griffon vulture is the highest-flying bird. One was recorded at 11,277 m (37,000 ft)—the altitude at which jets fly.

The folds of loose skin on the head are called lappets.

The king vulture is the showiest member of the vulture family. The skin around its neck can be orange, red, yellow, or purple.

The California condor is North America's largest bird, with a wingspan of up to 3.4 m (11 ft).

Back from the Brink

The California condor became extinct in the wild in 1987 because of habitat loss, poaching, and lead poisoning. Thanks to a conservation plan, it has been reintroduced to parts of Arizona and Utah, but it is still one of the world's rarest birds.

Hummingbirds

There are around 325 hummingbird species, all native to the Americas. These amazing little birds take their name from the humming sound of their fast-beating wings, which can flap up to 200 times a second. Hummingbirds have one of the highest heart rates of any animal—an average of 1,200 beats per minute.

The rufous hummingbird winters in Mexico and heads to its breeding grounds in Canada and Alaska in spring. It is found farther north than any other hummingbird.

The male rufous hummingbird has an iridescent orange-red throat patch.

The wings have a total span of just 11 cm (4.3 in), but they carry the rufous hummingbird on a 3,200-km (2,000-mile) migration twice a year.

Aerial Acrobatics

Hummingbirds are the only bird that can fly upside down and backward. Their top flight speed is 48 km/h (30 mph). Adaptations that make them more lightweight include fewer feathers and smaller feet. Their feet and legs are not strong enough to walk on.

The wings of a hovering hummingbird, such as this male golden-tailed sapphire hummingbird, move almost too fast to see.

RUFOUS HUMMINGBIRD

SELASPHORUS RUFUS
"REDDISH LIGHT CARRIER" BIRD

Habitat: Scrub, parks, gardens, woodlands, swamps, meadows; N and C America
Length: 8 cm (3.1 in)
Wingspan: 11 cm (4.3 in)
Weight: 4 g (0.1 oz)
Diet: Nectar, insects
Lifespan: Up to 5 years
Wild population: Unknown; Least Concern

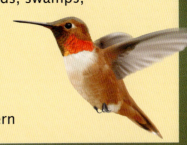

The long, thin beak is designed to probe flowers and snap up insects. It houses a long tongue that darts in and out up to 20 times a second as it slurps up nectar.

Constant Snacking

All hummingbirds eat nectar and pollen. They hover in front of a flower and lick out the nectar with their long, grooved tongue. A hummingbird can visit 2,000 flowers in a day and consume twice its own body weight. They also catch and eat tiny insects while on the wing.

A sword-billed hummingbird and two speckled hummingbirds consume nectar from an artificial feeder.

DID YOU KNOW? The bee hummingbird is the world's smallest bird. It weighs just 1.8 g (0.06 oz)—about the same as a paperclip.

Frogs

The frog has a large, sensitive ear behind each eye. It has keen hearing.

Frogs are by far the most common kind of amphibian—there are around 4,800 different species. They range in size from a tiny 7-mm (0.3-in) frog that lives on the floor of Papua New Guinea's rain forests (and holds the record for smallest vertebrate) to Africa's well-named 32-cm (12.6-in) goliath frog.

Frogs on the Move

Most frogs are strong swimmers and exceptional jumpers. Their legs have stretchy muscles that are pulled in when the frog is at rest. If an enemy approaches, the legs kick back and the muscles act as a spring to push the frog through the air.

Frogs jump horizontally rather than up into the air. Many species can leap more than 20 times their own body length.

The tree frog has sticky pads at the ends of its fingers and toes for extra grip.

DID YOU KNOW? Puerto Rico's common coqui frog is the world's noisiest amphibian. Males are just 3.4 cm (1.3 in) long, but their calls hit 100 decibels.

A frog blinks when it swallows its food. This pushes its eyes into the head, forcing the struggling insect down the frog's throat.

Skin Deep

Poison dart frogs live in Central and South American rain forests and come in eye-catching blues, reds, greens, oranges, yellows, and blacks. Their bright skin is a warning to predators that it tastes bad and contains toxic chemicals. The most poisonous, the golden poison frog, contains enough toxin to kill up to 20 people.

Bulging eyes can see about 280 degrees all around. This is useful because the frog cannot bend its neck.

Poison dart frogs are tiny. The largest species, this dyeing dart frog, is just 5 cm (2 in) long.

RED-EYED TREE FROG

AGALYCHNIS CALLIDRYAS
"BEAUTIFUL SHINING TREE NYMPH"
AMPHIBIAN

Habitat: Rain forests; C America
Length: Male 5 cm (2 in); female 7.5 cm (3 in)
Weight: Male 10 g (0.3 oz); female 15 g (0.5 oz)
Diet: Small insects, other invertebrates
Lifespan: Up to 5 years
Wild population: Unknown; Least Concern

Turtles

Turtles make up a family called chelonians—reptiles that have a protective shell of bone or cartilage. The ones that live in water have flippers for swimming. Turtles that live on land, often known as tortoises, have four short, powerful legs. Like all reptiles, chelonians cannot make their own body heat.

Tiny magnetic crystals in the turtle's brain let it use Earth's magnetic field to navigate.

Landlubbers

Tortoises range in size from the Cape speckled tortoise at around 100 g (3.5 oz) to the Galápagos giant tortoise at more than 400 kg (880 lb). They live in deserts, semi-arid zones, swamps, and rain forests. They dig deep burrows to avoid extreme temperatures.

The ornate box turtle lives in the semi-arid prairies of the American Midwest.

Coming up for Air

Sea turtles usually surface to breathe every five to 40 minutes, but they can stay underwater for hours when they are sleeping. Freshwater turtles take a breath every half-hour. Some species, such as the alligator snapping turtle, hibernate through the winter at the bottom of a pond. They hold their breath for months!

The alligator snapping turtle has a worm-like lure in its mouth that tempts fish to approach.

GREEN SEA TURTLE

CHELONIA MYDAS
"WET TORTOISE"
REPTILE

Habitat: Warm oceans; Near the equator
Length: 1.3 m (4.3 ft);
Weight: 150 kg (330 lb)
Diet: Young: jellyfish, marine invertebrates, crustaceans; adults: sea grass, algae
Lifespan: Up to 80 years
Wild population: Unknown; Endangered

Hard shell of modified bone is covered with plates of keratin (the material that makes our nails). It protects the turtle's organs.

The green sea turtle is the second largest of the seven sea turtle species after the leatherback.

Paddle-like front flippers power the turtle along. Some green sea turtles migrate 2,000 km (1,300 miles) from their nesting grounds to their feeding grounds.

The turtle cannot pull its flippers or its head into its shell.

DID YOU KNOW? Tortoises live longer than any other land animal. A giant tortoise called Adwaita was 255 years old when he died in a zoo in Kolkata, India, in 2006.

189

Sharks

Sharks are fish with skeletons made of tough, flexible cartilage instead of bone. They first appeared around 220 million years before the dinosaurs. Today, there are more than 500 species. Sharks have a reputation as fierce predators, but most species are harmless and shark attacks are rare.

All Shapes and Sizes

Most sharks—including the great white, tiger, blue, bull, mako, and reef sharks—have a sleek, streamlined body. Others are very different shapes. In deep waters, the frilled shark is long and eel-like, while the goblin shark is named for its unusual nose. The flattened bodies of angel sharks and wobbegongs suit life on the seabed.

The skin is as rough as sandpaper. It is covered with grooved, tooth-shaped scales that direct the flow of water over the shark's body and reduce drag.

The great white has an excellent sense of taste. It can detect a few drops of blood in the water from 5 km (3 miles) away.

There are ten species of hammerhead. These sharks have a T-shaped head with eyes far apart, which gives them a wide field of vision.

The shark has rows of sharp, triangular teeth up to 7.5 cm (3 in) long. As old ones are lost, new teeth move forward to take their place.

A torpedo-shaped body, pointed at each end, cuts down water resistance. The shark swims at 40 km/h (25 mph).

DID YOU KNOW? The Greenland shark is the world's longest-living vertebrate. It can live to be nearly 400 years old.

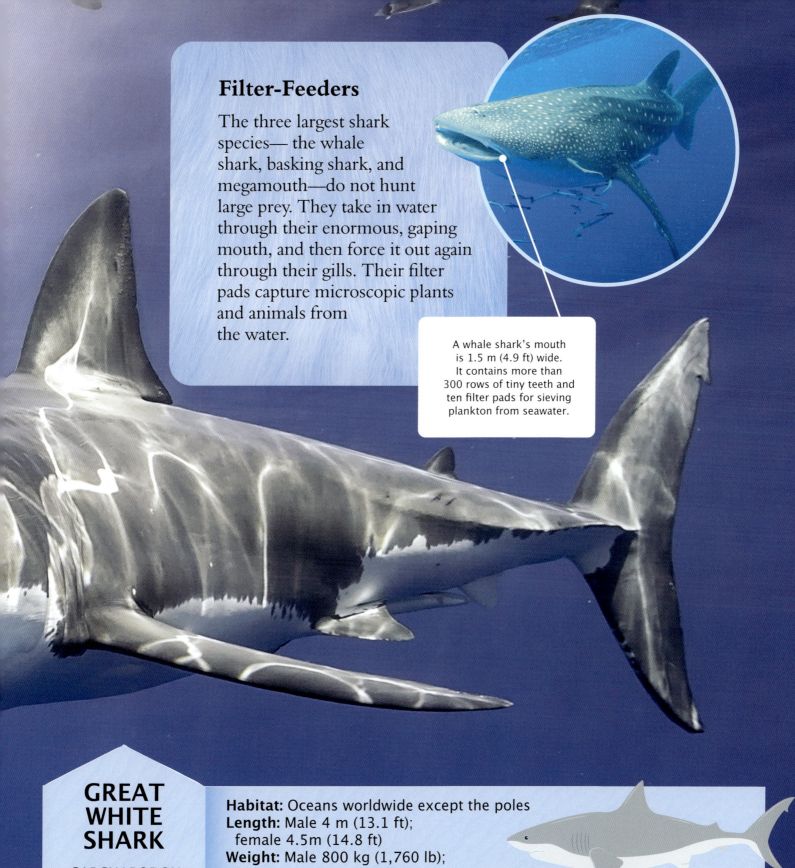

Filter-Feeders

The three largest shark species— the whale shark, basking shark, and megamouth—do not hunt large prey. They take in water through their enormous, gaping mouth, and then force it out again through their gills. Their filter pads capture microscopic plants and animals from the water.

A whale shark's mouth is 1.5 m (4.9 ft) wide. It contains more than 300 rows of tiny teeth and ten filter pads for sieving plankton from seawater.

GREAT WHITE SHARK

CARCHARODON CARCHARIAS
"POINTED TOOTH" FISH

Habitat: Oceans worldwide except the poles
Length: Male 4 m (13.1 ft); female 4.5m (14.8 ft)
Weight: Male 800 kg (1,760 lb); female 1,000 kg (2,200 lb)
Diet: Fish incl. sharks, turtles, marine mammals
Lifespan: Up to 70 years
Wild population: Unknown; Vulnerable

Seahorses

A horse-like head and snake-like tail make seahorses distinctive fish. Together with their close relatives, pipefish and seadragons, they form a family containing around 230 species—of which 120 are found in warm, shallow waters off the coast of Australia. They eat tiny crustaceans and are well-camouflaged among plants.

A male leafy seadragon turns yellow to show it is ready to mate. It also changes hue for camouflage.

Prehensile Tail

Seahorses are weak swimmers because they don't have the usual tail fin that pushes fish through water. They move by fluttering the small dorsal fin low down on their back. Easily swept away by strong currents, seahorses anchor themselves by wrapping their tail around a plant stem.

With its tail curled around a plant, this slender seahorse can take a break from swimming and rest.

When seahorse babies swim out of their father's pouch they are tiny, but fully formed.

Having Babies

Seahorse fathers give birth! The female lays as many as 2,000 eggs in a pouch on the male's belly. He provides oxygen and nourishment and, after about a month, the eggs hatch. Clouds of miniature seahorses swim off into the ocean. Only about one in 20 of these tiny fry will survive to adulthood.

Seadragons and pipefish swim horizontally through the water. Seahorses swim upright.

The seadragon's long, thin snout can suck up thousands of sea lice or other small crustaceans in a single day.

Leafy lobes disguise the seadragon so it looks like floating seaweed. They do not help it to swim.

LEAFY SEADRAGON

PHYCODURUS EQUES
"HORSE WITH SEAWEED SKIN" FISH

Habitat: Ocean; S and E Australlia
Length: Male 25 cm (9.8 in); female 20 cm (7.9 in)
Weight: Male 114 g (4 oz); female 90 g (3 oz)
Diet: Plankton, small crustaceans
Lifespan: Up to 10 years
Wild population: Unknown; Least Concern

DID YOU KNOW? The dwarf seahorse is the world's slowest fish. Even at its top speed, it travels only 1.5 m (5 ft) in an hour.

Cephalopods

Octopuses, squid, cuttlefish, and nautiluses belong to a group of animals called cephalopods (meaning "head-foots"). Cephalopods have a large head, big brain, and a set of arms for gathering food. There are around 800 species. The nautilus is the only living cephalopod with a shell.

The octopus's head lies between the arms and body. It has well-developed eyes, a large brain, and a beak-like mouth. The octopus's poisonous saliva paralyzes prey.

Close Cousins

Octopuses and squid both have eight arms, but the squid also has a pair of tentacles that it uses to grab prey. Many octopuses spend their time on the seabed, where they eat crabs, clams, limpets, and scallops. Squid live in the open ocean and hunt fish, crustaceans, and other squid.

The giant Pacific octopus can change its reddish-brown skin to blend in with its surroundings.

OCTOPUS

OCTOPUS VULGARIS
"COMMON EIGHT FOOT"
INVERTEBRATE

Habitat: Warm oceans worldwide
Length: 60 cm (2 ft)
Weight: 5.5 kg (12 lb)
Diet: Fish, mollusks, crabs, other marine invertebrates
Lifespan: Up to 18 months
Wild population: Unknown; Least Concern

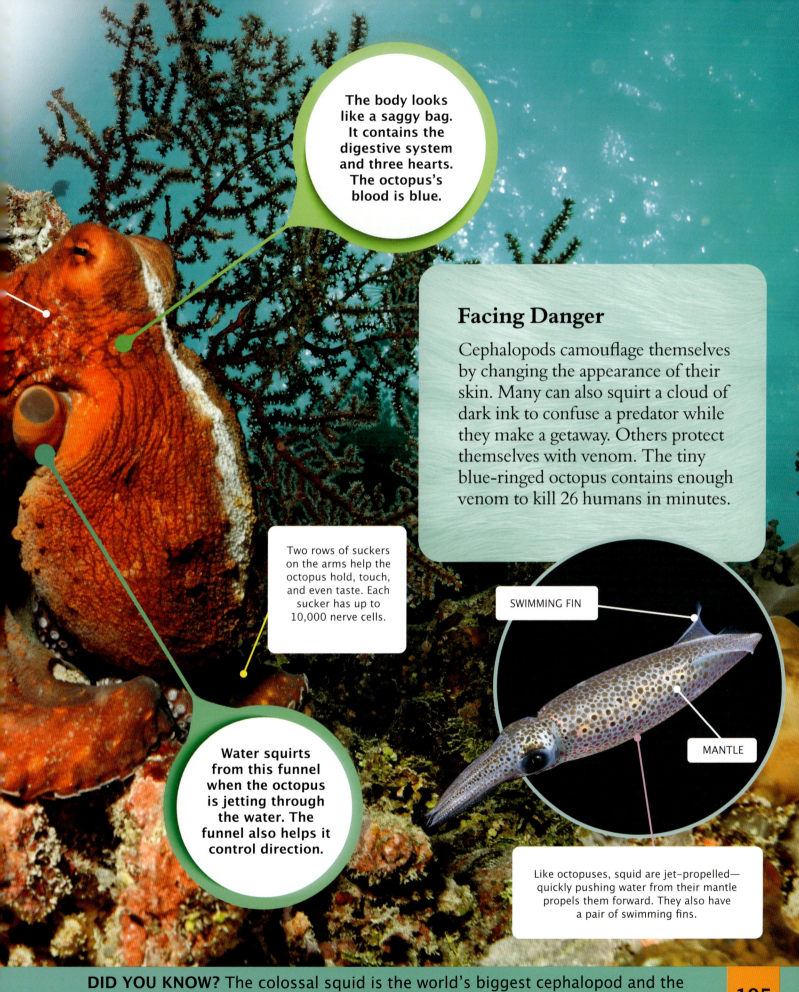

The body looks like a saggy bag. It contains the digestive system and three hearts. The octopus's blood is blue.

Facing Danger

Cephalopods camouflage themselves by changing the appearance of their skin. Many can also squirt a cloud of dark ink to confuse a predator while they make a getaway. Others protect themselves with venom. The tiny blue-ringed octopus contains enough venom to kill 26 humans in minutes.

Two rows of suckers on the arms help the octopus hold, touch, and even taste. Each sucker has up to 10,000 nerve cells.

SWIMMING FIN

MANTLE

Water squirts from this funnel when the octopus is jetting through the water. The funnel also helps it control direction.

Like octopuses, squid are jet-propelled—quickly pushing water from their mantle propels them forward. They also have a pair of swimming fins.

DID YOU KNOW? The colossal squid is the world's biggest cephalopod and the largest invertebrate. It is 14 m (46 ft) long and weighs up to 750 kg (1,650 lb).

Jellyfish

Jellyfish are not fish—they are invertebrates from the same family as anemones and corals. They have been around for around 650 million years and live in every ocean. Instead of a brain, a jellyfish has a net of nerves that helps it detect changes in its surroundings and find prey.

Dangerous Jellies

Jellyfish are predators. They eat whatever they can fit into their mouth, including plankton, crustaceans, fish eggs, fish, and other jellyfish. They paralyze or kill their prey with venom produced by cells on their trailing tentacles. They also use their tentacles to push the food into their mouth.

Life of a Jellyfish

Jellyfish have complicated life cycles. Adults gather—sometimes in their millions—in breeding swarms called blooms. They release eggs and sperm into the water. The fertilized eggs must go through four different life stages before they become medusas (adults). Many are eaten and never reach adulthood.

In a bloom, sometimes the bigger jellyfish turn cannibal and eat the smaller ones.

The box jellyfish is the world's most poisonous animal. The stings of some species can kill a person in minutes.

Twenty-four long maroon tentacles trail behind the jellyfish. They have venomous stings.

Four frilly, creamy-white "arms" surround the sea nettle's mouth. Like the tentacles, they have stinging cells.

The main part of the jellyfish is called the bell. The mouth is hidden under the bell.

PACIFIC SEA NETTLE

CHRYSAORA FUSCESCENS

"DARK INTO LIGHT OF CHYSAOR"

INVERTEBRATE

Habitat: Warm waters; E Pacific
Length of tentacles: 3 m (9.8 ft)
Width: 30 cm (1 ft)
Diet: Jellyfish, plankton, other marine invertebrates
Lifespan: Up to 6 months
Wild population: Unknown; Least Concern

DID YOU KNOW? Jellyfish bodies are 95 percent water. When jellyfish get stranded on a beach, they quickly dry up and disappear!

Spiders and Scorpions

A crab spider has eight eyes to see in all directions. It lies in wait, perfectly disguised, ready to ambush insect visitors to the flower.

Along with mites and ticks, scorpions and spiders are arachnids. There are at least 45,700 species of spider and 1,750 species of scorpions. They are eight-legged predators with no antennae or wings. Their body is split into two parts covered by an exoskeleton. All scorpions and most spiders have venom, but few are fatal to humans.

Super Spiders

All spiders spin silk, but not all build webs. From spiral orbs to tubes and funnels, spider webs are used to trap prey. Other spiders have different hunting methods. The trapdoor spider ambushes prey from a hidden lair, while the huntsman spider gives chase. Spiders range in size from a pinhead-sized orbweb to the massive goliath tarantula.

The leg-like pedipalps on either side of the jaws crush and tear up food.

The two front walking legs are also used to grasp bees, flies, and other prey.

The world's biggest spider, the goliath tarantula, can weigh 175 g (6.2 oz). It hunts mice, lizards, and small birds.

There are more than 2,000 species of crab spider. Many match the flowers where they hunt for insect prey each day.

Sting in the Tail

While spiders inject venom with their fangs, the scorpion produces venom from a stinger at the end of its curving tail. It stings to protect itself from predators. It can also stun struggling prey, but usually it saves its venom and kills prey with its powerful pincers.

Scorpions are tough survivors and are found in many harsh habitats. This yellow fattail scorpion lives in deserts in North Africa and the Middle East.

CRAB SPIDER

THOMISUS ONUSTUS
"STRING LOADED"
INVERTEBRATE

Habitat: Moors, deserts, grasslands; Europe, Asia, Africa
Length: Male 4 mm (0.16 in); female 7 mm (0.28 in)
Weight: Male 2.5 g (0.09 oz); female 3 g (0.11 oz)
Diet: Small invertebrates
Lifespan: Up to 4 months
Wild population: Unknown

DID YOU KNOW? The giant huntsman spider has the largest legspan of any spider. At 30 cm (1 ft) across, it is larger than most dinner plates.

Slugs and Snails

Slugs and snails are gastropods. Like cephalopods (see page 194), gastropods are mollusks. There are around 75,000 species, and a third of these live on land. The others live in the oceans and in fresh water. Slugs and snails are found worldwide, except in places of extreme cold. They have soft, slimy bodies and they move along slowly on a single, broad foot.

The spiral shell, made mostly of chalk, protects the snail from birds and other predators.

Almost the Same

Snails have a protective shell, but slugs do not. Slugs squeeze under logs or stones to stay safe and moist. Apart from that, slugs and snails are very similar. They feed mostly on plants and move slowly along a slime trail. They are also both hermaphrodite (part male and part female) so when they mate, each partner lays eggs.

The leopard slug eats dead plants and fungi, but it also hunts other slugs.

COMMON GARDEN SNAIL

CORNU ASPERSUM
"SPECKLED HORN"
INVERTEBRATE

Habitat: Gardens, farmland, meadows, forests; Europe, Asia, North Africa
Shell width: 3.5 cm (1.4 in)
Weight: 30 g (1 oz)
Diet: Plants
Lifespan: Up to 2 years
Wild population: Unknown; Least Concern

The radula (mouth) looks like a rough tongue. It is covered with tiny teeth for grating plant matter.

The snail has two pairs of tentacles. The longer pair of tentacles has a simple eye at the end.

Sea Slugs

Nudibranches are marine snails, but they are known as sea slugs because they shed their shell after their larva life stage. Many of the 2,300 nudibranch species are brightly patterned. Some just pretend to be poisonous and some really are—they may create their own toxins or take them in by eating other animals, such as sponges.

The variable neon slug is a nudibranch that lives in tropical waters. It grows to around 12 cm (4.7 in) long.

DID YOU KNOW? The African giant snail is the largest land-living gastropod: It can grow over 18 cm (7 in) long and 9 cm (3.5 in) wide.

Bees

Bees are insects. Like other insects, they have six legs, a three-part body, and antennae. Worldwide, excluding Antarctica, there are about 20,000 bee species. Most live alone, but honeybees and bumblebees form large colonies made up of a queen bee, hundreds of drones, and thousands of workers. The drones mate with the queen. The workers guard the nest, collect pollen and nectar, and care for young.

Breaking Away

When a bee colony becomes too large, the queen bee lays eggs that will develop into queens instead of worker bees. She leaves the nest with a large group of workers. The swarm flies to a suitable site to start a new colony. When they get there, the queen starts laying eggs that are already fertilized by the drones.

A swarm can contain hundreds or even thousands of honeybees.

Each leg is split into segments, so it is very flexible.

The bee has a pair of jointed antennae. They can touch, smell, taste, and pick up vibrations.

The bumblebee has two pairs of wings. They beat up and down so quickly that they make a buzzing noise.

GARDEN BUMBLEBEE

BOMBUS HORTORUM
"PLANT BUZZER"
INVERTEBRATE

Habitat: Grasslands, farmland; Europe, Asia, New Zealand
Length: 1.5 cm (0.6 in); queen 2 cm (0.8 in)
Weight: 2.5 g (0.09 oz); queen 4 g (0.14 oz)
Diet: Nectar, pollen
Lifespan: Up to 2 weeks; queen up to 1 year
Wild population: Unknown; Least Concern

Many plants need bees to pollinate them so they can produce fruit.

Female bumblebees can sting. Their sting is not barbed like a honeybee's, so it can be reused many times.

Finding Food

Honeybees carry nectar and pollen back to the hive. They mix nectar with saliva to make honey to feed the young. When bees find a good source of nectar, they tell the other workers where it is with an elaborate, waggling dance.

The hairy body picks up grains of pollen, which rub off on the next flower the bee visits. This is called pollination.

Bees store honey in hexagonal cells, which they build from beeswax. The cells also house eggs and larvae.

DID YOU KNOW? A healthy queen bee can lay as many as 2,000 eggs in a single day.

Chapter 8: The Human Body

Amazing Body

The body is a complex collection of about 37 trillion cells (see pages 148–149) that work together to create a living, thinking human being. Those cells are joined together to make tissues that have different properties. The tissues build into organs with specific jobs, from pumping blood to making signal-sending chemicals called hormones.

Body Systems

The body has systems to look after different functions. Bones and muscles provide support and movement. The brain and nerves gather information about our surroundings and help us respond. The heart and lungs provide muscles with fuel. The digestive system harvests energy from the food we eat. Other systems repair the body and keep it stable.

Some body systems involve an organ in a particular place, such as the lungs. Others, such as the nervous system, are spread throughout our body.

OTHER ELEMENTS
NITROGEN
HYDROGEN
CARBON
OXYGEN

Human Recipe

We are built from common chemical elements. Oxygen makes up 65 percent of our mass, 9.5 percent is lightweight hydrogen and 18.5 percent is carbon (a versatile element that builds the complex chemicals necessary for life). Nitrogen, calcium, and phosphorus account for 5.2 percent. The remaining 1.8 percent is made up of tiny amounts of other elements.

Most of our body's oxygen and hydrogen is locked up in water molecules (H_2O). Water makes up 55–60 percent of an adult's body weight, and it makes up even more in children.

| AMAZING DISCOVERY | **Scientist:** Andreas Vesalius
Discovery: Human anatomy
Date: 1543
The story: Brussels-born physician Vesalius pioneered the dissection of dead human bodies. He made countless discoveries and overturned mistaken ideas about human anatomy that doctors believed for almost 1,400 years. |

The brain tells the body what to do based on information gathered by the eyes, ears, and other sensory organs.

The systems of the body are always working, whether the body is at rest or doing something energetic.

The digestive system provides the energy to run. It gathers nutrients from food, which the blood carries to every cell.

Bones support the legs, and muscles make it possible for them to move. The directions that make the legs run come from the brain.

DID YOU KNOW? Most body cells can be seen only through a microscope, but an egg cell is visible with the naked eye at 0.1 mm (0.004 in) across.

Inside the Brain

The human brain is the most complex structure in all of nature. It is packed with 86 billion individual cells called neurons, which form a vast web of connections. These neurons send signals with little bursts of electric charge that are carried by a flow of chemicals washing around the brain.

How the Brain Works

Our brain is split into regions, and each is made up of neurons that are specialized to carry out particular tasks. Areas near the middle and bottom of the brain handle instinctive tasks and help regulate our body. The wrinkly outer layer of the brain, called the cerebral cortex, is in charge of more complex tasks such as thinking and sensory processing.

The cerebral cortex's wrinkles give neurons maximum space. The wrinklier the brain, the more processing it can do!

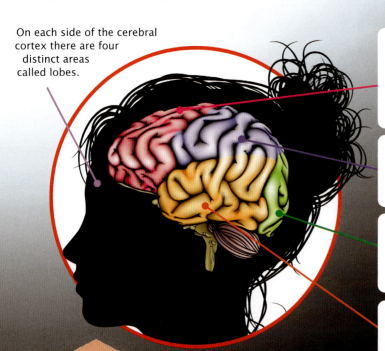

On each side of the cerebral cortex there are four distinct areas called lobes.

The frontal lobes look after emotions, thinking, memory, planning, language, and more.

The parietal lobes are concerned with the senses of taste and touch.

The occipital lobes are where we process information from our eyes.

The temporal lobes manage our hearing.

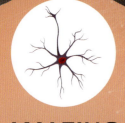

AMAZING DISCOVERY

Scientist: Santiago Ramón y Cajal
Discovery: The neuron doctrine
Date: 1888
The story: Spanish anatomist Ramón y Cajal used new techniques to study neurons under the microscope. He showed that the nervous system was made up of individual nerve cells that formed temporary connections when passing on chemical instructions.

DID YOU KNOW? Although the scalp has plenty of pain receptors, the brain does not contain any, so it cannot feel pain.

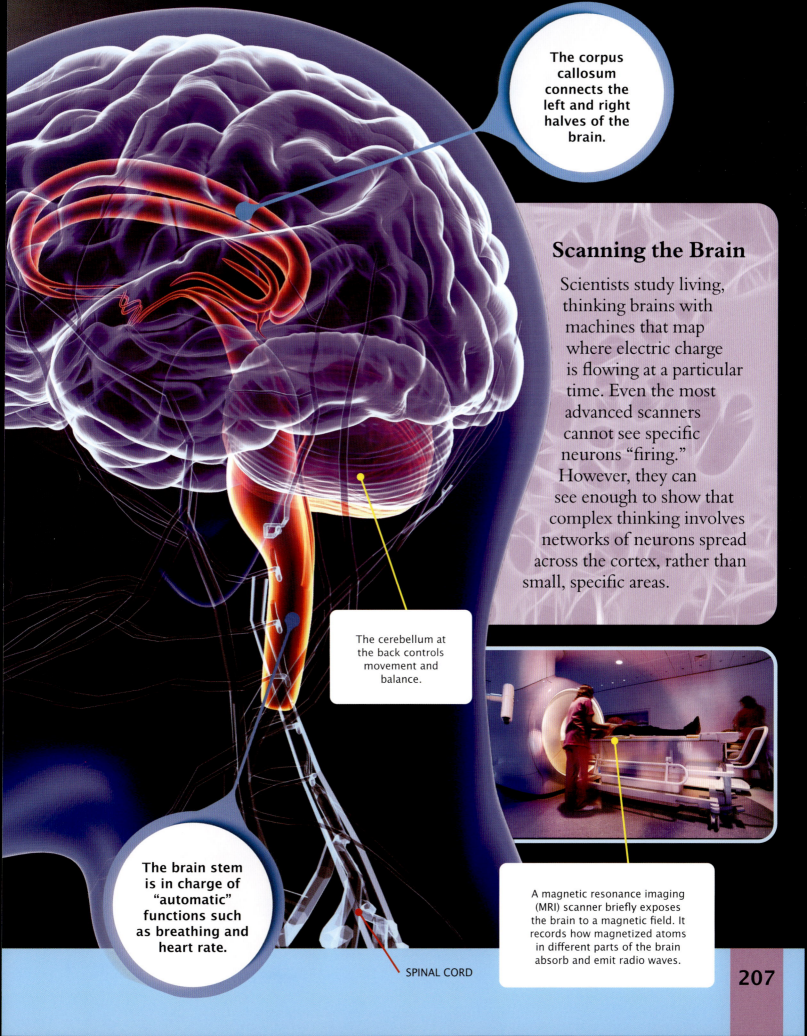

The corpus callosum connects the left and right halves of the brain.

The cerebellum at the back controls movement and balance.

The brain stem is in charge of "automatic" functions such as breathing and heart rate.

SPINAL CORD

Scanning the Brain

Scientists study living, thinking brains with machines that map where electric charge is flowing at a particular time. Even the most advanced scanners cannot see specific neurons "firing." However, they can see enough to show that complex thinking involves networks of neurons spread across the cortex, rather than small, specific areas.

A magnetic resonance imaging (MRI) scanner briefly exposes the brain to a magnetic field. It records how magnetized atoms in different parts of the brain absorb and emit radio waves.

207

Bone and Muscle

Bones are a special type of rigid, hardened tissue that supports the weight of the human body and gives it an overall shape. Cartilage is a tough but flexible connective tissue that holds the framework of bones together. Muscles attached to bones can pull in different directions so our body changes shape and can move.

Our Skeleton

Babies are born with 300 bones in their body, but as we grow some of these join together—most adults have 206. Bones get their toughness from a mineral called calcium phosphate. Despite their solid appearance, bones are spongy inside and filled with a tissue called marrow that produces the body's blood cells.

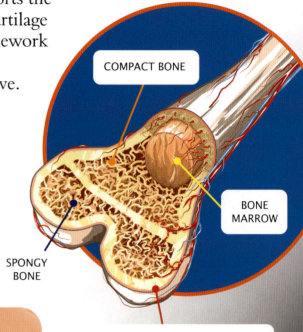

Most of our blood cells are manufactured by bone marrow in the large, ball-like ends of long bones such as the femur or hip bone.

Muscle Tissues

Muscles are made up of special cells that can reduce in length, creating a pulling force. Skeletal muscle is the most common type and it is made up of stringy bundles. Smooth muscle lines blood vessels and various body organs. Cardiac muscle is a special kind of muscle in the heart that can work without resting.

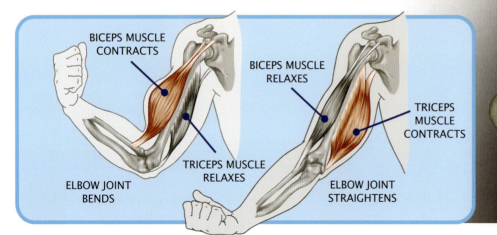

Together, the feet contain 52 bones—that is one-quarter of all the bones in the body.

Muscles can only pull, not push, so many skeletal muscles work together in opposing pairs. As one relaxes and the other contracts, they make a joint move.

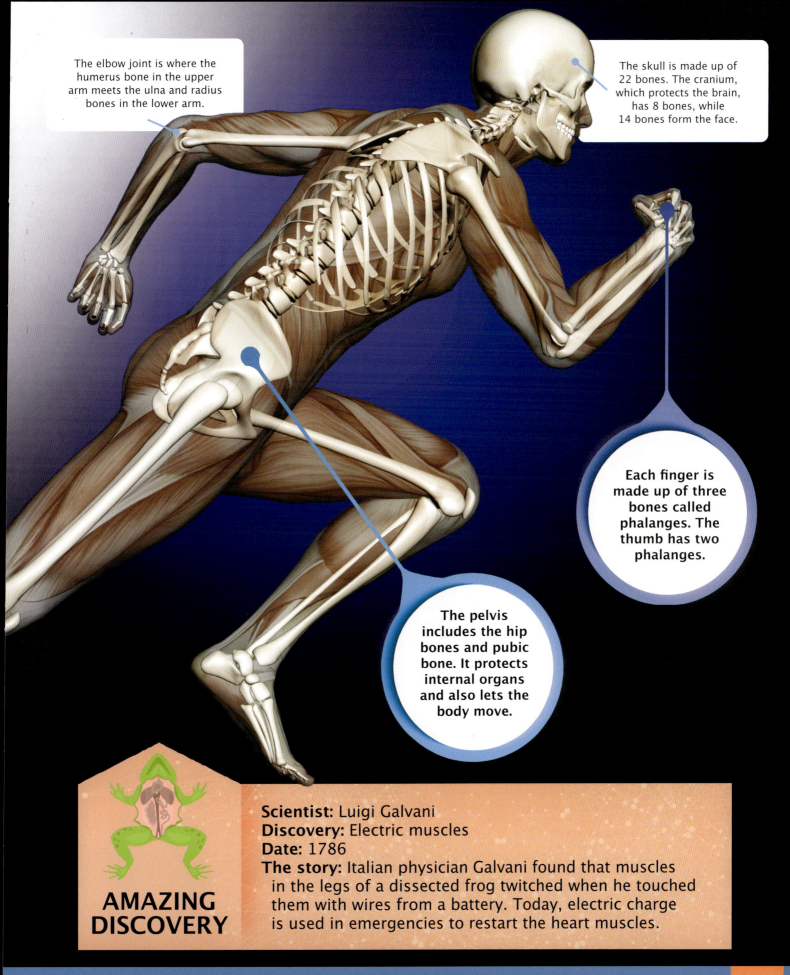

The elbow joint is where the humerus bone in the upper arm meets the ulna and radius bones in the lower arm.

The skull is made up of 22 bones. The cranium, which protects the brain, has 8 bones, while 14 bones form the face.

Each finger is made up of three bones called phalanges. The thumb has two phalanges.

The pelvis includes the hip bones and pubic bone. It protects internal organs and also lets the body move.

AMAZING DISCOVERY

Scientist: Luigi Galvani
Discovery: Electric muscles
Date: 1786
The story: Italian physician Galvani found that muscles in the legs of a dissected frog twitched when he touched them with wires from a battery. Today, electric charge is used in emergencies to restart the heart muscles.

DID YOU KNOW? The largest bone in the human body is the femur (thigh bone). The smallest is the stapes in the middle ear, which is just 3 mm (0.12 in) long.

Nervous System

The brain and spinal cord make up the central nervous system. They contain neurons—specialized nerve cells that carry information around the brain and between the brain and body. There are two other kinds of nerve cell—sensory nerves and motor nerves—which look after our senses and movement.

Signals and Synapses

Information travels from neuron to neuron as bursts of electrically charged chemicals. Signals cross tiny gaps between the neurons, called synapses, and enter the next neuron through one of its short tendrils, called dendrites. Signals leave the neuron along its one extra-long tendril, the axon, and cross synapses into other neurons.

On Two Levels

Part of the nervous system works automatically without us having to think about it. It controls organs and body functions and sends signals to relax the body or prepare it for action. The other part of the nervous system handles tasks that require more complex thought, such as interpreting senses and moving muscles.

The spinal cord is the highway between the body and the brain. Nerves branch off it to every part of the body.

When it is tapped by the doctor's hammer, the knee jerks involuntarily. This is a reflex action. Nearby nerve cells make the knee jerk without waiting for directions from the brain. Reflexes help to protect the body from harm.

The axon is like a long, very thin wire. It carries outgoing electrical signals from the neuron.

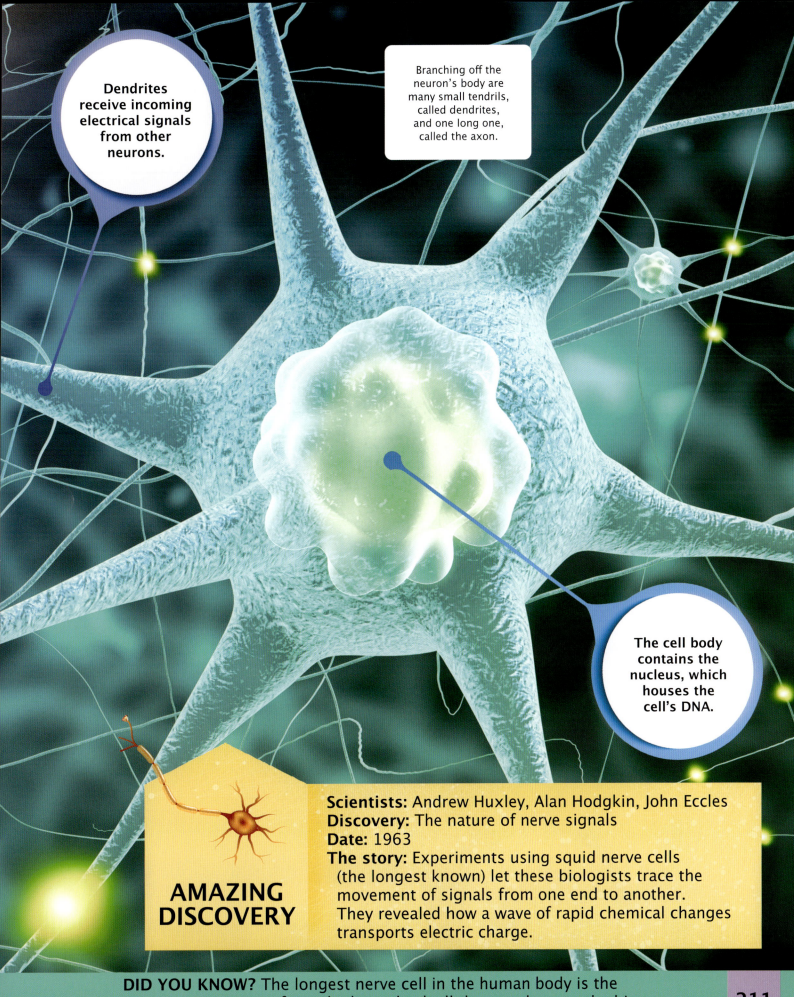

Skin and Hair

Just like the heart or liver, the skin is an organ—a part of the body with a particular job. Its layers have nerves, hairs, and glands that protect the body's delicate inner tissues, keep its temperature steady, and let us touch.

Skin Structure

The skin has three layers. The outer epidermis is made of cells with no blood supply and creates a waterproof barrier. The middle dermis has a rich blood supply and many sense receptors. The inner hypodermis lies directly over muscles, bones, and organs. It stores the body's fuel reserves in the form of fat.

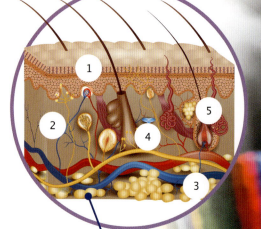

This cross-section of the skin shows its three layers: the epidermis (1), dermis (2), and hypodermis (3). The dermis contains hair follicles (4) and sense receptors (5).

Every follicle contains two pigments. The exact mix decides how dark or light the hair is.

Hairs are thin shafts of a protein called keratin. They grow out of roots called follicles in the dermis layer of the skin.

As we age, the skin becomes less elastic. It develops lines and wrinkles.

Hair

Compared to most mammals, humans have very little hair, but it still does important jobs. Head hair protects us from sunburn and losing body heat. Eyebrows, eyelashes, and nose and ear hairs stop microbes, dust, and parasites from entering the body. Some hairs help with our sense of touch, too.

In the epidermis, older skin cells push closer to the surface. They flatten, dry out, and eventually flake off.

Hair and skin keep our temperature steady. Hairs help sweat evaporate off our skin and cool us down. They can also stand on end to trap a layer of air close to the skin that warms us up.

AMAZING DISCOVERY

Scientist: Ibn Sina (Avicenna)
Discovery: Skin creams
Date: 1025
The story: Persian philosopher Ibn Sina wrote about skin conditions in his medical handbook of 1025. He recommended the use of zinc oxide, a chemical compound that is still used today to soothe rashes.

DID YOU KNOW? Our body sheds 30,000–40,000 skin cells every minute!

Digestive System

Like all animals, humans need to harvest energy from food to survive. This process is called digestion. A series of organs, linked to one another along a tube called the gastrointestinal tract (gut), break down the food, remove its useful nutrients, and get rid of any waste.

The liver produces bile that helps to digest fats and remove cholesterol and other waste products.

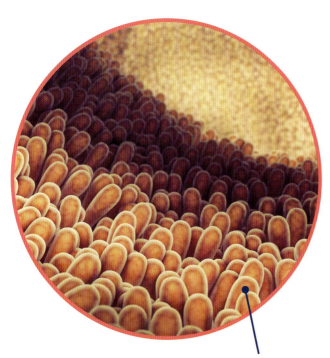

The small intestine is lined with thousands of tiny protrusions called villi. Digested nutrients pass through their thin walls and into the bloodstream.

In and Out

When we swallow, chewed-up food squeezes down a tube called the gullet or oesophagus to the stomach. Here, strong muscles mush up the food and gastric juices begin to break it down. The intestines absorb the nutrients from the food into the bloodstream, leaving behind waste that is pushed out of the rectum.

The large intestine processes the watery waste that leaves the small intestine. It absorbs water back into the bloodstream and creates solid waste—poop.

AMAZING DISCOVERY

Scientist: Jan Baptiste van Helmont
Discovery: Chemical digestion
Date: 1662
The story: Van Helmont argued against a popular idea that heat was responsible for breaking down food in the stomach. He argued that digestion is mostly done by chemical agents—what modern scientists call enzymes.

DID YOU KNOW? The small intestine is about 6 m (20 ft) long. The large intestine is only about 1.5 m (5 ft) long, but it is much wider.

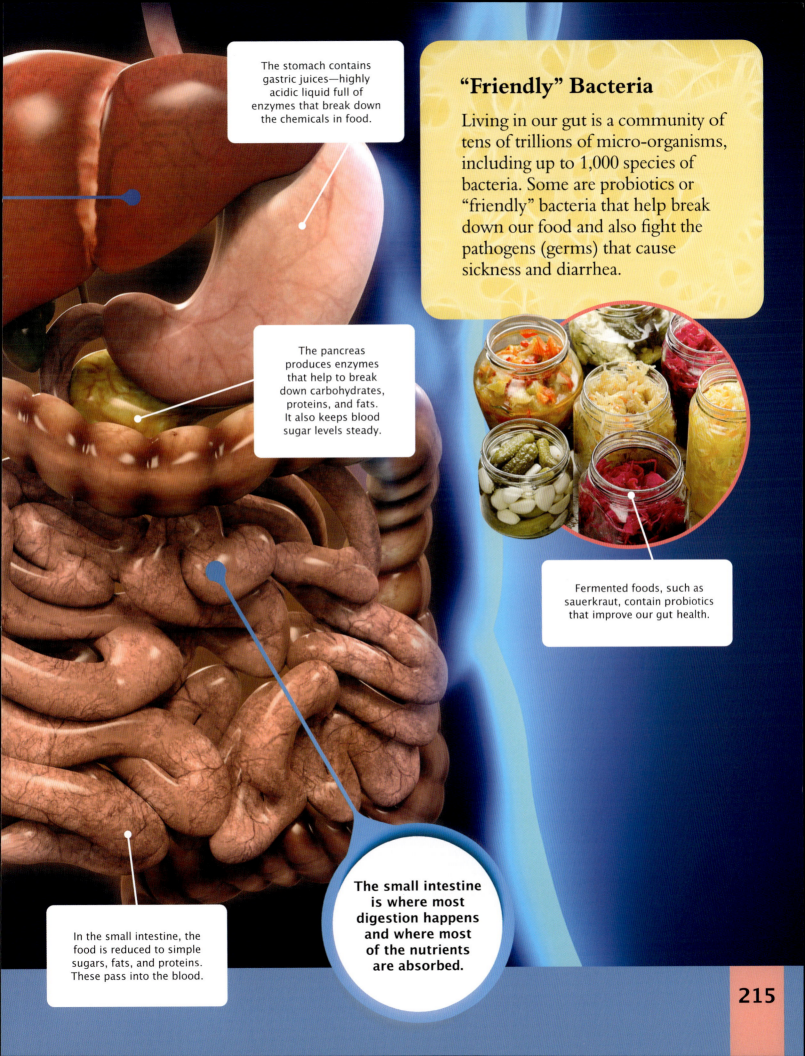

The stomach contains gastric juices—highly acidic liquid full of enzymes that break down the chemicals in food.

"Friendly" Bacteria

Living in our gut is a community of tens of trillions of micro-organisms, including up to 1,000 species of bacteria. Some are probiotics or "friendly" bacteria that help break down our food and also fight the pathogens (germs) that cause sickness and diarrhea.

The pancreas produces enzymes that help to break down carbohydrates, proteins, and fats. It also keeps blood sugar levels steady.

Fermented foods, such as sauerkraut, contain probiotics that improve our gut health.

In the small intestine, the food is reduced to simple sugars, fats, and proteins. These pass into the blood.

The small intestine is where most digestion happens and where most of the nutrients are absorbed.

Heart, Blood, and Lungs

Blood is the body's transport system. It moves many different chemicals and other materials around our body pumped by a powerful muscle, the heart. The blood's most important job is to carry oxygen from the lungs to the muscles so they can work.

Blood is made up of a watery liquid called plasma. Most of it is made up of red blood cells. There are also white blood cells that fight disease and platelets that help blood to clot (stop bleeding after an injury).

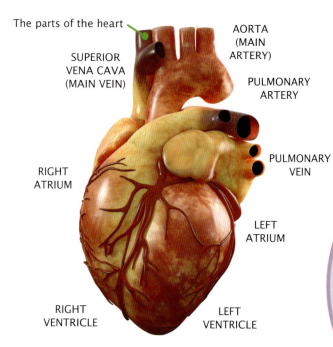

The parts of the heart: AORTA (MAIN ARTERY), SUPERIOR VENA CAVA (MAIN VEIN), PULMONARY ARTERY, PULMONARY VEIN, RIGHT ATRIUM, LEFT ATRIUM, RIGHT VENTRICLE, LEFT VENTRICLE

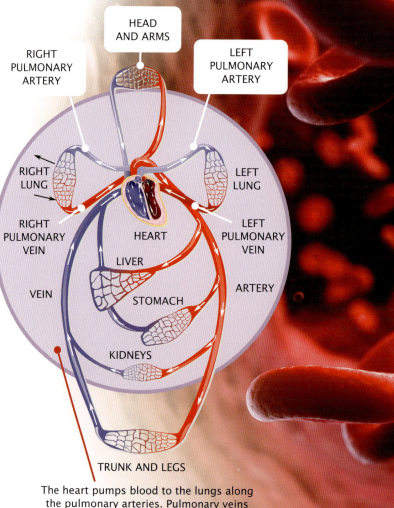

The heart pumps blood to the lungs along the pulmonary arteries. Pulmonary veins carry the oxygen-rich blood (red) back to the heart. Arteries take blood to every part of the body, and veins carry oxygen-poor blood (blue) back to the heart.

Circulatory System

The heart is a hollow, muscular pump. It has two halves, left and right. Each half has an upper chamber, the atrium, and a lower chamber, the ventricle. During each heartbeat, the left atrium receives oxygen-rich blood and the left ventricle pumps it to the body. At the same time, the right atrium receives oxygen-poor blood, and the right ventricle pumps it to the lungs.

DID YOU KNOW? By some measures, the lungs are the body's largest organ—if their surface was spread out flat, it would cover about the same area as a tennis court.

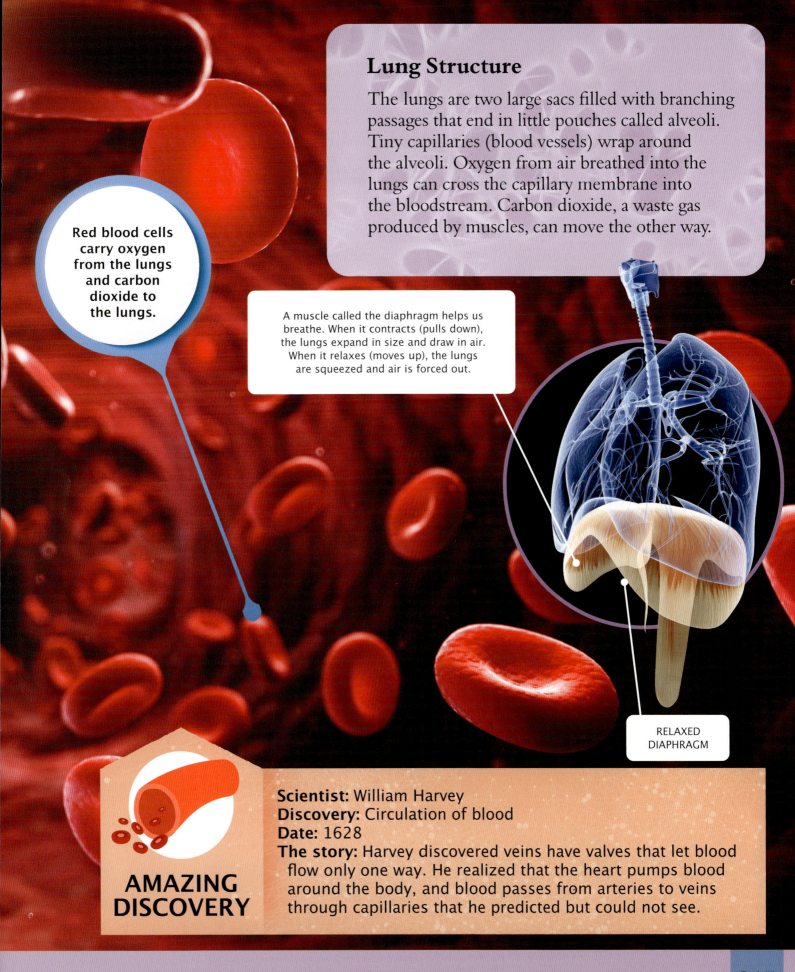

Lung Structure

The lungs are two large sacs filled with branching passages that end in little pouches called alveoli. Tiny capillaries (blood vessels) wrap around the alveoli. Oxygen from air breathed into the lungs can cross the capillary membrane into the bloodstream. Carbon dioxide, a waste gas produced by muscles, can move the other way.

Red blood cells carry oxygen from the lungs and carbon dioxide to the lungs.

A muscle called the diaphragm helps us breathe. When it contracts (pulls down), the lungs expand in size and draw in air. When it relaxes (moves up), the lungs are squeezed and air is forced out.

RELAXED DIAPHRAGM

AMAZING DISCOVERY

Scientist: William Harvey
Discovery: Circulation of blood
Date: 1628
The story: Harvey discovered veins have valves that let blood flow only one way. He realized that the heart pumps blood around the body, and blood passes from arteries to veins through capillaries that he predicted but could not see.

The Liver

No wonder the liver is the heaviest organ! It is our in-built "chemical factory," and it is responsible for more than 500 different functions. One of its jobs is storing, processing, and releasing the nutrients from food—even though it is not directly part of our digestive system.

Hardworking Cells

The liver is made up of lobules, hexagonal groups of cells arranged around a central vein. These cells, called hepatocytes, process nutrients, secrete bile (see below), store vitamins and minerals, and break down toxins, such as alcohol.

Bitter Brew

Bile is a bitter, greenish-brown fluid that digests fats. It travels along the hepatic ducts to be stored in the gall bladder, a pouch below the liver. When food enters the small intestine, the gall bladder squeezes bile into the bile duct, which leads into the duodenum.

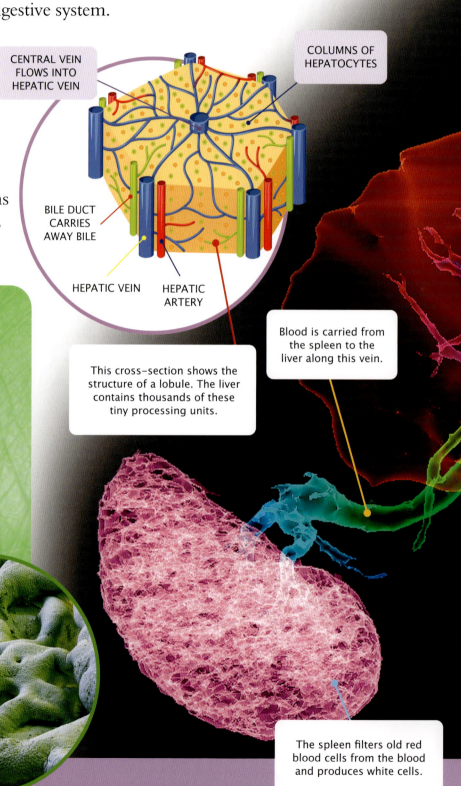

CENTRAL VEIN FLOWS INTO HEPATIC VEIN

COLUMNS OF HEPATOCYTES

BILE DUCT CARRIES AWAY BILE

HEPATIC VEIN

HEPATIC ARTERY

This cross-section shows the structure of a lobule. The liver contains thousands of these tiny processing units.

Blood is carried from the spleen to the liver along this vein.

This scan magnifies the gall bladder's wrinkled lining. Each bump is a cell.

The spleen filters old red blood cells from the blood and produces white cells.

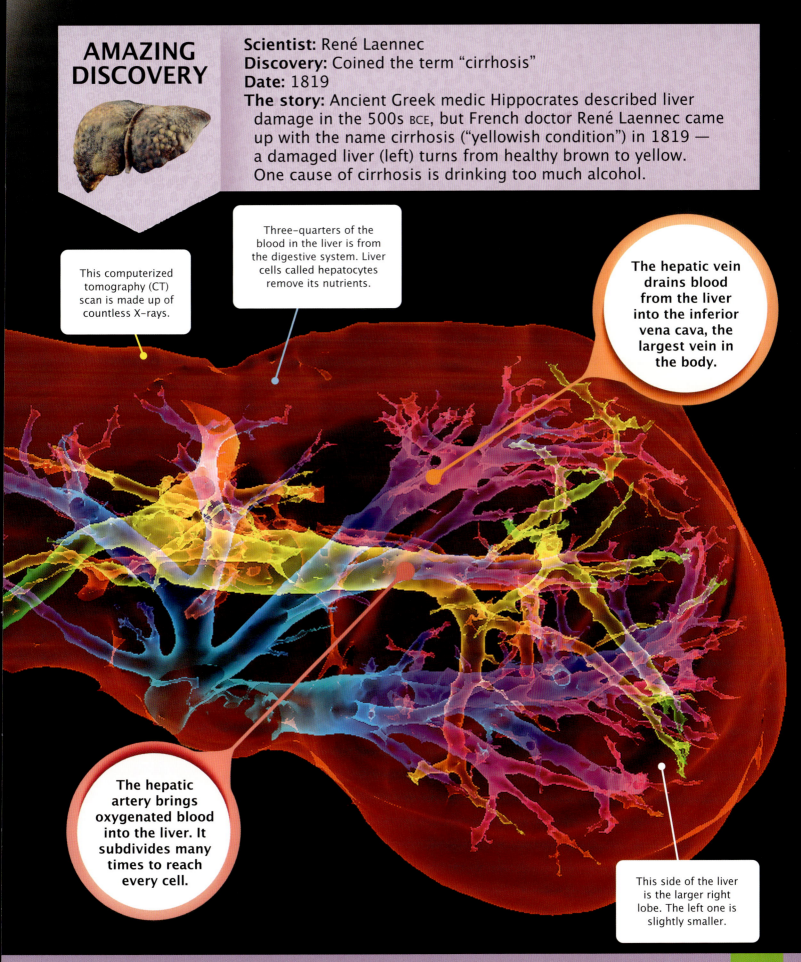

AMAZING DISCOVERY

Scientist: René Laennec
Discovery: Coined the term "cirrhosis"
Date: 1819
The story: Ancient Greek medic Hippocrates described liver damage in the 500s BCE, but French doctor René Laennec came up with the name cirrhosis ("yellowish condition") in 1819 — a damaged liver (left) turns from healthy brown to yellow. One cause of cirrhosis is drinking too much alcohol.

This computerized tomography (CT) scan is made up of countless X-rays.

Three-quarters of the blood in the liver is from the digestive system. Liver cells called hepatocytes remove its nutrients.

The hepatic vein drains blood from the liver into the inferior vena cava, the largest vein in the body.

The hepatic artery brings oxygenated blood into the liver. It subdivides many times to reach every cell.

This side of the liver is the larger right lobe. The left one is slightly smaller.

DID YOU KNOW? The liver can repair itself and regenerate (grow back). Up to 65 percent of it can be removed and it will regrow in about three months.

Kidneys and Urine

Over a lifetime, we produce about 42,000 l (11,000 gallons) of urine.

Chemical reactions in our body produce waste. For example, when the liver breaks down proteins, a substance called urea is created. Our kidneys get rid of the body's waste as urine.

Inside the Kidneys

The kidney's outer layer, the cortex, has millions of microscopic structures called nephrons. They filter the blood and reabsorb useful substances, such as glucose. The waste (urine) collects in narrow tubes in the kidney's middle layer, the medulla. It travels through the funnel-like renal pelvis and into the ureter (the duct leading to the bladder).

Every nephron has a cluster of capillaries that brings and takes away blood. It also has tubules (microscopic tubes) that absorb substances and form urine.

The kidney adjusts the body's water content. If we are dehydrated, the body retains water. We produce only a small amount of concentrated urine.

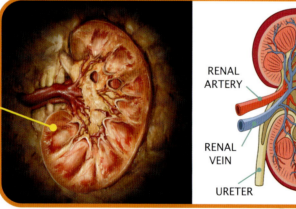
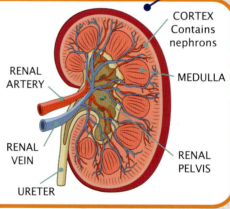

CORTEX Contains nephrons
RENAL ARTERY
MEDULLA
RENAL VEIN
RENAL PELVIS
URETER

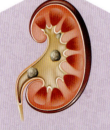

AMAZING DISCOVERY

Scientists: I Fernström and B Johansson
Discovery: A new way to remove kidney stones
Date: 1976
The story: Uric acid or calcium can build up in the kidney to form "stones." If they get stuck, they cause pain and infection. Surgeons Fernström and Johansson came up with a removal technique: They inserted a fine plastic tube through the skin and used it to drain the kidney.

DID YOU KNOW? Urine is 95 percent water. Its other ingredients include urea and salts, such as chloride, sodium, and potassium.

URINARY SYSTEM
1. KIDNEY   3. BLADDER
2. URETER   4. URETHRA

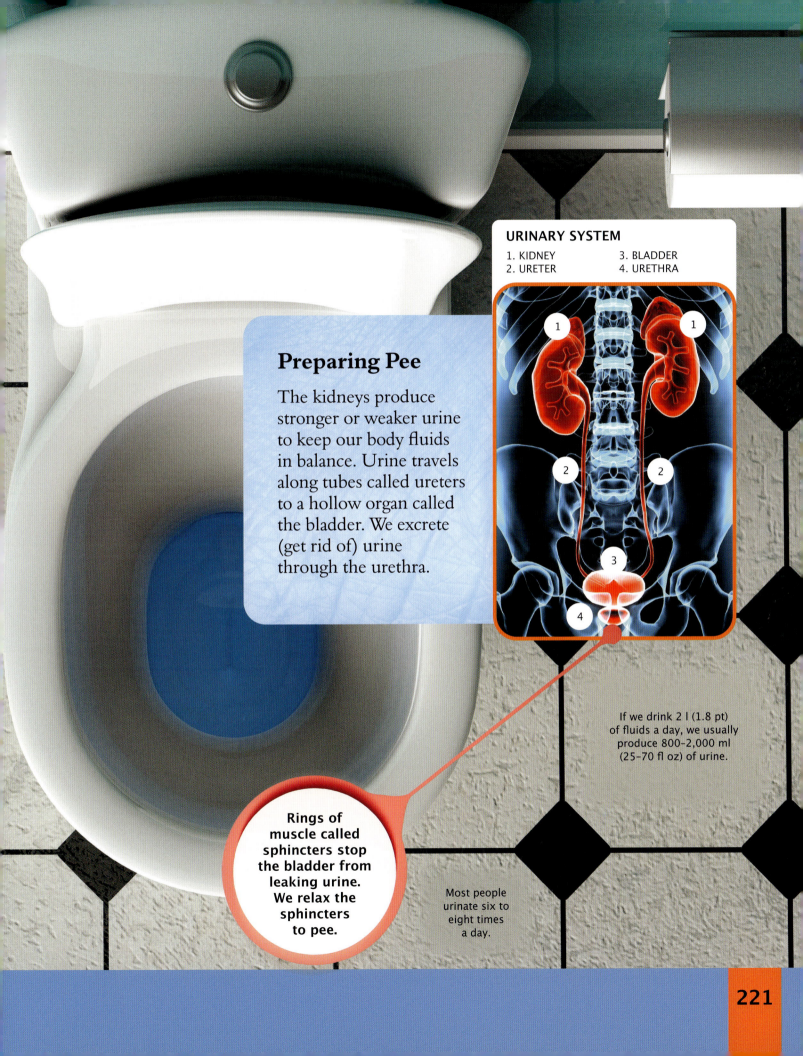

Preparing Pee

The kidneys produce stronger or weaker urine to keep our body fluids in balance. Urine travels along tubes called ureters to a hollow organ called the bladder. We excrete (get rid of) urine through the urethra.

If we drink 2 l (1.8 pt) of fluids a day, we usually produce 800–2,000 ml (25–70 fl oz) of urine.

Rings of muscle called sphincters stop the bladder from leaking urine. We relax the sphincters to pee.

Most people urinate six to eight times a day.

Making Babies

It takes nine months for a fertilized egg to grow into a baby that is able to survive outside its mother's body. During this time, a special organ in the woman's tummy, called the uterus or womb, provides the developing fetus with all that it needs to grow and develop.

Within the uterus, the fetus is protected inside a fluid-filled bag called the amniotic sac.

From Fertilization to Fetus

Each month between a woman's teens and early fifties, one of her ovaries releases a tiny egg. Made up of just one cell, it carries half the genetic information needed to produce another human. If it is fertilized with sperm from a man, it receives the other half of genetic material. Then it can begin to divide and become a more complex embryo. At eight weeks, it becomes a fetus.

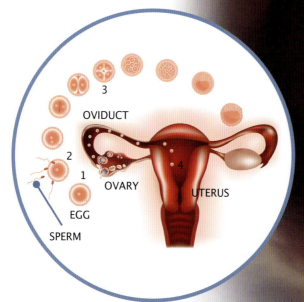

This diagram shows an egg's journey from ovary to uterus. A sperm fertilizes the egg as it moves down the oviduct and its cells start dividing over and over. Fertilization makes the uterus lining thicken to receive the embryo. Safe in the uterus, it can develop into a baby.

1. EGG
2. FERTILIZATION
3. CELL DIVIDES
4. EMBRYO IMPLANTS INTO UTERUS LINING

AMAZING DISCOVERY

Scientists: Patrick Steptoe and Robert Edwards
Discovery: In vitro fertilization (IVF)
Date: 1977
The story: To help a couple who couldn't conceive, these doctors put the father's sperm into the egg in a laboratory (*in vitro* fertilization, or IVF) and implanted the embryo in the mother's uterus. This was the first "test tube" baby.

The umbilical cord brings oxygen and food to the baby and takes away waste. It is connected at one end to what will become the baby's belly button, and at the other end to a spongy disk called the placenta.

An average baby weighs 2.7–4.1 kg (6–9 lb) at birth and is around 52 cm (20.5 in) long.

A Baby is Born

In the ninth month of pregnancy, the baby usually turns so that its head presses the cervix (uterus opening). The pressure encourages the uterus to begin a series of contractions (squeezes) that increase over time. Eventually, the cervix opens and the baby is pushed along the birth canal into the outside world.

Human babies are the most helpless in the animal kingdom and need constant care. For several months, they must rely entirely on their mother's milk before eventually moving on to solid foods.

DID YOU KNOW? In the last 10 weeks of pregnancy, women need to eat about 10 percent more food.

Fighting Disease

Our body is under constant attack from tiny organisms called pathogens that cause disease, and it has different ways to defend itself. Waterproof skin, protective hairs, and sticky mucus form the first barrier against intruders. If any pathogens do make it through, the immune system is ready to attack.

Soldier Cells

Our immune system is made up of different types of white blood cells that can fight off invaders—neutrophils, eosinophils, basophils, lymphocytes, monocytes, and mast cells. They can engulf and digest harmful bacteria, viruses, and other microbes, or attack them with chemical weapons. Lymphocytes and monocytes work together using messengers called antibodies.

Our body can "remember" pathogens it has encountered before. Lymphocytes target them with tailor-made antibodies.

The two main types of pathogens are simple single-celled organisms called bacteria and viruses—capsules of rogue genetic information that can invade and reprogram our own cells.

VIRUS

BACTERIUM

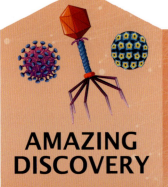

AMAZING DISCOVERY

Scientists: Dmitri Ivanovsky and Martinus Beijerinck
Discovery: Viruses
Date: 1892–1898
The story: When Russian botanist Ivanovsky investigated a disease damaging tobacco crops, he discovered that the infection was caused by something far smaller than a bacterium. A few years later, Beijerinck named these tiny infectious agents viruses.

DID YOU KNOW? Scientists have studied about 5,000 viruses, but there are probably millions. More than 200 of them can cause the common cold.

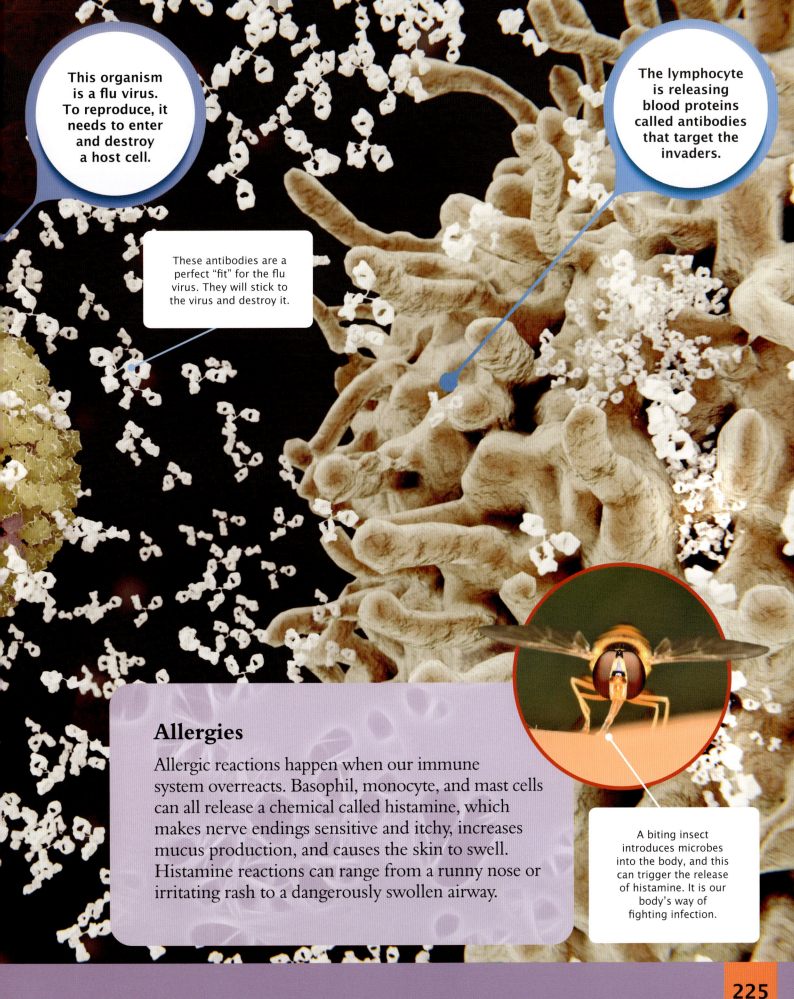

This organism is a flu virus. To reproduce, it needs to enter and destroy a host cell.

The lymphocyte is releasing blood proteins called antibodies that target the invaders.

These antibodies are a perfect "fit" for the flu virus. They will stick to the virus and destroy it.

Allergies

Allergic reactions happen when our immune system overreacts. Basophil, monocyte, and mast cells can all release a chemical called histamine, which makes nerve endings sensitive and itchy, increases mucus production, and causes the skin to swell. Histamine reactions can range from a runny nose or irritating rash to a dangerously swollen airway.

A biting insect introduces microbes into the body, and this can trigger the release of histamine. It is our body's way of fighting infection.

Touch

Hot or cold, soft or hard, rough or smooth, itchy or tickly … We feel different sensations thanks to sensors in our skin called touch receptors. We have four types. Touch helps us understand and interact with what is around us. It also helps us to avoid harm.

Types of Touch Receptor

Mechanoreceptors detect pressure, vibrations, and texture; thermo-receptors sense temperature; nociceptors feel pain; and proprioceptors in muscles and joints tell us where our body is in relation to the environment. Our touch sensors send signals to the brain whenever we come into physical contact with something. Our lips and fingertips have the most touch sensors.

Touch receptors help us work out the size, shape, texture, and temperature of things.

The lips are some of the most sensitve parts of the body.

This model resizes the parts of the body according to how much brain space is used processing their sensory data.

Our fingertips have up to 100 pressure receptors per 1 cm³ (0.06 cu in).

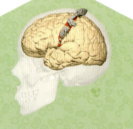

AMAZING DISCOVERY

Scientist: Wilder Penfield
Discovery: Functional anatomy of the brain
Date: 1951
The story: Brain surgeon Wilder Penfield operated on patients under local anesthetic. To limit harm when removing diseased parts, he used an electric probe to activate brain cells and asked patients what they felt. Penfield used their responses to map the brain, including the somatosensory cortex (left) that processes touch signals.

DID YOU KNOW? A very rare condition, congenital analgesia, means some people feel no pain. It sounds nice, but it puts them in great danger.

Skin sensors in the hands are linked to a large area in the brain's somatosensory cortex.

Feeling Pain

Nociceptors send pain signals to the brain in response to injuries, wounds, or extreme temperatures. Some signals do not reach the brain. If an immediate reaction is needed to avoid further harm, the spinal cord triggers a reflex arc— we pull away at once.

A scrape does not put us in immediate danger, so it does not trigger a reflex response. The nociceptor signals travel all the way to the brain.

We learn to control how we react to pain when we are children. The sensation can be overwhelming.

Eyes and Sight

The eye is a sensor that detects patterns of light. It turns light into nerve signals using more than 100 million light-sensitive nerve cells. These nerve signals travel along the optic nerve to the brain, where we use them to make a virtual model of the world around us.

Journey Through the Eye

Light enters the eye through a hole called the pupil. The lens and cornea focus light onto tissue at the back of the eye, the retina, which has a layer of light-detecting cells. Rod cells allow vision in dim light and cone cells detect fine detail and hues. The retina also has layers of neurons that send signals to the brain.

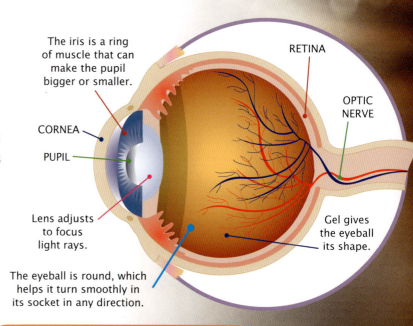

The iris is a ring of muscle that can make the pupil bigger or smaller.

CORNEA
PUPIL

Lens adjusts to focus light rays.

The eyeball is round, which helps it turn smoothly in its socket in any direction.

RETINA

OPTIC NERVE

Gel gives the eyeball its shape.

Visual Tricks

We do not always "see" the world as it actually is. We see what our brain interprets from the data. To make quicker sense of the data, the visual cortex takes shortcuts based on certain rules. However, this can lead to false interpretations or optical illusions.

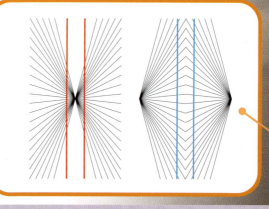

The red and blue lines seem to bend because the brain interprets the black lines as "distance."

AMAZING DISCOVERY

Scientist: Patricia Bath
Discovery: Improved cataract surgery
Date: 1981
The story: Ophthalmologist (eye doctor) Patricia Bath cofounded the American Institute for the Prevention of Blindness. She invented the Laserphaco Probe, a pioneering device and technique for cataract surgery. It removes cataracts with a laser, making it easier to insert a new lens and restore people's vision.

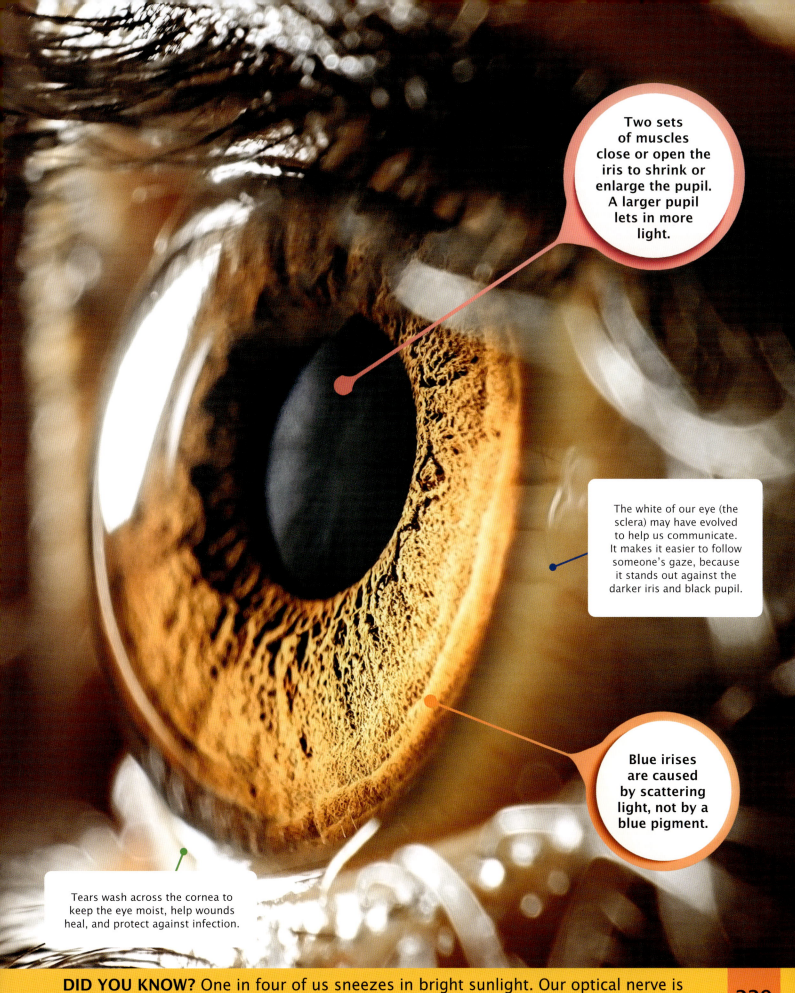

Two sets of muscles close or open the iris to shrink or enlarge the pupil. A larger pupil lets in more light.

The white of our eye (the sclera) may have evolved to help us communicate. It makes it easier to follow someone's gaze, because it stands out against the darker iris and black pupil.

Blue irises are caused by scattering light, not by a blue pigment.

Tears wash across the cornea to keep the eye moist, help wounds heal, and protect against infection.

DID YOU KNOW? One in four of us sneezes in bright sunlight. Our optical nerve is in the same bundle as the nerve that carries sense signals to and from the nose.

Ears and Hearing

Our ears collect sound waves from our surroundings and turn them into nerve signals that travel to the auditory cortex. This part of the brain translates the nerve signals so we hear noises, speech, or music and can tell if they are quiet or loud, high or low, sweet or harsh.

Inside the Ear

The ear lobe funnels sound waves along the ear canal to a thin layer of tissue called the tympanum (eardrum). Like the skin of a musical drum, the eardrum vibrates. The vibrations pass through three tiny bones called ossicles. The last of these, the stapes, is attached to a thin layer of tissue called the oval window. From here, the sound vibrations enter the inner ear, which is made up of the snail-shaped, fluid-filled cochlea and the semicircular canals.

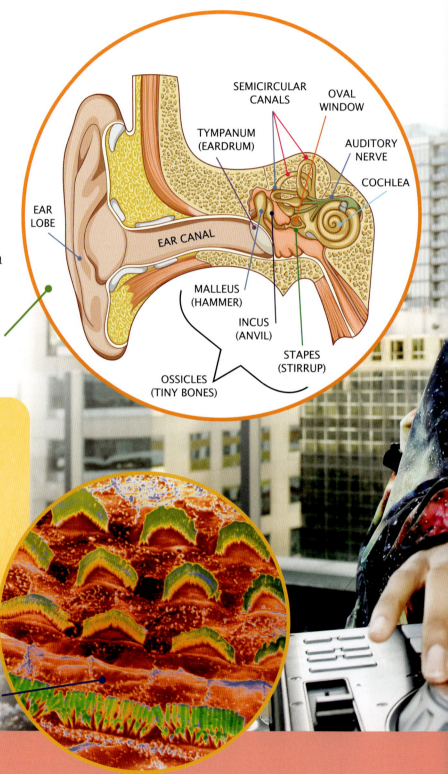

Sound travels as vibrations through the air-filled middle ear and fluid-filled inner ear, where it is turned into electrical signals.

Hairs for Hearing

The organ of Corti, inside the cochlea, contains sound-sensing hairs. They translate the vibrations made by sound waves into electrical impulses and transmit them to the brain along the auditory nerve.

The organ of Corti has up to 20,000 outer hairs arranged in V-shapes in three rows. It also has one row of around 3,500 inner hairs that lead to the auditory nerve.

AMAZING DISCOVERY

Scientist: Miller Reese Hutchison
Discovery: First electric hearing aid, the Acousticon (left)
Date: 1902
The story: In 1895, US inventor Hutchison designed an electric hearing aid for a friend, but it was too big to be practical. By 1902, he shrunk it to create a portable hearing aid, the Acousticon. It used a carbon microphone, like the ones in early telephones, to make sounds louder.

We have auditory areas on both sides of the brain.

Headphones let us listen to sounds privately without disturbing others. They also block out noise from our environment.

Loudness is measured in decibels (dB). Sounds above 85 dB can permanently damage our hearing.

An adult hears sounds in the 20–20,000 Hz range. We lose our ability to detect higher-pitched sounds with age.

DID YOU KNOW? Dogs have hearing four times more sensitive than humans, so what we hear at 10 m (33 ft) away, they can hear at 40 m (130 ft) away.

Smell and Taste

Our primitive ancestors were more tuned in to smell and taste than we are today. They relied on those senses to find a partner or food to eat, and to avoid fire, dangerous animals, or poisonous foods.

Smelly Science

The smell receptors in our nose detect many different smell molecules, from rose petals to freshly baked cakes and from sour milk to burning plastic. When smell molecules bind to a receptor, it sends a signal to the olfactory bulb for processing. From here, signals move along the olfactory tract higher into the brain. Scientists believe there are 10 primary smells. Just like paints, they mix together to make different smells.

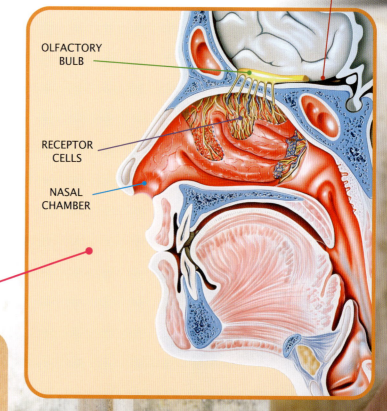

OLFACTORY TRACT
OLFACTORY BULB
RECEPTOR CELLS
NASAL CHAMBER

Smell is the only sense that is "wired in" to the brain. Signals travel directly from the receptor cells to the olfactory bulb.

A Matter of Taste

Taste buds in our mouth, tongue, and throat detect molecules from food and drink and send taste data along nerves to the brain. But our experience of taste is not based only on taste receptors. Our brain adds in information gathered by our senses of sight and smell. If food looks or smells yucky, it will taste disgusting to us, too.

This scan shows some of the taste buds on the surface of the tongue. Each one is a cluster of 50 to 75 taste receptors.

Chapter 9: Dinosaurs and Relatives

Dinosaurs and Relatives

Millions of years ago, reptiles called dinosaurs walked the Earth. The first dinosaurs lived around 233 million years ago. About 66 million years ago, all the dinosaurs were wiped out after a giant space rock, called an asteroid, hit Earth, filling the sky with dust for up to a year. This killed many plants, the plant-eating dinosaurs that fed on them, and finally the meat-eating dinosaurs.

Dinosaurs

Around 312 million years ago, reptiles were the first four-legged animals to spend all their time on land. Reptiles have scaly skin, breathe air, and usually lay shelled eggs on land. Unlike other reptiles, dinosaurs walked with their back legs beneath their body rather than sprawled to the sides. This meant they could run faster. Over time, some meat-eating dinosaurs started to grow feathers, which are made of the same hard material, keratin, as scales. Birds are the descendants of these feathered dinosaurs.

A lizard's legs stretch to the sides, but a dinosaur's strong legs are directly beneath its body.

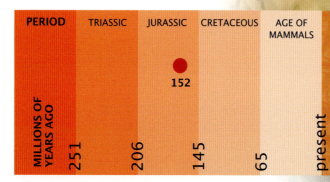

Name: *Allosaurus* (AL-uh-SAWR-us)
Family: Allosauridae
Height: 5 m (16.5 ft)
Length: 12 m (40 ft)
Weight: 2.7 tonnes (3 tons)

DINOSAUR PROFILE

Flying Reptiles

The pterosaurs were cousins of the dinosaurs. Although some dinosaurs later developed wings, the pterosaurs were the first reptiles in the air, around 228 million years ago. Pterosaur (pronounced "teh-roh-sore") means "wing lizard."

Like all pterosaurs, *Pteranodon* had wings that were flaps of skin stretching from its legs to its extra-long fourth finger.

Thick, sturdy legs supported its heavy bulk.

Allosaurus had long claws for gripping flesh.

Allosaurus fed on carrion or its own kills.

DID YOU KNOW? Over millions of years, around 1,000 dinosaur species evolved, two-thirds of them plant-eaters and the rest meat-eaters or omnivores (with a mixed diet).

Tyrannosaurus

One species of dinosaur is more famous than any other: *Tyrannosaurus rex*, or "king of the tyrant lizards." It inhabited North America between 68 and 66 million years ago. For a long time, it was the largest known land carnivore (meat-eater). Today, that title goes to *Spinosaurus* (see pages 238–239).

Search for Meat

Tyrannosaurus had two forward-facing eyes, allowing it to judge distance and speed when tracking prey. It could also move fairly quickly, thanks to its muscular back legs. Once it reached its prey, it tore into its flesh with powerful jaws. *Tyrannosaurus*'s teeth could easily crush through bone. Teeth were different sizes, but the longest were around 15 cm (6 in).

One *Tyrannosaurus* sinks its teeth into another's neck.

Life in a Pack

Trackways in Canada show that—at least some of the time—*Tyrannosaurus* hunted in packs. As in wolf packs today, rival males probably fought each other to be pack leader. *Tyrannosaurus* would have used its fearsome jaws not only to kill prey, but to attack rivals.

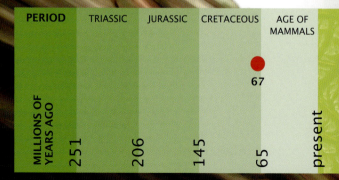

Name: *Tyrannosaurus* (Tye-RAN-uh-SAWR-us)
Family: Tyrannosauridae
Height: 5.5 m (18 ft)
Length: 12 m (39 ft)
Weight: 6.1 tonnes (6.7 tons)

DINOSAUR PROFILE

DID YOU KNOW? *Tyrannosaurus*'s 1.2-m- (4-ft-) long jaw contained up to 60 serrated (jagged-edged) teeth that were perfect for slicing through flesh.

Spinosaurus

The largest and longest carnivorous dinosaur, *Spinosaurus* was a theropod, like *Tyrannosaurus* and *Archaeopteryx*. Dinosaurs in this large group usually walked on their two back legs. *Spinosaurus*'s pointed, crocodile-like snout was perfectly shaped for snapping up fish, but this theropod also fed on dinosaurs and other land animals.

Species and Specimens

Only a handful of fairly complete *Spinosaurus* specimens have been found—and one of those was destroyed in bombing raids on Munich, Germany, during World War II. Most dinosaur experts recognize just one species, which they call *Spinosaurus aegyptiacus* ("Egyptian spine lizard").

Sail or Hump?

Most paleontologists believe that the spines along *Spinosaurus*'s back held up a large sail of skin. A few have another theory—that the spines supported a fatty hump, like a camel's. Either structure could have helped *Spinosaurus* to attract a mate. Among modern reptiles, such as frilled lizards, features like these are often shown off at mating time.

Spinosaurus had a series of tall spines sticking out of its backbone. Most experts agree this supported a sail.

PERIOD	TRIASSIC	JURASSIC	CRETACEOUS	AGE OF MAMMALS
MILLIONS OF YEARS AGO	251	206	145 ● 105	65 — present

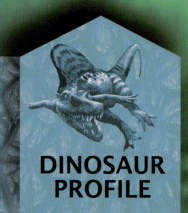

DINOSAUR PROFILE

Name: *Spinosaurus* (SPY-nuh-SAWR-us)
Family: Spinosauridae
Height: 6 m (20 ft)
Length: 16 m (52.5 ft)
Weight: 9 tonnes (9.9 tons)

Archaeopteryx

Birdlike *Archaeopteryx* lived in what is now southern Germany around 150 million years ago. *Archaeopteryx*'s arms had developed into wide, strongly muscled wings, while the feathers on its tail and wings had evolved to be long and stiff. These features meant that this dinosaur could make short flights.

Germany in the Late Jurassic

The landscape where *Archaeopteryx* lived was made up of low-lying islands among bodies of water, called lagoons. These lagoons had become separated from the nearby Tethys Ocean. When they dried up, the mud turned into limestone. Creatures that had sunk to the bottom were preserved as fossils.

Unlike modern birds, *Archaeopteryx* had clawed fingers.

Archaeopteryx was about the same size as a raven. It hunted frogs, lizards, dragonflies, and beetles.

Archaeopteryx's teeth were sharp and cone-shaped.

Flapping its wings while it was running helped *Archaeopteryx* to move faster.

PERIOD	TRIASSIC	JURASSIC	CRETACEOUS	AGE OF MAMMALS

150

MILLIONS OF YEARS AGO: 251, 206, 145, 65, present

Name: *Archaeopteryx* (Ar-kee-OP-ter-ix)
Family: Archaeopterygidae
Length: 30 cm (12 in)
Wingspan: 50 cm (20 in)
Weight: 1 kg (2.2 lb)

DINOSAUR PROFILE

Jurassic dragonflies were huge, with wingspans up to 75 cm (30 in).

Archaeopteryx means "ancient wing."

Bird or Dinosaur?

The first feathered dinosaur ever discovered, *Archaeopteryx* was nicknamed the "first bird." It was clearly an early ancestor of birds because of its wing and tail feathers. However, it also had reptilian features—a long, bony tail, large hand claws, and jaws lined with sharp teeth.

This *Archaeopteryx* skeleton was preserved in limestone.

DID YOU KNOW? The first *Archaeopteryx* fossil was found in 1859—the same year that Charles Darwin published his theory of evolution by natural selection.

Sauroposeidon

In 1994, a few fossilized neck bones were discovered by a dog walker in Oklahoma, USA. They belonged to *Sauroposeidon*. At 18 m (59 ft) high, it was the tallest known dinosaur, and almost as heavy as the biggest known dinosaur of all, *Argentinosaurus*, a plant-eater that weighed up to 75 tonnes (83 tons).

Hot and Humid

Plant-eating (herbivorous) *Sauroposeidon* lived around the shores of what is now the Gulf of Mexico. At that time, the landscape was made up of rain forests, river deltas, and wetlands. The climate was tropical (hot and humid all year round) or subtropical (with hot, wet summers and short, mild winters).

Ground Shaker

Sauroposeidon was named after Poseidon—the Greek god of earthquakes—because its huge bulk would have made the ground shake. *Sauroposeidon* was a sauropod, a group of large, long-necked, long-tailed plant-eaters. The area's top predator was *Acrocanthosaurus*, which preyed on young *Sauroposeidon*.

Fossilized *Sauroposeidon* footprints have been found in Texas, USA.

Like other sauropods, *Sauroposeidon* lived in herds.

DINOSAUR PROFILE

PERIOD	TRIASSIC	JURASSIC	CRETACEOUS	AGE OF MAMMALS
MILLIONS OF YEARS AGO	251	206	145 — 110	65 — present

Name: *Sauroposeidon* (SAWR-oh-puh-SIGH-don)
Family: Titanosauridae
Height: 18 m (59 ft)
Length: 34 m (112 ft)
Weight: 55 tonnes (60 tons)

The estimated neck length was 12 m (39 ft). The largest neck bone, or vertebra, was a record-breaking 1.2 m (4 ft) long.

Vegetation included palms, tree ferns, and magnolias.

Sauroposeidon juveniles may have lived with the herd for protection.

DID YOU KNOW? *Sauroposeidon* may have evolved to be large so that it had room for a huge stomach and intestines to get all the nutrients out of the plants it ate.

Parasaurolophus

One of the hadrosaurs, or duck-billed dinosaurs, herbivorous *Parasaurolophus* lived across North America around 75 million years ago. It was thought to be a close relative of another hadrosaur, *Saurolophus* ("crested lizard"). *Parasaurolophus* means "like *Saurolophus*."

The crest made its calls travel farther.

Loud Caller

Saurolophus's crest was mostly solid, while *Parasaurolophus*'s was hollow. It had tubes leading to and from the nostrils and amplified the dinosaur's calls (made them louder). This would have helped with signaling danger to the rest of the herd.

Parasaurolophus went up on two legs to run or look out for danger.

***Parasaurolophus*'s short, stout legs helped it to push through thick undergrowth.**

Parasaurolophus grazed on all fours.

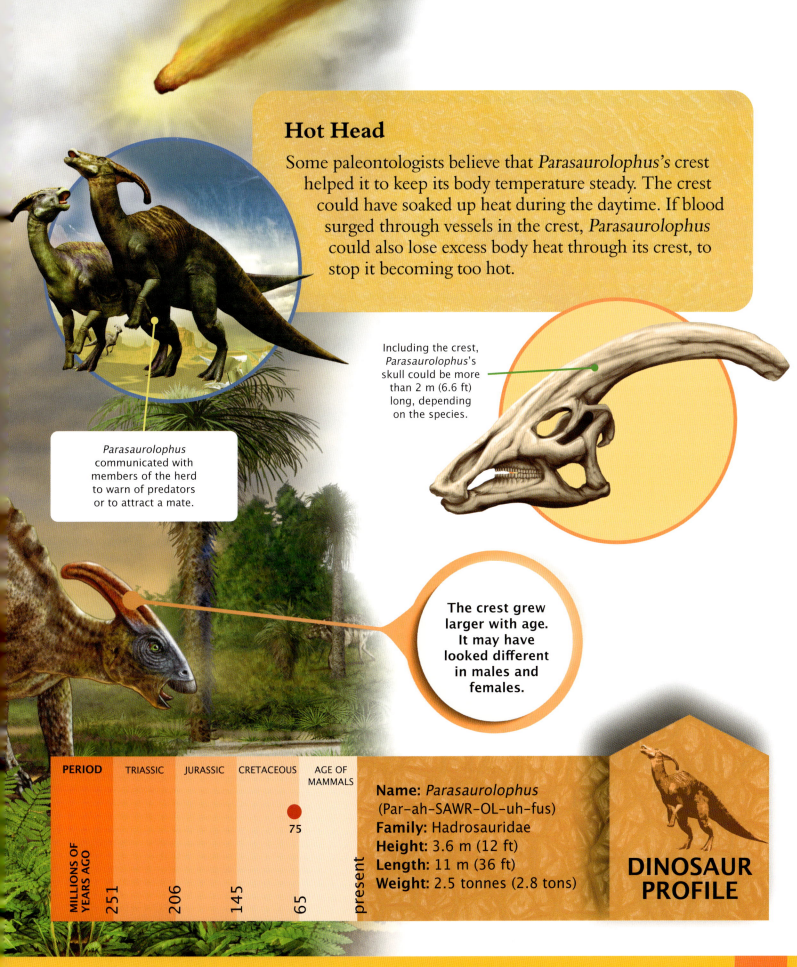

Hot Head

Some paleontologists believe that *Parasaurolophus*'s crest helped it to keep its body temperature steady. The crest could have soaked up heat during the daytime. If blood surged through vessels in the crest, *Parasaurolophus* could also lose excess body heat through its crest, to stop it becoming too hot.

Including the crest, *Parasaurolophus*'s skull could be more than 2 m (6.6 ft) long, depending on the species.

Parasaurolophus communicated with members of the herd to warn of predators or to attract a mate.

The crest grew larger with age. It may have looked different in males and females.

DINOSAUR PROFILE

Name: *Parasaurolophus* (Par-ah-SAWR-OL-uh-fus)
Family: Hadrosauridae
Height: 3.6 m (12 ft)
Length: 11 m (36 ft)
Weight: 2.5 tonnes (2.8 tons)

PERIOD	TRIASSIC	JURASSIC	CRETACEOUS	AGE OF MAMMALS
MILLIONS OF YEARS AGO	251	206	145	65 — present

75

DID YOU KNOW? At least three species of *Parasaurolophus* have been identified. The first, *Parasaurolophus walkeri*, was discovered as long ago as 1920.

Triceratops

One of the biggest ceratopsians, *Triceratops* lived 68 to 66 million years ago in North America. Ceratopsians walked on four legs and had beaks for cropping plants, neck frills, and horns. *Triceratops* had three horns—a longer pair over its eyes and a shorter one on its nose.

> The neck frill might have helped *Triceratops* keep its temperature steady. It was also for display.

Skull Features

Triceratops's skull was massive. Its horns and neck frill were both used for display—showing off to possible mates, fighting rivals, and perhaps even allowing herd members to identify each other. The dinosaur also used its horns to defend against predatory tyrannosaurs.

Triceratops's skull was around 2 m (6.6 ft) long—about a quarter of its total body length.

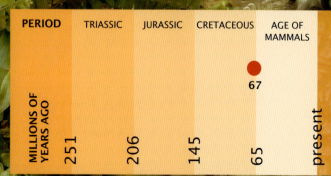

PERIOD	TRIASSIC	JURASSIC	CRETACEOUS	AGE OF MAMMALS
MILLIONS OF YEARS AGO	251	206	145	65 — present

67

Name: *Triceratops* (Try-SEH-ruh-tops)
Family: Ceratopsidae
Height: 3 m (10 ft)
Length: 8.5 m (28 ft)
Weight: 8 tonnes (8.8 tons)

DINOSAUR PROFILE

Triceratops had up to 800 cheek teeth. Cycads and palms quickly wore them down, but they were constantly being replaced.

Social Groups

For more than a century, all the *Triceratops* fossils were of solitary animals. Then, in 2009, paleontologists found three juveniles together. It is possible that *Triceratops* lived in social groups, just as African elephants do. Like them, *Triceratops* was a plant-eater and could have used its bulky body to knock down big bushes.

Each brow horn was around 1 m (3 ft) long.

Triceratops used its brow horns to fight rival males.

The beak-like mouth could snap tough plant stems.

DID YOU KNOW? Some fossils of *Triceratops* skulls have *Tyrannosaurus* bite marks, but it is possible that the tyrannosaurs bit the massive beasts only after they were dead.

Stegosaurus

Stegosaurus was a stegosaur, a group of plant-eaters with tough bony plates and spiked tails. *Stegosaurus* lived in North America and Europe. It had diamond-shaped plates down its back and a small head, containing a small, simple brain.

Lethal Weapon

The group of spikes at the end of a stegosaur's tail is called a thagomizer. It was *Stegosaurus*'s only protection against predators. The dinosaur swung and flicked its tail, hoping to hit an attacker and inflict serious damage.

Stegosaurus's skull was long and narrow.

Unlike other known stegosaurs, *Stegosaurus*'s plates were staggered instead of in pairs.

All about Plates

Early reconstructions of *Stegosaurus* had its plates flat on top of its body—that is how the dinosaur got its name, which means "roofed lizard." Paleontologists now know that the plates stood upright, making the dinosaur look bigger than it was. They were almost certainly for display, as they did not cover enough of the dinosaur's body to help in an attack.

Stegosaurus probably used its plates to show off to other members of the same species.

248

PERIOD	TRIASSIC	JURASSIC	CRETACEOUS	AGE OF MAMMALS	
MILLIONS OF YEARS AGO	251	206 • 153 / 145	65	present	

Name: *Stegosaurus* (STEG-uh-SAWR-us)
Family: Stegosauridae
Height: 2.75 m (9 ft)
Length: 9 m (30 ft)
Weight: 5 tonnes (5.5 tons)

DINOSAUR PROFILE

Stegosaurus's skull housed a hotdog-shaped brain.

Ornitholestes hunted in packs.

Stegosaurus could not move fast because of its short front legs. Its top speed was 7 km/h (4.3 mph).

Ornitholestes was a 12.6-kg (27.8-lb) theropod that lived in North America at the same time as *Stegosaurus*.

DID YOU KNOW? *Stegosaurus*'s plates were up to 60 cm (23.6 in) tall and made of bone covered by tough horn.

249

Quetzalcoatlus

Named after Quetzalcoatl, the feathered serpent god of Aztec mythology, *Quetzalcoatlus* was a pterosaur that lived at the end of the Cretaceous Period. Its wingspan was up to 11 m (36 ft), making it the largest of the 150 known species of pterosaur.

On the Lookout

Quetzalcoatlus had a long neck and good eyesight. On land it walked on all fours, looking for carrion or small animals to eat. Flight used a lot of energy. Wherever possible, *Quetzalcoatlus* glided rather than flapping its wings.

The wing membrane was thin but tough; it was just 23 cm (8 in) thick at the elbows.

Taking Off

Smaller pterosaurs could launch themselves into the air by running along on their back legs, like birds. Larger ones, such as *Quetzalcoatlus*, were too heavy for that and needed to start from a four-legged position. Their front legs were much stronger than their back ones, and could give enough of an upward thrust to make the animal airborne.

Pterosaurs did not have feathers. However some, perhaps including *Quetzalcoatlus*, had fuzzy filaments called pycnofibers covering their bodies.

DID YOU KNOW? *Quetzalcoatlus* belonged to a family called the azhdarchids, which includes some of the largest flying animals of all time.

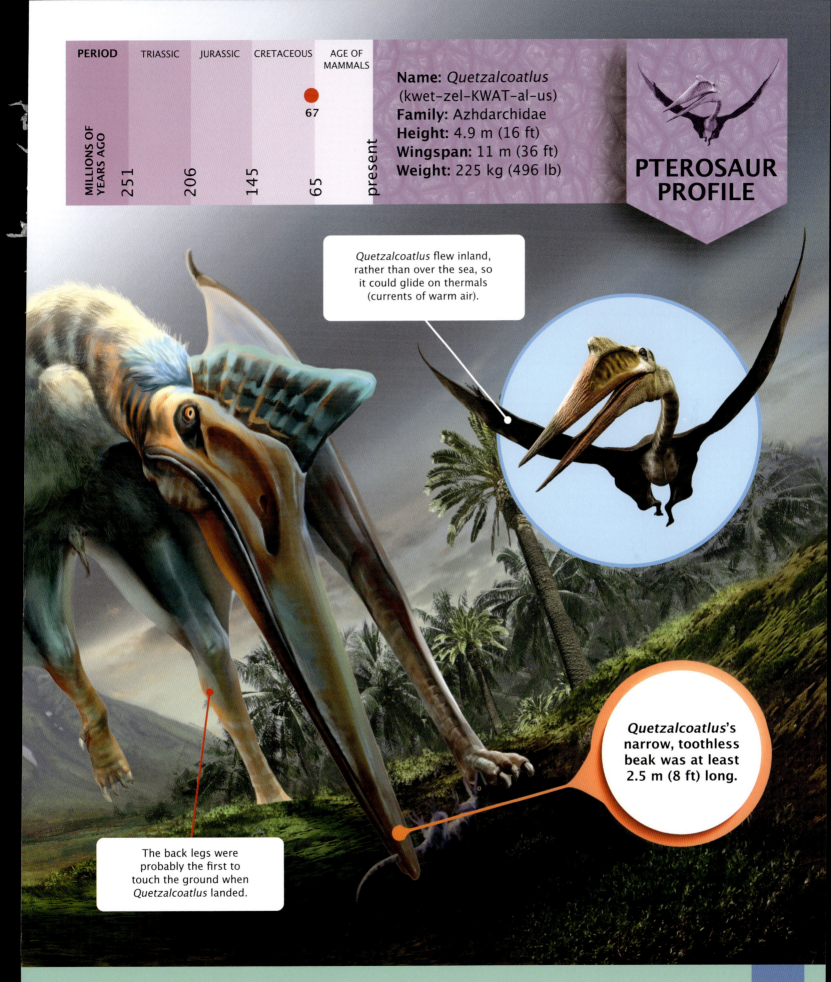

PERIOD	TRIASSIC	JURASSIC	CRETACEOUS	AGE OF MAMMALS
MILLIONS OF YEARS AGO	251	206	145	67 • 65 — present

Name: *Quetzalcoatlus* (kwet-zel-KWAT-al-us)
Family: Azhdarchidae
Height: 4.9 m (16 ft)
Wingspan: 11 m (36 ft)
Weight: 225 kg (496 lb)

PTEROSAUR PROFILE

Quetzalcoatlus flew inland, rather than over the sea, so it could glide on thermals (currents of warm air).

Quetzalcoatlus's narrow, toothless beak was at least 2.5 m (8 ft) long.

The back legs were probably the first to touch the ground when *Quetzalcoatlus* landed.

251

Glossary

ALLOY
A mixture of two or more metals, or of a metal and a non-metal.

AMPHIBIAN
An animal that is born in water and breathes underwater using gills when young. As an adult, it usually breathes air using lungs and lives on land or in water.

AMPLITUDE
The height of a wave.

ANALOG
Using signals or information that are in a physical form, such as electric current or radio waves.

ATOM
The smallest unit of an element.

BINARY
A base-2 system of numbering—it has only two numbers, 0 and 1.

BIRD
An animal with a beak, wings, and feathers. Females lay hard-shelled eggs on land.

CELL
The smallest unit of a living body.

CHEMICAL BOND
A connection formed between two or more atoms that can only be broken by a chemical reaction.

COMPOUND
Elements bound together by chemical bonds.

CRYSTAL
A solid with atoms or molecules arranged in a regular pattern.

DIGITAL
Using signals or information that are in a coded form, usually binary.

DNA (deoxyribonucleic acid)
A substance that carries genes and is found in the nucleus of cells.

ELECTRIC CHARGE
A property of some forms of matter that means they can be influenced by electromagnetism.

ELECTRICITY
A flow of electric charge from one place to another.

ELECTROMAGNETISM
A force that influences all particles that carry electric charge or a magnetic field.

ELECTRON
A negatively charged subatomic particle.

ELECTRONICS
A technology that uses the flow of very small electric currents to store, send, and alter information.

ELEMENT
A substance that is made entirely from one type of atom.

ENERGY
What allows us to do work. Its forms include heat and light.

ENZYME
A protein that controls a chemical reaction.

EVOLUTION
The process by which living organisms gradually change over very long periods of time.

EXTINCT
Describes an animal or plant that has disappeared forever.

FISH
A water-living animal that takes oxygen from the water using gills and usually has fins.

FORCE
A push or pull on an object that changes its movement.

FOSSIL
The preserved remains of an ancient animal or plant.

FRICTION
A force between moving objects, where their surfaces rub against each other, slowing them down.

GAS
A phase of matter in which atoms or molecules are widely separated and move freely.

GENE
An instruction on a section of a DNA molecule that is needed to make the structures and provide the functions that a living organism requires.

GRAVITY
A force that draws objects that have mass toward each other.

INVERTEBRATE
An animal without a backbone, such as a crab, spider, or insect.

ISOTOPE
One of two or more special forms of atom belonging to the same element, but having varying numbers of neutrons.

LIQUID
A phase of matter in which atoms or molecules are loosely bound together but can move freely.

LOGIC GATE
Part of a circuit in a computer that decides whether to allow current through, based on binary numbers.

MAGNETIC FIELD
A form of electromagnetism created around, and felt by, electrical conductors and metals with certain properties.

MAMMAL
An animal that grows hair and feeds its babies on milk.

MATTER
Anything that has mass and occupies space.

MINERAL
A solid chemical compound, often with a crystal structure, formed in water or the ground.

MOLECULE
The smallest unit of a compound, made up of two or more atoms bonded together.

NEUTRON
A subatomic particle with no charge, located inside the nucleus.

NUCLEUS
The middle of an atom, where its positive electric charge and nearly all of its mass are concentrated in a cluster of subatomic particles called protons and neutrons.

ORGAN
A collection of tissues in a complex living thing that carries out a special function.

PALEONTOLOGIST
A scientist who studies fossils.

PHASE
The way the atoms or molecules of a substance are arranged.

PHOTOSYNTHESIS
A chemical reaction used by plants to make food from sunlight, carbon dioxide, and water.

PREDATOR
An animal that hunts and eats other animals for food.

PREY
An animal that is hunted and eaten by other animals for food.

PROTON
A positively charged subatomic particle, located inside the nucleus.

QUANTUM PHYSICS
A branch of physics that describes how subatomic particles behave.

RADIOACTIVE
Relating to atoms whose nuclei are unstable and break apart, releasing high-energy particles.

RADIO WAVE
A moving wave of electromagnetic radiation with much less energy than light.

REACTION
A chemical process that breaks apart chemical bonds within molecules, moves atoms around, and creates new molecules.

REPTILE
An animal with a dry, scaly skin that usually lays eggs on land.

ROCK
A solid material found in nature, made up of a mix of minerals.

SCAVENGE
To eat carrion or leftover kills from other hunters.

SOLID
A phase of matter in which atoms or molecules are tightly bound together and cannot move freely.

SPECIES
One particular type of living thing. Members of the same species look similar and can produce offspring together.

STAR
A huge ball of gas that releases energy, forcing small atomic nuclei together to form larger ones.

STRONG NUCLEAR FORCE
A powerful force that holds subatomic particles together in the nucleus of an atom.

SUBATOMIC PARTICLE
Any particle smaller than an atom.

SUPERCONDUCTOR
A material that conducts electricity without losing its energy as heat.

SYSTEM
A group of linked organs, such as those in the digestive system, that work together to do a task.

TECTONICS
The very slow movement and rearrangement of blocks of Earth's outer rocky crust.

TISSUE
A collection of cells that carries out a function in a living organism.

WAVE
A moving disturbance that carries energy from one place to another.

WORK
The process of moving energy from one place to another, usually through a force.

Index

absolute zero 33, 67
actinides 16–17
aircraft 13, 28, 88–89
algae 144
alkali earth metals 16–17
alkali metals 16–17
allergies 225
alligators 138
Allosaurus 234–235
alloys 11, 89
alternating current (AC) 20, 80
amphibians 152–153, 186–187
amplitude 30
anteaters 132
antibodies 224–225
apes 178–179
Arabian oryx 130
Archaeopteryx 240–241
archeology 108–109
Archimedes 79
Asteroid Belt 43, 52–53
asteroids 42, 43, 48, 52–53, 234
astronauts 29, 73
atmosphere 95, 112–113
atomic bonds 15
atomic mass 16, 17, 22
atomic number 16
atoms 8, 11, 14–15, 16–17, 18–19, 20, 22–23, 90–91, 92
aurorae 44, 112–113
axles 78–79

Babbage, Charles 84
babies 222–223
bacteria 144, 148, 215, 224
Bartoshuk, Linda 233
basic metals 16–17
bats 172–173
batteries 20
bears 128–129, 166–167
Beaufort Scale 126–127
bees 202–203
Bernoulli, Daniel 13
Big Bang 66–67
biomes 128–139
birds 136–137, 138–139, 140, 152–153, 161, 182–185, 234, 240–241
bits 82, 83
black holes 29, 59, 60–61, 65
bladder 221
blood 208, 215, 216–217, 218–219, 220
body systems 204

boiling point 8
bones 208–209
boreal forests 128–129, 134
brain 206–207, 210–211, 226, 227, 228, 230, 232
buffalo 133

cacti 131
camels 130–131
cancer 92–93
carbon 18, 92, 204
carbon dioxide 110, 111, 113, 142, 143, 154, 217
Carnot, Sadi 32
cars 80–81
Cassini 54
catalysts 18
cats 162–163
CD players 82–83
cellphones (mobile phones) 38, 84, 86
cells 146–149, 204, 206, 208, 210–211, 216–217, 218, 222, 224–225
Ceres 52
Chandra X-ray Observatory 60
cheetahs 26, 162
chemical energy 24, 32, 81
chemical reactions 16, 18–19, 32, 70, 97, 144, 150, 220
chimpanzees 6, 178
chlorine 15
chromosomes 147
climate change 113, 142–143
climate zones 128–129
clouds 122–123, 127
coal 110–111, 142, 143
combustion 18
comets 42, 43
compounds 14, 15, 96
computers 82, 84–85, 86
condensation 8
condors 183
conduction of electricity 20
conduction of heat 11, 32
conifers 129, 134, 150–151
convection 13, 32
Copernicus, Nicolaus 68
coral reefs 19, 128, 129, 144–145
cosmic microwave background radiation (CMBR) 66, 67
cougars 134
cows 26, 140
crabs 138
craters 46, 48
Crick, Francis 147
crocodiles 158–159
crops 140–141
crystals 10–11, 96, 104–105

Dalton, John 15
dark energy 66, 67
Darwin, Charles 156–157, 158
deposition 8
deserts 128, 130–131

digestive system 214–215
dinosaurs 108, 109, 161, 234–249
direct current (DC) 20
DNA (deoxyribonucleic acid) 146–147, 211
dodos 155
dolphins 170–171
drag 25, 89, 190
dwarf planets 42, 52

ears 206, 230–231
Earth 28, 34, 42–43, 48–49, 67, 94–111
earthquakes 94, 100–101, 103
Earth's layers 94–95
Earth's magnetic field 44, 94, 188
ecosystems 154–155
Eddington, Arthur 41
Einstein, Albert 40–41
electric charges 18, 22, 23, 122, 206, 207, 209, 210
electric circuits 20
electricity 18, 20–21, 33, 34–35, 80–81, 82–83, 86, 90
electrolysis 18, 19
electromagnetic force 20, 21, 23, 34
electromagnetic radiation 36–37, 38–39
electronics 82–86
electrons 15, 16, 17, 18, 20, 22, 82, 122
elements 14–15, 16–17, 90, 96–97, 204
elephants 135, 174–175
energy 8, 18, 20, 24, 30, 32–39, 66, 80–81, 90–91
engines 80–81, 89
entropy 32
enzymes 214, 215
equinoxes 114–115
erosion 118
escape velocity 25
evaporation 8
event horizons 61
Everest, Mount 102–103
evolution 156–161
exoplanets 62–63
expansion of the Universe 64, 65
eyes 206, 228–229

Faraday, Michael 34
farming 140–141
fireworks 18
fish 128, 152–153, 190–193
Fleming, John Ambrose 82
forces 24–29, 34–35, 78
forests 128–129, 134–135, 142
fossils 108–109, 156, 160, 237, 239, 241, 245, 246, 248
foxes 164–165
Franklin, Rosalind 147
freezing 8
frequency 30
friction 24, 25, 28
frogs 186–187
fuels 80, 81, 89, 110–111, 142, 143
fungi 144, 154–155

254

galaxies 58–59, 64–65
Galilei, Galileo 24, 54, 68
gall bladder 218
Galvani, Luigi 209
gamma rays 38, 39
Ganymede 54
gases 8–9, 12–13
Geiger, Hans 23
genes 146–147, 158, 159, 222
geological periods 160
geostationary orbits 74
geysers 9
giraffes 176–177
glaciers 118, 119, 142, 143
global warming 110–111
gold 96, 106
gorillas 178
grasslands 128, 132–133
gravitational lensing 41
gravity 24–29, 40–41, 43, 49, 60–61, 66
gunpowder 18

Hahn, Otto 91
hail 122
hair 212–213
halogens 16–17
Harvey, William 217
Hawking, Stephen 60
heart 208, 216–217
heat 8, 11, 12, 13, 18, 32–33, 38, 44
helicopters 88
helium 54, 58
Herschel, William 39
Hertzsprung, Ejnar 58
Hippocrates 219
Hooke, Robert 28, 148
horses 133
howler monkeys 134–135
Hubble, Edwin 65
humans 108–109, 161, 178
hummingbirds 184–185
hurricanes 126–127
Hutton, James 99
Huygens 76
Huygens, Christiaan 31
hydrogen 22, 23, 54, 58, 204

igneous rocks 98, 99, 101
immune system 224–225
induction 34
Industrial Revolution 78
infrared 32, 38, 39
insulation of heat 11
interference 30
International Space Station (ISS) 41, 72–73
Internet 86
intestines 214–215
invertebrates 152–153, 194–203
in vitro fertilization (IVF) 222
ions 18
iron 10, 14, 34–35, 95, 96, 97, 106, 107
isotopes 90

Jedlik, Ányos 81
jellyfish 196–197
joules 25, 33
Jupiter 42–43, 53, 54–55

kangaroos 180
kidneys 220–221
kinetic energy 24, 32, 80–81
kingdoms of life 144
koalas 180–181
Kuiper Belt 43

Laennec, René 219
lanthanides 16–17
lasers 87, 90–91, 93, 228
lava 8, 98, 99, 101
Lavoisier, Antoine 19
laws of motion 26–27, 71
leap years 116
Leavitt, Henrietta Swan 65
lift, force of 13, 28, 88
light 31, 33, 36–37, 38, 41, 44, 87
lightning 33, 122
light-years 59
liquids 8–9, 12–13
Linnaeus, Carl 145
lions 163
liver 214, 218–219
Lomonosov, Mikhail 19
longitudinal waves 31
Lovelace, Ada 84
low Earth orbit 74
lungs 216–217

maglev trains 20–21
magnetic resonance imaging (MRI) scans 207
magnetism 14, 20–21, 34–35, 80–81, 94
magnification 37, 68
mammals 152–153, 162–181
mangrove forests 138–139
Mars 42–43, 50–51
Marsden, Ernest 23
marsupials 180–181
mass 28–29, 40–41
matter 8–9
Meitner, Lise 91
melting 8
melting point 8, 11
Mendel, Gregor 159
Mendeleev, Dmitri 17
Mercury 42–43, 46
mercury 8
metals 10, 11, 14, 16–17, 20, 34–35, 96, 97, 106–107
metamorphic rocks 98, 108, 110
meiosis 149
Meteosat 10 74–75
microscopes 37, 92, 148, 206
microwaves 38
midnight sun 117
Milky Way 58–59, 67

minerals 96–97, 104–105
mining 96–97, 106–107
mitosis 149
mixtures 14
Mohorovicic, Andrija 94
molecules 8, 15, 18–19
momentum 26
Moon, the 28, 48–49
moons 48–49, 51, 54, 56–57
motors 80–81
mountains 102–103
muscles 208–209, 216, 217

nanotechnology 92–93
natural gas 110–111, 142, 143
neon 37
Neptune 42–43, 56–57
nervous system 210–211
neurons 206, 207, 210–211
neutrons 22, 23, 90, 91
Newcomen, Thomas 78
New Horizons 77
Newton, Isaac 26–27, 28, 36, 40, 71
newtons 25
Newton's cradle 32
noble gases 16–17
non-metals 16–17
nuclear energy 90–91
nuclear fission 90, 91
nuclear fusion 17, 58, 90–91
nuclei, atomic 22–23, 90

oceans 118
octopuses 194–195
oganesson 17
okapis 177
Oort Cloud 43
optical fibers 87
orangutans 178–179
orbits 28, 42–43
ores 97
organic chemistry 18
organs 204
Ørsted, Hans-Christian 21
owls 140
oxygen 14, 96, 97, 104, 152, 154, 204, 216–217, 223
ozone layer 112

pancreas 215
pandas 167
Parasaurolophus 244–245
peat 110–111, 138
Penfield, Wilder 226
penguins 136–137
Penzias, Arno 67
periodic table 16–17
petroleum (oil) 110–111, 142, 143
phases of matter 8–9
phases of the Moon 48

255

Phobos 51
photosynthesis 150, 151, 154
physics 24
plants 144, 150–151, 161
plate tectonics 98–103
Pluto 43
polar bears 136, 143, 166–167
polar regions 128, 136–137, 143
pollen 150, 202–203
potential energy 32
power stations 21, 90
precipitation 119, 122–123
pressure 12
prisms 36, 39
prokaryotes 144, 148
protoctists 144
protons 16, 20, 22, 23, 122
Proxima Centauri 62
Pteranodon 235
pterosaurs 235, 250–251
puffins 138

quarks 23
quartz 10–11, 104
Quetzalcoatlus 250–251

radar 46, 47, 125
radioactivity 90
radio waves 38, 66, 75, 77, 86–87
rain 119, 122–123
rain forests 128, 134–135
reactants 18
red shift 64
reflection 37, 68–69
reflexes 210, 227
refraction 37, 68–69
reindeer (caribou) 136, 137
relativity, theories of 40–41
renewable energy 81
reproduction 222–223
reptiles 138, 152–153, 158–159, 188–189, 234–251
rice 140–141
rings, planetary 54, 56
rockets 24–25, 70–71
rocks 96–99
rollercoasters 27
rovers 50
Russell, Henry Norris 58
Rutherford, Ernest 23

salt 10, 15
satellites 74–75, 86–87
Saturn 42–43, 56–57
Saturn V rocket 70
sauropods 242–243
Sauroposeidon 242–243
scorpions 198–199
seahorses 192–193

seals 168–169
seasons 114–115
seawater 19
sedimentary rocks 98, 108, 110
semiconductors 82
semi-metals 16–17
senses 210, 226–233
sharks 190–191
Shockley, William 82
silver 106–107
singularities 61
skin 212–213, 227
slugs 200–201
smell 232–233
snails 200–201
snow 122–123
sodium 15
solar panels 72
solar prominences 44
Solar System 42–43
solar wind 44
solids 8–9, 10–11
solstices 116
solutions 18, 19
sound waves 30, 31, 33, 230–231
Space Launch System 70–71
space probes 47, 54, 76–77
space stations 29, 41, 72–73
space-time 40–41, 66
species 144–145
spiders 198–199
Spinosaurus 238–239
Sputnik 1 74, 75
squid 194–195
starfish 138
stars 44–45, 58–59, 60, 64
steam power 78
steel 11, 35
Stegosaurus 248–249
strong nuclear force 23
subatomic particles 22–23
sublimation 8
sulphur 14–15, 104, 105
Sun 28, 32, 36, 38, 39, 42, 43, 44–45
sunspots 44, 45
supernovae 58, 64

taste 206, 232–233
telescopes 37, 38, 68–69
theropods 234–241
Thomson, James 9
thrust 25
thunder 122
tides 49
tigers 162–163
time zones 116
tissues 204, 208
Titan 56, 76
tornadoes 124–125
tortoises 156–157, 188
touch 206, 212, 226–227
transformers 21

transistors 82
transition metals 16–17
transverse waves 31
trees 134, 142, 150–151
Triceratops 246–247
trilobites 108
tropical cyclones 126–127
tundra 128, 136, 137
tungsten 11
turbines 80–81, 90
turtles 145, 188–189
Tutt, J.W. 159
Tyrannosaurus 236–237

ultraviolet (UV) 38, 39
Universe, the 64–65, 66–67
uranium 90–91
urine 220–221

V-2 rocket 70
valves 82
van Helmont, Jan Baptiste 214
variable stars 64
velocity 24, 26, 27
Venus 42–43, 46–47
Vesalius, Andreas 205
Vesta 53
viruses 224–225
viscosity 12
visible spectrum 36, 39
volcanoes 46, 47, 50, 100–101
voltage 21
Voyager 2 76–77
vultures 182–183

Wallace, Alfred Russel 157
walruses 169
water 8–9, 30–31, 118–119, 204, 220
water cycle 119
Watson, James 147
wavelengths 30, 36, 38
waves 30–31
weather 120–127
weather satellites 74–75
Wegener, Alfred 100
weight 29
weightlessness 29
wetlands 138–139
whales 170–171
wheels 78–79
white blood cells 224
white dwarfs 58
wildebeest 158
Wilson, Robert 67
winds 112, 121, 124–127
wireless technology 86–87
work 24, 25, 32, 78
Wright, Orville and Wilbur 89

X-rays 38, 60, 219

zebras 158–159